AVRO
VULCAN

The Avro 698 prototype, VX770.

The Avro 698 prototype, VX770. First flight was made on August 30 1952 and the aircraft subsequently went to A&AEE for trials. It exploded and crashed at Syerston on September 20 1958, killing its crew.

AVRO
VULCAN

Robert Jackson

Patrick Stephens
Wellingborough, Northamptonshire

First published in 1984
First paperback edition published in 1987

British Library Cataloguing in Publication Data

Jackson, Robert, *1941-*
  Avro Vulcan.
  1. Vulcan (Jet bomber)
  I. Title
  623.74'63   UG1242.B6

  ISBN 1-85260-010-1

*Patrick Stephens Limited is part of the
Thorsons Publishing Group*

Printed and bound in Great Britain.

Contents

The Avro 698 prototype, VX770.

Acknowledgements

It is always hard to provide a comprehensive list of acknowledgements in a work of this kind, made up as it is of the reminiscences and comments of so many individuals. I wish, however, to single out the following for special mention: Air Commodore Ron Dick, not only for agreeing to write the Foreword, but also for supplying much valuable comment and advice; Air Commodore Henry Probert and his staff at the Air Historical Branch, MoD (RAF), and particularly Humphrey Wynn, without whose help the appendix to this book would have been impossible to complete; Alan Todd, for delving into his files time and again to check dates and references; Dr Bob McManners, for supplying the drawings; and finally, two former Vulcan men who flew 'backside first to nowhere' in the rear cockpit: Roger Bagnall, AEO, and Dick Wright, navigator. One last point, which I make to prevent the pens of IX Squadron personnel bursting into flames. I have referred to the Squadron by the Arabic numeral '9' throughout the text purely for ease of reading.

Foreword
by Air Commodore Ron Dick, RAF,
Former OC IX Squadron

In contributing to Robert Jackson's admirable history of the Vulcan, I am conscious that I am not among those best qualified to do so. My association with the big delta was limited to two tours with IX Squadron; one as a flight commander at Coningsby and later as the CO when the Squadron was based in Cyprus. Many Vulcan operators served in the 'Lincolnshire Air Force' for the best part of a quarter century and may therefore feel that I am a 'sprog' and inadequate as their representative. However they view my qualifications, I am sure that they will find Robert Jackson's book to be wholly admirable in its account of an aircraft which played such a significant part in the lives of a whole generation of RAF aircrew.

By any standards the Vulcan has been quite remarkable. It has served with distinction not only its original guise as the backbone of Britain's nuclear deterrent, but in roles as diverse as low level strike/attack, maritime reconnaissance, air-to-air tanker and engine test-bed. It has caught the eye as the star of countless air shows and has been a dramatic ambassador for the Royal Air Force in every corner of the world.

Most Vulcan crews grew to respect the Vulcan for its remarkable capabilities and its generally excellent handling characteristics. They enjoyed the occasional training flight to exotic places and they were proud of the attention attracted by their aircraft and its startling performance. This is not to say that Vulcan rapture was always unmodified. The crew compartment could be claustrophobic and uncomfortable. When overseas trips were rare, the long high-level navigation exercises could be boringly repetitive; indeed, rear crew members often threatened to record their experiences in a book called 'Backside First to Nowhere'. Pilots lulled into thinking of the Vulcan as an 'old lady' could be shocked by her savage behaviour if not treated with due respect during an assymmetric approach. There was also for some the unsettling thought, almost subconscious and seldom expressed, that, in an emergency, some crew members were more equal than others, since only the pilots had ejection seats.

Warts and all, the Vulcan has been an aircraft to be reckoned with. Robert Jackson has painted a comprehensive picture of the challenges, frustrations and achievements which were a part of creating and operating an aeroplane which began as an aerodynamic adventure and developed into the most durable element of the 'V' force. Dramatic in concept and realization, the Vulcan has most thoroughly earned its prominent place in the history of the Royal Air Force. Its story is well worth the telling.

Left *Vulcan B 2s sweep low over the RAF Ensign during a flypast at RAF Waddington.*

Chapter 1

A new shape in the sky

During the first week of September 1952 the crowds which flocked daily to the SBAC Show at Farnborough thrilled to the sight of a new aircraft which was the sensation of the display. No details of its performance or dimensions had so far been released; nothing was known of it apart from its company designation, and the fact that it had flown for the first time only days earlier. But those who witnessed the fighter-like performance of the Avro Type 698, the great white delta-winged prototype of Britain's latest jet bomber, knew that nothing like it existed anywhere else in the world; they were seeing a supreme achievement of British aviation technology, an aircraft which, seven years after the end of the Second World War, would once again give Royal Air Force Bomber Command unparalleled striking power.

Almost exactly 20 years earlier, other crowds in another country had also thrilled to the performance of a very different kind of aircraft. The occasion had been the Rhön Gliding Championships in Germany, and the aircraft in question had been a little glider built by the Horten Brothers of Bonn. Weighing only 440 lb and with a wing span of 41 ft, it had been brought out from under its security wraps to take part in the championships, from which it emerged the outright winner. The link between Horten's little glider and Avro's Type 698 was more than merely tenuous. Between the two designs lay two decades of advanced and adventurous aerodynamic research, most of it undertaken in Nazi-dominated Germany, without which the Avro delta would never have come to fruition so quickly from its original conception; for the Horten glider was an all-wing design too, the forerunner of a series of projects which, by 1945, were aerodynamically years ahead of any similar designs under study in either Britain or the United States.

After the original Horten glider, the H-1, came the H-2, which was developed under conditions of strict secrecy. In fact, following the seizure of power by the Nazi Party in 1933, with its renewed emphasis on re-creating Germany as a leading military power, there had come a security clampdown on any aircraft projects with military potential; scientists at the Reichsluftministerium, the German Air Ministry, had not been slow to realise the revolutionary quality of the H-1's design and on the RLM's orders, the H-1, which had already attracted a great deal of publicity, had been destroyed, together with a number of all-wing models. Consequently, flight-testing of the Horten H-2, which flew in both glider and powered versions in 1934, was not reported outside official circles. The H-2 spanned 54 ft and had an all-up weight of 830 lb in its unpowered version, and all-round flight characteristics were better than those of the earlier model.

The next variant, the H-3, flew at Berlin-Tempelhof just before the outbreak of the Second World War, and was the first Horten design to feature metal skinning in part of the wing covering. Metal skinning was used more extensively in the H-4 (also designated

Left *Roly Falk, Avro's chief test pilot, amazed Farnborough crowds by upward-rolling the Vulcan at the 1955 SBAC show. He is seen here in the cockpit of one of the Avro 707 research aircraft.*

RLM-251) which flew at Königsberg-Neumas in 1941; it weighed 750 lb and had a sink rate of only half a metre (1 ft 9 ins) per second. Another glider was also built at the same time to explore the use of lightweight plastic known as Tronal as a covering for the wing surfaces, but this experiment ended in disaster when the aircraft stalled on a test flight and went into a violent spin, breaking up and killing its pilot. A similar accident befell the next flying wing, the Ho-5 (the company was now using the first two letters of the Horten name to prefix its type number) which also broke up in flight.

Horten had little success with subsequent all-wing designs; the Ho-6, which had new high-aspect-ratio wings, was abandoned, while the Ho-7, which was powered by two 240 hp Argus Aslo-C engines and which was tested late in the war, proved to be directionally unstable. Nevertheless, all the flying-wing research undertaken by Walter and Reimar Horten since their original little H-1 in 1932 now culminated, in the closing months of the war, in the design of a very advanced combat aircraft: the Ho-9 fighter-bomber.

The prototype of this radical machine, the Ho-9V1, was built under the direction of the Luftwaffe's Sonderkommando 9 at Göttingen and was based on the design of the Ho-5. It was intended to power the machine with two 1,760 lb thrust BMW 003A-1 turbojets, but as these were not available for installation, the first Ho-9 was completed as a glider and test flown at Oranienburg in the closing weeks of 1944. The second prototype, the Ho-9V2, was completed with two 1,890 lb thrust Junkers Jumo 004B turbojets and flew for the first time in January 1945. The V2 version was destroyed in an accident after only two hours of flight testing, but the results obtained had been encouraging and an order was placed for 30 production machines.

The prototype production aircraft, the Ho-9V3, was built at the Gothaer Wagenfabrik at Friedrichsrode, where all subsequent production machines were to have been constructed under the designation Go 229, but it was only partially completed when the war in Europe ended. The airframe was captured by United States forces in May 1945 and subsequently shipped to the USA, but no further work was carried out on it and the machine was never flight tested.

Most of the detailed models and drawings of the later Horten designs were destroyed before they could fall into Allied hands. From remaining data, however, it was estimated that the production Go 229 would have had a maximum speed of 590 mph at sea level, an initial climb rate of 4,300 ft per minute, and an operational ceiling of 52,000 ft. Armament was to have comprised four 30 mm Mk 108 cannon and a 4,400 lb bomb load, and loaded weight was estimated at 18,700 lb. Wing span was 52 ft 6 ins and the wing area 566 sq ft. Estimated endurance was in excess of four hours in the fighter configuration. Landing speed was only 90 mph, and the estimated take-off run, fully laden, was 3,000 ft (the Messerschmitt Me 262 jet fighter needed 5,500 ft). The design was fitted with what would later be termed 'elevons', a combination of elevators and ailerons, which were then a novel feature.

The Horten brothers were by no means alone in their experiments with all-wing aircraft in wartime Germany. Another leading designer in the field was Dr Alexander Lippisch, who was responsible for the radical Messerschmitt 163 rocket fighter which saw operational service on a limited scale in the closing months of the war. Lippisch's later design studies were in many ways less orthodox than the Hortens', and some of them embodied a delta-wing planform. This was tested first of all on a series of models in wind tunnels (here again, German designers were at an advantage in having access to supersonic wind tunnel facilities, which existed neither in the USA nor in Britain during the war) and, as a result, Lippisch constructed a delta-wing research glider known as the DM-1. This was not ready for flight-testing before American forces overran the Lippisch factory at Wiener Wald in 1945, but the aircraft (and Lippisch) were taken back to the

United States. Further wind tunnel tests were undertaken by the NACA, and subsequently Convair, in consultation with the German designer, were asked to build an experimental turbojet-powered delta based on his research findings. This emerged in September 1948 as the XF-92A; it was the world's first delta-wing jet to fly, and was the forerunner of the Convair F-102 Delta Dagger.

In Germany, Lippisch also designed a number of piston-engined all-wing aircraft, including the twin-engined Messerschmitt 329 fighter derived from the rocket-powered Me 163 and the Me 265 fighter-bomber. Of the two, only a solitary prototype of the Me 329—the Me 329V-1—was built and test flown as a glider at Rechlin before the end of the war. By this time, early in 1945, Lippisch was concentrating on turbojet-powered delta-wing studies, the first of which was the P 11; this was to have been powered by two Junkers Jumo 004 turbojets buried in the delta wing and fed via wing root intakes. Two vertical tail surfaces were to have been fitted to the straight trailing edge of the wing. Maximum speed was estimated, perhaps optimistically, as 645 mph at 19,500 ft, with a cruising speed of 528 mph and a still-air range of 1,860 miles.

The second of Lippisch's delta-wing designs, the P 12, was to have used a ramjet engine burning solid fuel in the form of small pieces of brown coal carried in a wire mesh container mounted in the intake duct at a slight angle to the airflow. The idea was that oxygen in the airstream, passing through the solid fuel and ignited by a gas burner, would mingle with more oxygen passing through the unobstructed upper part of the duct to form carbon dioxide. The necessary speed for the ramjet to work would have been achieved by an auxiliary rocket motor. A more advanced version of this unorthodox aircraft, the P 13A, was at a very advanced design stage when the war ended, although construction of a prototype was never started.

Alexander Lippisch was the true originator of the practical delta-wing concept, although British, French and American designers had investigated the aerodynamic value of all-wing designs before and during the war (the French contribution, of course, having been curtailed by the armistice in 1940). The major British exponent of the field was Armstrong-Whitworth Aircraft Ltd, who began serious design studies in May 1943; these culminated in a small two-seat all-wing research glider, the AW 52G, which made its first flight on March 3 1945. Aerodynamic characteristics were good, and the glider was followed by two full-size AW 52s, one powered by two Rolls-Royce Nene turbojets and the other by Derwents. The Derwent-powered aircraft went out of control and crashed in 1949; test pilot Jo Lancaster escaped by using his ejector seat, the first Briton to do so.

In the United States, Northrop Aircraft Incorporated had amassed a vast background of experience in the design of all-wing aircraft since 1941, when the company had initiated a 'flying wing' bomber project. The first of Northrop's all-wing bombers was designated XB-35, and two prototypes were ordered by the USAAF for evaluation in 1942. Construction of the first prototype, which was powered by four Pratt and Whitney Wasp radial engines driving eight-blade 'pusher' contra-rotating propellers, was begun in January 1943, and in the meantime Northrop built four 60-foot-span one-third scale flying models to provide flight data. The full-size aircraft eventually flew on June 25 1946, and although some trouble was experienced with the propeller governing mechanisms and the engine reduction gears, the flight characteristics appeared to vindicate Northrop's faith in the all-wing concept and the company was allocated funds for the construction of a pre-production batch of 13 more aircraft.

The bulk of the research into all-wing designs undertaken by Armstrong-Whitworth and Northrop was carried out before the war's end, and therefore did not benefit at this stage from captured German material; material which, despite determined German efforts to destroy much of it, still remained intact in large quantities at locations all over

Germany and became the object of a race between the Allies in which the British came a poor second, and in some cases a poor third. There were two reasons for this: one was geographical, the other a matter of supreme American initiative. The principal geographical problem, as far as the British were concerned, was that the route of their advance in the closing weeks of the war lay through northern Germany, an area from which most secret research facilities had long since been removed to the more secure mountainous regions of central and southern Germany. This placed them precisely in the path of the American advance, so it was hardly surprising that the bulk of the material was destined to fall into American hands. Apart from that, long before the end of the war, every branch of the United States armed forces had formed its own team of specialists, given the task of ferreting out secret material and the scientists responsible for it within its own area of responsibility. The British had a comparable organisation, but nothing on the American scale. The USAAF team was led by a Lieutenant Morton Hunt who, in May 1945, went into the Dessau area of central Germany with specific orders to remove everything of aeronautical research value before the territory became part of the Soviet occupation zone. In less than a week Hunt and his men removed a staggering quantity of documentation, as well as a number of key scientists and their entire households. The scientists included Dr Lippisch and Dr von Dopp, designer of a supersonic wind tunnel used by Junkers in advanced flight research. There was no trouble in persuading any of the scientists to leave; all Hunt needed to do was to point out that the Russians would be occupying the area in a few days' time. The scientists and engineers were eventually concentrated at Fort Bliss, in Texas, and were employed almost immediately in assisting American experts to sift through the mass of captured paperwork.

Aeronautical material, including airworthy aircraft, captured by the British was assembled at the Royal Aircraft Establishment, Farnborough, under the direction of a team of experts from the Aerodynamics Flight headed by Captain Eric M. Brown, RN. The captured aircraft, including jets like the Me 262, He 162 and Arado 234, were pooled and selected examples flight tested before being ferried to No 6 Maintenance Unit at RAF Brize Norton to await disposal. The reports compiled by the RAE staff on the performance and aerodynamic characteristics of individual machines, together with translations of captured technical data, were subsequently circulated among the various British aircraft manufacturers, and were to have a profound effect on the future course of high-speed aerodynamic research.

Yet such research progressed slowly in Britain during the immediate post-war years; there was a far greater sense of urgency in the United States, fostered not only by the availability of substantial research and development funds, but also by the recognition of a growing threat from Soviet Russia to the security of the western world. At the war's end in 1945 the Soviet Air Force had no true strategic bombing capability, but a year later the picture was beginning to change. In the autumn of 1944, three American B-29 Superfortress bombers had made emergency landings in Russian territory following attacks on targets in Japan, and within two years the Russians succeeded in building and flying a copy, the Tupolev Tu-4, neatly shattering all US Intelligence estimates that the Russians would not have a strategic bomber until the early 1950s. In 1946, when the Tu-4 made its first flight, the standard long-range bomber of the US Strategic Air Command was still the B-29; admittedly, a replacement was on the way in the shape of the giant Convair B-36, the first bomber in the world with a truly global capability, but this was still a piston-engined type and was not sufficiently advanced to give Strategic Air Command a clear lead over whatever new designs the Russians might produce as a result of their experience with the B-29/Tu-4. The first XB-36 flew in August 1946, and Strategic Air Command anticipated deliveries of the first production machines a year later.

WD280 *was the first Avro 707A and was flown for the first time by Roly Falk on June 14 1951. The 707A was designed for high-speed research and continued work of this type in Australia after 1956. It is now preserved in Melbourne.*

Meantime, Boeing, Convair, Martin and North American had all submitted designs in response to a USAAF specification for a medium jet bomber. Two were selected, of which the first was North American's B-45 Tornado. Powered by four General Electric turbojets, the prototype XB-45 flew for the first time on March 17 1947, and the first production examples entered USAAF service during the following year.

Nevertheless, the B-45 was a very conventional design—far more conventional in many ways than Convair's mighty B-36—and did not employ any advanced aerodynamic concepts. In any case, its still-air range was restricted to about 1,200 miles, so it was a tactical rather than a strategic bomber. Strategic Air Command's hopes, therefore, were pinned on the design submitted by the Boeing Aircraft Company, which had been initiated in September 1945 as the Model 450. The aircraft was a radical departure from conventional design, featuring a thin, flexible wing—heavily based on wartime German research data—with 35 degrees of sweep and carrying six turbojets in underwing pods, the main undercarriage being housed in the fuselage. Basic design studies were completed in June 1946, and the aircraft made its first flight as the XB-47 Stratojet on December 17 1947. It would eventually enter service with Strategic Air Command in 1951. With the advent of the B-47, SAC had the capability to deliver nuclear weapons to virtually any target inside the Soviet Union, at speeds and altitudes that would have made the aircraft almost impossible to be intercepted by the current generation of Soviet jet fighters. The B-47, in fact, marked the true beginning of the western world's nuclear deterrent force.

In 1946, when the prototype of the futuristic XB-47 was under construction, the heavy bomber squadrons of Royal Air Force Bomber Command were just starting to be equipped with the Avro Lincoln, descended from the famous Lancaster. Powered by four Rolls-Royce Merlin engines, the Lincoln had a top speed of only 290 mph—nearly 100 mph slower than the B-29—and an operational ceiling of only 22,000 ft. Conceived in 1943 as a Lancaster replacement, it was a classic example of a policy that had been followed by British aircraft designers throughout the war years, a policy that had called for the development and refinement of existing designs rather than the initiation of new ones. The logic behind this thinking was not difficult to see. In 1944 the sustained bombing offensive mounted by the RAF and USAAF was steadily bringing the German war economy to a standstill; precision daylight attacks by the USAAF, combined with 'area' attacks by the RAF at night, were at last achieving the desired result. When the British Air Staff had formulated the specification for the two principal heavy bombers then in service, the Lancaster and the Halifax, it had been decided to sacrifice range, speed and altitude in favour of a maximum bomb load. Both types were therefore able to carry a respectable tonnage of bombs (22,000 lb maximum, in the case of the Lancaster) over medium ranges, which meant that the potential destruction that could be wrought by individual aircraft was far greater than that of their American contemporaries, the B-17 Flying Fortress and the B-24 Liberator, whose capacity bomb load over even short ranges was less than half that of the British machines.

Bomber Command's destructive potential in 1944 was therefore adequate for the task in hand, and even if the war were to have dragged on for another two or three years that task would have remained much the same, even if the Command's main effort had been switched to the Pacific Theatre, against Japan. So the Avro Lincoln, which could carry a 14,000 lb bomb load over a range of 2,250 miles, was selected to meet the requirements of Air Staff Specification B 14/43, and there was no reason to suppose that it would fall short of any operational task that would be demanded of it in the foreseeable future.

In the summer of 1945, a RAF heavy bomber force—Tiger Force—based on several squadrons of Lincolns was being readied for operations against Japan when, on August 6, a single atomic bomb dropped by a B-29 wiped the town of Hiroshima off the map, to be closely followed by a second which destroyed Nagasaki. Overnight, the well-tried policies which had enabled Bomber Command to devastate Germany's industrial cities were turned upside down; a single aircraft could now obliterate a city with one bomb. Such an aircraft, however, had to possess sufficient speed and altitude to escape the devastating effects of its own atomic weapon. No aircraft in the world other than the B-29 could have carried out the nuclear attacks on Hiroshima and Nagasaki; the Lancaster and the B-17 could not have done so, and neither could the Lincoln, the aircraft which was now destined to form the main equipment of Bomber Command's heavy units during the immediate post-war years.

At the beginning of 1946, despite the obvious need for a strategic jet bomber capable of nuclear weapons delivery to replace the Lincoln, the British Ministry of Supply had yet to issue a specification for such an aircraft. The only jet bomber specification so far issued, in fact, was B 3/45, and this was written around a tactical aircraft designed for the radar bombing role with conventional weapons; it was eventually to materialise in the English Electric Canberra, the prototype of which flew on May 13 1949.

One of the problems that bedevilled British thinking on the design of a strategic jet bomber at this stage was that there was, as yet, no clear idea of the configuration of the weapon such an aircraft would have to carry. Despite the fact that British scientists had been instrumental in initiating the Allied atomic bomb project during the war, and had collaborated fully with the Americans in bringing an operational weapon to fruition, the

Americans chose to make no exception in the case of the British when, in August 1946, they clamped down on the release of nuclear information to other nations under the terms of the McMahon Act. This meant, simply, that any nuclear weapons carried by future British bombers would have to be of indigenous design.

Fortunately, Britain still had access to supplies of uranium from various sources; also fortunately, nuclear research had been progressing in Canada, independently of that undertaken in the USA. In September 1945, at Chalk River, about 150 miles west of Ottawa, a small nuclear reactor built under the direction of an Anglo-Canadian team went critical for the first time, the first to do so outside the USA, and the knowledge gained in this and subsequent experiments was pooled with that of the British scientists who had worked on the American atomic bomb project. This success was followed, in October 1945, by a recommendation of the Joint Chiefs of Staff that Britain should begin to develop her own nuclear weapons, although no political decision was forthcoming at that time.

Nevertheless, some progress towards this ultimate goal was made on January 29 1946, when the Prime Minister, Clement Attlee, appointed Lord Portal as Controller of Atomic Energy. An Atomic Energy Bill was drafted, transferring control of the British atomic energy project from the Department of Scientific and Industrial Research to the Ministry of Supply. The design and construction of a plutonium reactor had already been approved in December 1945; the necessary theoretical studies were to be carried out by a team under Professor (later Sir John) Cockcroft, Portal's Director of Research, who set up his headquarters on an old airfield site at Harwell, near Oxford. At the same time, a Research Team directed by the Deputy Controller, Christopher Hinton, established itself in an old munitions factory at Risley, in Lancashire, and work started in May 1946 to turn a disused poison gas factory at Springfields, near Blackpool, into a uranium metal plant.

The government finally took the decision to embark on an independent British nuclear weapons programme in January 1947, and to run the military side of things brought in William (later Lord) Penney, Chief Superintendent of Armament Research at the Ministry of Supply. Penney had been deeply involved with the American atomic bomb project, and had been one of two British observers of the atomic attack on Nagasaki (the other was Group Captain Leonard Cheshire, VC). Working closely with Penney was a ten-man team of RAF weapons specialists led by Wing Commander J.S. Rowlands.

In the meantime, anticipating the government's decision to go ahead with a nuclear weapons programme, the Air Staff, under the chairmanship of the CAS, Lord Tedder, had drafted a requirement for a British atomic bomb and also for an aircraft which would be capable of delivering it to its target. The bomb configuration was based on that of the 10-ton 'Grand Slam', used on a limited scale by Bomber Command in the closing months of the war; the proposed weapon would be of similar length, in other words about 25 ft, but would be lighter, weighing some 10,000 lb. In this respect—and also in its projected explosive power of about 22 kilotons—it was similar to the Nagasaki bomb, which was also a plutonium weapon, although the British bomb would be far more streamlined and aerodynamically clean.

The first specification for a new jet bomber, B 35/46, which was issued by the Ministry of Supply on January 7 1947 and which was based on the Air Staff's Operational Requirement 229 dated December 17 1946, was formidable in its demands. It required an aircraft which would be capable of carrying a 10,000 lb weapons load over a still-air range of 3,350 nautical miles at 500 knots, with an over-the-target ceiling of 50,000 ft; it would also have to carry a 20,000 lb bomb load over shorter ranges. For this purpose, and also to accommodate the envisaged nuclear weapon, its weapons bay would have to measure 25 ft in length by 5 ft in diameter. It was to have a five-man crew, accommodated in a jettisonable pressure cabin; pressure would be maintained at 9 lb per square inch—equivalent to an altitude of 8,000 ft above sea level—during cruise to the target at 45,000 ft, reducing to 3.5 lb per square inch over the target to reduce the risk of explosive decompression if the cabin should be damaged by enemy fire.

On January 9 1947, Avro, Armstrong-Whitworth, Bristol, English Electric, Handley Page and Short Brothers were all invited to submit tenders. Handley Page appeared to be a step ahead of the rest, for in June 1945 their chief designer, Reginald Stafford, had gone on a mission to Germany to gather information on high-speed aerodynamic research, with particular reference to tail-less designs. (The company had, in fact, built and flown an experimental tail-less aircraft, the Manx, in 1943.) In October, Stafford's deputy, Godfrey Lee, had also gone to Germany to study all-wing data on behalf of the Royal Aircraft Establishment and to gather as much material as still remained on advanced high-speed designs, particularly those of the Arado company, which had built the world's first jet bomber, the Ar 234. With the help of this valuable information, the Handley Page team at Cricklewood set about designing a tail-less jet bomber with a wing swept at an angle of 45 degrees and tipped with vertical fins and rudders. This design had been submitted to the Ministry of Aircraft Production as early as June 1946, six months before B 35/46 was issued, and when Handley Page was asked to tender for that specification it was logical that Stafford's team should seek to meet the requirement with a more advanced version of the earlier project. Handley Page considered both delta and swept wing planforms, neither of which seemed to offer an ideal solution, so they decided to combine the two and designed a wing featuring three different degrees of sweep, ranging from 53 degrees at the root to 22 degrees at the tip. Once again, the idea was based on a wing designed by the Arado firm in 1944. The wing was married to a lengthy fuselage surmounted by a tall, swept fin and rudder on top of which was set a crescent-shaped tailplane, and the design was given the type number HP 80.

The designs submitted by Armstrong-Whitworth, Bristol and English Electric never progressed beyond the project stage, but the submission of Vickers-Armstrongs (Aircraft) Ltd at Weybridge showed considerable promise. Like Handley Page, Vickers had been involved in jet bomber design studies for some time—since 1944, in fact. These studies had been undertaken in parallel with work on the development of a new piston-engined bomber, the Windsor, which early in 1945 seemed fair set to join the Avro Lincoln as Bomber Command's second new 'heavy'. Three prototypes had flown, four more were under construction, and 300 production aircraft were on order. Then, suddenly, jet engine technology made the piston-engined bomber obsolete overnight, and the Windsor programme was cancelled. Vickers therefore channelled their resources into the development of their jet bomber design. Designated Vickers Type 660, it was a relatively conventional aircraft, employing well-tried aerodynamic principles; the problem was that its performance did not match up to what was required by B 35/46, so it was rejected. But the design was saved by its conventional nature, which meant that the aircraft could be 'built quickly, with few unknown aerodynamic characteristics to be sorted out, and in the end a new specification—B 9/48—was written around it, with Vickers receiving an 'Instruction to Proceed' with the building of two prototypes in April 1948. The Type 660 was regarded as an interim aircraft, an insurance against the failure of more radical designs submitted by other manufacturers, but it was to become much more than that. As the Vickers Valiant, it was destined to be the mainstay of Bomber Command's nuclear strike force during the 1950s.

The design submitted by Short Brothers was also conventional, but this was really in response to another specification, B 14/46, which was issued in August 1947. This was also in the form of an insurance against the failure of the more advanced designs, and the requirement was for an aircraft with the same range as B 35/46, but with a lower ceiling of 45,000 ft and a speed of 390 knots instead of 500. Short Brothers' answer to this was the SA 4 Sperrin, the prototype of which eventually flew in August 1951. Had the need arisen, there is no doubt that this aircraft could have been manufactured very quickly as a Lincoln replacement, and would have effectively stopped a dangerous gap. As it was, only two prototypes were built, and these were used to carry out a variety of trials in connexion with the strategic bomber programme, including the testing of bomb shapes to determine the ballistic properties of future nuclear weapons.

Meanwhile, in January 1947, A.V. Roe and Company at Chadderton, Manchester, had begun preliminary work on a design—or series of designs—in a bid to fulfil the Air Staff's OR 229. At that time, the design office at Chadderton was preoccupied with the Avro Tudor airliner and an uprated maritime version of the Lincoln known as the GR 3; this would eventually become the Shackleton. The six-man design team in the firm's Projects Department was led by Stuart Davies, who had assumed the post of chief designer when the previous incumbent, Roy Chadwick, was elevated to the position of technical director. Davies summed up the formidable problems confronting his team:

'It was obvious from the start that no conventional aircraft, as we then knew them, would do the job the Air Staff were asking for. We knew something about swept-back wings even in those days—we gathered quite a lot from the Germans on that score—and it was obvious that any successful bomber would have to have a fair amount of sweep-back on its wings. We went ahead with our preliminary sketches, and it became increasingly obvious that we were going to exceed the maximum all-up weight by a considerable amount. The first idea we produced was an aircraft three times as big as the machine the Air Staff wanted—and we could still not see how we could get the performance they required. The next stage in our thinking turned against the Air Staff's requirements. Are they ridiculous? Have they made a mistake to ask for all those qualities in one aircraft? These were the sort of questions we asked ourselves. Then we started to think again and studied projects embodying thin swept-back wings and low wing loading in various configurations. The high specified cruising speed more or less fixed these design features at values which for a conventional aircraft meant more structure weight than we could afford, and as this meant a corresponding reduction in payload the concept was rendered quite uneconomical. Stalemate seemed to have been reached until, as our next step, we investigated the possibility of using the tips of our highly-swept wing for longitudinal control. This seemed to be a move in the right direction, for it meant elimination of the weight and drag of the tailplane. But we were still faced with a wing design which seemed too large and too heavy for what it had to do.'

The preliminary series of Avro designs culminated in one which featured a wing with 45 degrees of sweep and swept tail surfaces, but as Davies pointed out the weight penalty here was enormous—greatly in excess of the 100,000 lb limit imposed by B 35/46. The gross weight, in fact, would have been nearly twice that, and the performance of the projected aircraft would have been much lower than required. There were four options open to the Avro team. The first was a relatively conventional design for high speed and long range, with a thin wing incorporating a sharp sweepback angle and large span; for reasons mentioned above, such a design would be expensive to build, almost three times as big as the one required by the specification, and prohibitively heavy. The second option envisaged a similar aircraft dimensionally, in which the function of the tailplane was replaced by wingtip controls, but this introduced a spate of mechanical complications, and the wing was still too large and heavy. The third option was to consider a smaller aircraft, with the same wing area as the first two designs. In this case, a reduction in wing span also meant a reduction in weight, which was a step in the right direction, but the

The Avro 707B, VX790, was the second in the 707 series and was similar to the prototype, VX784. Designed for low-speed trials, it flew for the first time on September 6 1950.

problem remained of where to stow the payload, undercarriage and fuel tanks; the available space would not give the aircraft sufficient range to meet the demands of B 35/46.

By this time, Stuart Davies and Robert Lindley (who was in charge of the Projects Office and who years later was to become deeply involved in the McDonnell Aircraft Corporation's Mercury space capsule programme) were firmly convinced that the answer lay with an all-wing design; it was a conclusion that had taken four or five weeks of hard work to reach. The projects team had studied all available German material in this particular area, and had also drawn on the results of the tail-less research carried out by Armstrong-Whitworth, as well as on knowledge gained from working on designs for a jet-engined civil transport known as the Brabazon 3, which never progressed beyond the project stage. In addition, the Avro men had been observing with interest the progress being made in the United States by the Northrop Company and their all-wing XB-35; because of problems with the piston engines, plans were afoot to convert the existing XB-35s to turbojet power under the designation YB-49.

'The outstanding difficulty,' said Davies, 'was the excessive weight of the wing, and a series of exercises was undertaken to reduce the span of the wing and so the weight. At the same time we had to make sure that we did not upset unduly the inter-relation of other factors, including sweepback, thickness and wing area. So we reduced the weight by reducing the span, and, as this reduced the area, which we didn't want to do, we put the area back by filling in the space between the swept-back wing and the fuselage. The result of all this logical thinking was the delta.'

It was indeed logical; the delta configuration now made it possible to bury the engines, fuel and undercarriage in the wing, which was still slim enough to achieve the necessary high performance and was structurally a much simpler proposition than the designs considered so far. Roy Chadwick, who had gone down with shingles, came back to work and liked the delta idea immediately; he was very much an advocate of all-wing designs, and had made some studies in the field before the war.

Further calculations began to show that there was every likelihood of the delta design meeting the Air Staff requirement, and from March 1947 the aircraft began to take firmer shape on the drawing board under the project designation Avro Type 698. Nevertheless, it was still a long way from what it would eventually become before a prototype made its first flight. In this early configuration, the crew compartment, surmounted by a perspex blister, was built into the apex of the triangle formed by the delta wing; there was no projecting nose. The powerplants were to be four Bristol BE 10 engines, two buried in the thick centre section of the wing on either side of the centreline; the bomb bays were to be situated outboard, between the engines and the main undercarriage, and there was provision for one weapons bay on either side to serve as a housing for extra fuel tanks, if needed. The wings were tipped with small, swept fins and rudders, and double elevons ran along the length of the trailing edge. The flying controls were based on the system fitted to the Armstrong-Whitworth AW 52 research aircraft, which had yet to fly in its jet-powered version.

Given the radical nature of the design, the management of A.V. Roe took a courageous step in giving their full backing to the project team, who in May 1947 submitted detailed drawings to the Ministry of Supply. The Ministry were cautiously interested, and the Projects Department went on to produce more intricate documents dealing with various aspects of the new design's structure while the official tender for the job was prepared. A hard fight lay ahead, and Roy Chadwick plunged into the thick of it valiantly, hammering home the merits of the Avro design in the offices of both Air Ministry and Ministry of Supply in the face of fierce competition and often criticism from his fellow designers at Vickers and Handley Page. There is little doubt that Chadwick's tremendous reputation in the aeronautical design field helped to carry him through round after round; a man who had designed the Lancaster would clearly not give his approval lightly to, nor fight so hard for, a concept that had only a marginal chance of success.

In the summer of 1947 things were at last starting to move more rapidly towards the fulfilment of B 35/46. On July 28 there was a tender design conference at the Ministry of Supply; the progress made so far by the contending companies was reviewed, and the real competition narrowed down to Handley Page and Avro. Then, just a few weeks later, came a terrible blow which threatened to jeopardise Avro's chances: Roy Chadwick was killed when the prototype of the Tudor 2 airliner, *G-AGSU*, crashed on take-off at Woodford because of an aileron malfunction, the controls having been fitted the wrong way round. For a few critical weeks, Ministry interest in the Avro project waned, for it was felt in some circles that Chadwick's untimely death might have an adverse effect on further development work. However, Chadwick's place as technical director was filled by William S. Farren, a man who had been a former director of the RAE at Farnborough and who had, like Chadwick, the highest reputation in the aeronautical world. He carried on the fight Chadwick had begun, and his efforts contributed greatly to the MoS decision, on November 27 1947, to accept the Avro tender. The decision came as an enormous relief to the Avro team, for a week earlier, on November 19, Handley Page had been awarded a prototype contract for their HP 80.

This was followed, on January 1 1948, by an Instruction to Proceed with the building of two Avro 698 prototypes. This meant simply that, although there was not yet a firm commitment to issue a production contract, the Ministry would allocate funds for further development work. 'It was their job to "shoot the thing down" if they could,' Stuart Davies said later. 'Experts in all branches of aeronautical science examined our documents, and word came through to the company at the end of 1947 "Go ahead and build a prototype". It was a bold decision, and I believe the Air Staff at that time showed foresight in demanding the high performance in their requirements; and courage in placing an order when no previous delta-wing aircraft had flown.'

In the weeks before the ITP was issued, the Type 698 had undergone radical design changes. Following extensive wind tunnel tests at Farnborough, the design team had recognised a need to reduce the thickness/chord ratio of the delta wing, which ruled out the original intention of mounting the four Bristol BE 10 engines in superimposed pairs. It was therefore decided to relocate the engines side by side, which in turn cancelled out the weapons bays in the wings; a single weapons bay was now designed to fit into a ventral bulge under the wing centreline. The reduction of the thickness/chord ratio also led to the emergence of a fuselage, with a nose projecting some distance ahead of the wing and housing the crew compartment, the radar and some of the fuel. The engines were still served by large circular air intakes; exhaust was by way of four paired jet pipes, with a short rear fuselage cone between them.

The control system underwent changes, too. In the spring of 1948 the designers were investigating the possibility of using moveable wingtips to achieve lateral control, but in the summer of that year the idea of wingtip controls was abandoned, and the wingtip fins themselves were deleted in favour of a more conventional centrally-mounted fin and rudder. Apart from reasons of aerodynamic stability, the designers considered that a central fin would provide a convenient mounting for a tailplane, should one be needed. Along the trailing edge of the delta wing, the elevons were split up into separate ailerons and elevators. The engine intakes also underwent redesign, losing their big circular configuration and becoming rectangular. By September 1948, when Avro and various associated companies were hard at work on the design of the systems that were to be incorporated in the Type 698, the design was well on its way to being finalised.

During 1948, the Avro team had been much preoccupied by the fact that a pure delta aircraft had never been flight-tested, and hardly any information was available on the likely characteristics of such a design at either high or low speeds, or for that matter at altitudes of up to 50,000 ft, at which the bomber would be expected to operate. Only a matter of weeks after receiving the ITP, the Advanced Bomber Project Group within the company had therefore decided to build a small-scale delta research aircraft, powered by a single engine, to carry out low-speed handling trials, and a larger twin-engined delta to investigate handling characteristics at speeds of up to 0.95M and altitudes of up to 60,000 ft.

Specification E 15/48 was written around the first aircraft, construction of which was started in the summer of 1948. It was designated Avro Type 707 and was powered by a Rolls-Royce Derwent turbojet. It was a very simple design, with considerable emphasis on economy; the main undercarriage, for example, came from an Avro Athena trainer, while the cockpit canopy and nosewheel unit were taken from a Meteor.

In September 1948, while the Avro 707 was building, the company had second thoughts about the twin-engined high-speed model, which was to have been designated Avro 710 and powered by a pair of Rolls-Royce Avons. Confidence in the way the full-scale Type 698 was progressing was building up all the time, and it was now decided that it would not be necessary to build scale models to investigate the whole of the flight envelope. The 710 was therefore dropped after consultation with the ministry, and the requirement was altered to encompass two low-speed 707s, one high-speed 707A and a full-size Type 698, stripped of all but the most essential equipment. After more consideration, however, the stripped-down 698 was also deemed unnecessary, and the programme now concentrated on the 707s as a build-up to the flight of the first prototype 698.

The first Avro 707, serialled *VX784*, was completed at Woodford in August 1949, and after some ground running and taxiing trials was dismantled and taken to the Aeroplane and Armament Experimental Establishment at Boscombe Down, where it was put together again and made ready for its first flight. This was scheduled for September 3, but had to be postponed because of a crosswind component which was outside the aircraft's limits, and it was not until 19:30 hours on September 4 that *VX784* finally took to the air in the hands of Flight Lieutenant Eric S. Esler, deputy chief test pilot on the A&AEE. The little aircraft handled well, and during the next two days Esler made two more flights totalling two and a half hours, after which the 707 was flown to Farnborough to take part in the static display at that year's SBAC show. It was then returned to Boscombe Down for the installation of data measuring equipment, which was checked out during the aircraft's third flight in the last week of September.

So far, the flight characteristics of the 707 had proved to be quite unremarkable; the only real difference between the delta and the other types Esler had flown seemed to be that the 707 needed a fair length of runway before unstick speed was reached. It therefore came as a profound shock to both Avro and the A&AEE when, on September 30, the aircraft crashed near Blackbushe, killing Esler. The true cause of the accident was never fully established, although it was suspected that the 707's airbrakes had locked in the 'fully out' position following a malfunction in one of the control circuits, resulting in a low-speed stall at low altitude. What was important, from the technical point of view, was that the delta configuration had in no way been responsible for the crash.

Meanwhile, building of the second Type 707, *VX790*, went ahead. This was a much more refined aircraft than the first prototype, incorporating a redesigned airbrake system, modified elevators and an ejector seat. The installation of new data measuring equipment required a redesigned nose, so to save time and expense the nose originally intended for the 707A high-speed variant was quickly built and installed. Like the first 707, *VX790* had a main undercarriage taken from an Avro Athena, but the nosewheel unit had belonged to a Hawker P1052 research aircraft.

Like its predecessor, *VX790* was taken by road to Boscombe Down in August 1950 and made ready for flight testing. The first flight was.scheduled for the evening of September 5 and was to be made by Wing Commander R.J. 'Roly' Falk, who had recently joined Avro as chief test pilot after a spell as experimental test pilot with Vickers-Armstrongs Ltd. Before that, in 1943, he had been Chief Test Pilot at the RAE, Farnborough. However, by the time preparations for the flight were completed darkness was falling, so the flight had to be postponed. The runway lights were switched on and Falk contented himself with carrying out some taxi trials, culminating in a short 'hop' of a few yards. The first flight proper was made the following day, and lasted 15 minutes; it presented no problems, and Falk, impressed by the way the 707B handled, immediately telephoned Sir Roy Dobson, managing director of A.V. Roe and Co, and Air Marshal J.N. Boothman, the Controller of Supplies (Air), to obtain permission for the aircraft to appear in the static display at the 1950 SBAC show. This was granted, and the little blue 707B, with Falk at the controls, appeared over Farnborough just as the first day's display was ending, bringing a halt to the homeward progress of the crowds as he circled overhead to allow the giant Bristol Brabazon to clear the runway before making his approach to land.

After remaining at Farnborough for a week, the 707B went back to Boscombe Down to take up its flight test programme, which was carried out both at the A&AEE and Dunsfold.

The aircraft's flight characteristics were investigated over the entire speed range of 80–350 knots, and during these trials it was found that the aircraft's dorsal air intake suffered from air starvation at high speed. The cause of this was discovered to be turbulence from the cockpit canopy, and modifications had to be made before the complete flight envelope could be probed. The machine also tended to oscillate in the pitching plane as a result of out-of-phase movement of the manually-operated elevators; this was something which would not manifest itself in the full-size Type 698, which had power-operated controls. Another modification was to the nosewheel leg, which was lengthened by 9 ins to increase the angle of incidence between the fuselage and the ground, enabling the elevators to 'bite' earlier in the take-off run and so reduce the unstick distance.

Much of the information gleaned from the 707B flight test programme had no relevance whatsoever to the Type 698 development; but some useful contributions were made, and as a result of flight experience with the 707B a number of design changes were incorporated in the 698, including a reduction of fin area and the angling of the jet pipe nozzles to compensate for longitudinal stability and trim variations with different power settings. The 707B completed about 100 hours of research flying for Avro until September 1951, after which it was sent to Boscombe Down to take part in other research programmes.

In the meantime, the first detailed drawings of the Type 698 had been passed over to the factory in May 1950, Avro having received a firm contract for the building of two 698s in July 1948, but now the whole programme was subjected to a series of delays. One reason was that the Avro design office was heavily involved in work on the Avro Shackleton, which was desperately needed by Coastal Command; the other was that work on the 698 had actually overtaken the 707 research programme, which had been intended as a preliminary to the production of a full-size aircraft. The high-speed 707A, which was intended to provide valuable data on the upper reaches of the delta flight envelope, was still a long way from making its first flight at the end of 1950, even though the decision to build it (to Specification E 10/49) had been taken that summer. By the time the 707A eventually flew at Boscombe Down on July 14 1951, however, metal for the 698 was already being cut, and subsequent design changes had nothing to do with the 707 programme, with one important exception. For example, some redesign of the 698's wing, involving the blending of the engine air intakes into the wing root, came as a result of wind tunnel tests at Farnborough, while the engines themselves had changed; the company, realising that the proposed Bristol BE 10 power plant (later named Olympus) would probably not be ready in time, was considering the Armstrong Siddeley Sapphire and the Rolls-Royce Avon as possible alternatives, and this too meant the redesign of various systems.

Nevertheless, it was decided to go ahead with the 707A programme on the pretext of testing the new wing and intake design, and this aircraft—*WD280*—was certainly much closer in configuration to the full-size 698 than the earlier 707s had been, having wing root intakes, ailerons and elevators to scale and servo tabs and balances to assist the manual controls. In the course of its working life for Avro the 707A put in some 92 hours of research flying, most of which, as previously stated, had no bearing on the design of the 698. The one important exception was that the airframe was found to vibrate badly at high speed and altitude; this was eventually cured by putting a 'kink' in the leading edges of the delta wing, but by the time the solution was found the 698 was already in production and the leading edges of the first 16 aircraft had to be scrapped. Had the 707A flown earlier, as part of a properly synchronised flight research programme, this costly flaw would have been discovered and rectified before it was too late.

The 707A prototype remained in the United Kingdom until 1956, flying in various RAE research programmes, after which it was shipped to Australia to take part in further aerodynamic research there. It was later sold off privately and put on display in Melbourne. Two more aircraft in the 707 series were built by Avro; the first, another 707A (*WZ736*) was used by the RAE for automatic throttle development. In 1967, it went to the aircraft museum at RAF Finningley, in Yorkshire. The second aircraft, the 707C (*WZ744*) had been originally designed as a prototype two-seat, side-by-side delta trainer and flew for the first time on July 1 1953, afterwards being used in the development of power controls and electronic systems by the RAE. It was also withdrawn in 1967, and went to the museum at RAF Cosford, near Wolverhampton.

Although, from a development point of view, the contribution made by the 707 programme had been disappointing, mainly because the whole business had been poorly timed, the flight research—apart from Esler's tragic crash—had gone relatively smoothly, and had been of immeasurable value in vindicating the delta concept. In the United States, Northrop's all-wing designs had suffered far worse fortunes: both prototypes of the YB-49 jet bomber had exploded in mid-air during testing, killing their crews, and the programme had been abandoned.

Meanwhile, in 1951, construction of the prototype Avro 698 had got under way, after a further three-month delay caused by a need to redesign the wing root. Wind tunnel tests at the RAE had revealed that the induced drag on the wing designed by Avro, which was constant in section, would be sufficient to bring about a marked reduction in planned performance at high speed and altitude, as the fuselage airflow was creating uneven pressure distribution over the wings. This was cured by making the wing section thickest at the root leading edge instead of further aft, but the redesign was a major operation involving some 200 draughtsmen.

Gradually, despite all the snags, the great delta wing of the Type 698 took shape at Woodford, while the rest of the airframe was built at Chadderton. There remained, however, the problem of the engines. The proposed powerplant, the Bristol BE 10 (Olympus), had been ground tested at Patchway for the first time on May 6 1950; with a thrust of 11,000 lb it was then the most powerful turbojet in the world, and plans to manufacture it under licence in the United States were already advanced. But in the spring of 1952 the engine was still being ground run, and Avro, in the knowledge that the BE 10 would not be ready in time, selected the 6,500 lb st Rolls-Royce Avon RA 3 engine to power the 698 instead.

Under wraps, the various bits and pieces of the 698 that were built at Chadderton were transported to Woodford on low-loaders to be married to the wing. The fuselage sections caused some transport problems as they negotiated the streets of Stockport, but there were no mishaps and good progress was made with the final assembly of the prototype. Everyone involved with the project, from top to bottom, worked like a slave to get the aircraft ready to fly in time for the 1952 SBAC Show, and also to beat Handley Page's HP 80 into the air. It was known that the Handley Page design was nearing completion, and the Avro team was spurred to still greater efforts when, in August 1952, it was learned that the Ministry of Supply had issued production contracts for an initial batch of 25 of each type.

The effort was not in vain. In the last week of August 1952 the great delta, resplendently beautiful in its gleaming white paintwork, broken only by the Royal Air Force roundels and the serial number, *VX770*, was rolled out of the big assembly hangar at Woodford for the first time. It did not yet have a name. That would come, officially, a month later, when the identity bestowed upon the new bomber would, appropriately, be that of the Roman god of fire and destruction: Vulcan.

Chapter 2

Testing and development: the B 1

It had taken Avro just 28 months to build the prototype 698, a remarkably short time in which to produce such a revolutionary aircraft, especially in view of the delays that had beset the programme. Now, with participation at Farnborough in mind, ground running and taxiing trials with *VX770* were completed in equally record time, and on August 30 1952 the prototype was ready for flight. Roly Falk, Avro's chief test pilot, tells the story of that occasion in his own words:

'It was a large aircraft and was, of course, unlike anything of its size which had flown before. My experience on the 707s had, however, given me the greatest confidence. One fast taxi run was sufficient to satisfy me with regard to ground handling, wheel shimmy and nosewheel lifting speed. I wished to reduce the number of taxi runs to a minimum, in order to avoid the risk of over-heating the brakes. When I was at the end of the runway ready for take-off, I noticed a large number of seagulls on the ground in front of me, and a car was sent to frighten them away so that there could be no possible risk of them either hitting the windscreen or going into the air intakes. A short run and the aircraft lifted smoothly into the air, the undercarriage up when well clear of the ground in case of any unexpected change of trim and a climb to about 10,000 ft, some preliminary manoeuvres in order to get the feel of the controls and that was sufficient for the first flight. After descending, the speed was reduced in circuit of the airfield and the undercarriage lowered.

'As the undercarriage was going down, Flying Control from Woodford called up and told me that something had come adrift from underneath. There was no indication whatsoever in the cockpit that anything had gone wrong and I continued to orbit the airfield, at the same time asking for another aircraft to be sent up to look at the underside of the Vulcan to see what had occurred. Frantic activity was taking place on the ground, the weaving crowd of sightseers looking just like a disturbed ant heap. But as far as I was concerned the aircraft was flying well and the undercarriage operated satisfactorily, so there was no cause for alarm.

'Shortly afterwards, a Vampire and a 707 joined me and both came close underneath to see what had occurred. The trouble was that a maladjusted fairing panel behind one of the undercarriage legs had broken off. [In fact, both panels had separated, and the problem was one of weakness rather than maladjustment. This information was still classified when Falk made this verbal report in 1955.] Reassured by this news, I joined circuit again, descended and landed. Although the landing run was short, the braking parachute was streamed. This has been my practice on all first flights of these aircraft, for it saves both brake wear and proves the mechanism.

'From the start, the Vulcan was laid out with a view to simple operation, both on the ground and in the air. The cockpit was arranged in such a way that the complexity necessary in a modern aircraft was reduced as much as possible. For this reason, there did not appear to be any necessity for a crew of more than one on the early flights. In fact, only one seat was fitted. In some quarters surprise was expressed at this unusual decision, but as all the controls required in flight—even in emergency—were within reach of the

The two Vulcan prototypes, VX770 and VX777, as they appeared at the 1953 Farnborough Show, accompanied by all four Avro 707s.

pilot, the Vulcan could in this respect be considered in the same light as a single-seater. [Another point here, also classified at the time, was that *VX770* had not yet been fitted with cockpit pressurisation, which was why Falk restricted his altitude during the maiden flight to 10,000 ft.]

'Further flights were made as soon as possible and the required flying hours were completed just in time to fly to Boscombe Down and appear in the air over the SBAC Show. Unfortunately, for security reasons, clearance could not be given for a landing to be made at Farnborough for the 1952 display. In the few hours' flying which I did before the display I was able to satisfy myself that the handling of the Vulcan came fully up to the high standard that we had been led to expect from our trials on the 707. And I think that anybody who witnessed the aircraft flying at the display that year would confirm that it set an entirely new standard of manoeuvreability for an aircraft of this size.'

The Type 698 was in fact flown to Boscombe Down on September 1, and from there made five appearances over Farnborough during the week that followed. It was accompanied to the show by the all-blue Type 707B, *VX790*, and the all-red 707A, *WD280*. The impression created by the great white delta was dramatic, and gave the Press plenty of scope for enthusiastic comment: 'Greatest All-Rounder' and 'World-Beater' were two of the milder descriptions which appeared in the headlines on the day after it made its first appearance. Speculation was rife over the name which would be given to the Type 698. The Vickers 660, which had flown in 1951 and which was to become the first of the RAF's V-bombers, had already been named Valiant, so the general assumption was that the Avro design would be given a name beginning with an 'A'. Among the names proposed were Albion, Apollo, Avenger and Assegai, but then the matter was settled by the Chief of Air Staff, Sir John Slessor, who ruled that the names of the Avro and Handley Page aircraft were to begin with 'V'. So the Avro 698 became the Vulcan, and the HP80—which flew on Christmas Eve, 1952—the Victor.

After appearing at Farnborough, the Type 698 was grounded for a few weeks to enable some necessary modifications to be carried out. These included the strengthening of the main undercarriage fairings, some repositioning of instruments, the installation of cockpit pressurisation and a second ejection seat. Flying resumed at the end of October;

principally, this involved handling and systems tests. By the end of January 1953 *VX770* had accumulated 32 hours' flying time and the preliminary test phase was pretty well complete, insofar as the limited power of the Avon engines would allow. For high-speed, high-altitude trials, it was clear that more powerful engines would be needed; since the Olympus was not yet operational—although it had completed its ground running tests in a Vulcan rig and had flown in a Canberra test-bed—*VX770* was grounded again in May 1953 to be fitted with 7,500 lb thrust Armstrong Siddeley Sapphire 6 turbojets. During this period, ground tests were carried out on a revised wing fuel system, which was designed to maintain a constant centre of gravity with shifts of the fuel load.

With this work completed, *VX770* resumed flying in July 1953, the test work including stress gauging, drag measurements, engine handling and the proving of the fuel system. By this time, a Royal Air Force liaison team was working closely with Avro in the test programme; it was headed by Squadron Leader Charles C. Calder, who in March 1945, while flying with No 617 Squadron, had captained the first Lancaster to drop a 22,000 lb 'Grand Slam' bomb on an enemy target, the Bielefeld Viaduct. Calder had gone to Avro's in December 1952 and had made his first flight in the Vulcan on February 18 1953, with Roly Falk as first pilot. The trip lasted about an hour and Calder handled the aircraft for 20 minutes. Later, he said: 'I had heard various rumours regarding the Vulcan's stalling characteristics, and I was determined to find out for myself. So I asked Roly if he would stall the machine. This he promptly did. To my surprise, the aircraft behaved in such a docile manner that I felt there must be some catch in it. Roly must have read my thoughts, for he immediately released the controls and said, "Now you do it!" I stalled the aircraft twice before I was finally convinced.'

Meanwhile, the second prototype Vulcan, *VX777*, was nearing completion at Woodford. This aircraft had a longer nose section than *VX770* to simplify retraction of the nosewheel unit, which had a telescopic oleo on the first prototype, and there was a new bomb-aiming blister under the cockpit. Since this machine was intended for high-altitude trials it carried full pressurisation, and since it was also to be used for navigation and bombing trials it was fitted with the Navigation and Bombing System (NBS) Mk 1, which was a very advanced development of the wartime H2S Mk IV radar. The system was based on the H2S Mk 9A, which had been developed by EMI to meet a very demanding specification that required twice the accuracy at twice the height and twice the speed of the Mk IV. The radar information registered by the Mk 9A was fed into a miniaturised electro-mechanical computer, developed by British Thomson-Houston and known as the Navigation and Bombing Computer (NBC) Mk 2; this kept a constant check on the position, track and groundspeed of the aircraft, and could be locked in to take over automatic control of the bomber during the final run-in to the target, as well as releasing the weapons automatically.

Finally, *VX777* was the first Vulcan to be equipped with the long-awaited Olympus engines; these were the Mk 100 version, developing 9,750 lb thrust, and under their power Roly Falk took the aircraft on its maiden flight on September 3 1953. Like its predecessor, *VX777* had an all-white paint finish, and made an even finer spectacle when it appeared over Farnborough a few days later accompanied by *VX770* and all four Avro 707s, the latter finished in red, orange, blue and silver.

VX777 went to Boscombe Down immediately after Farnborough Week to begin its trials, but it would be a long time before it was in a position to explore the upper speed and altitude ranges of the flight envelope. First of all, the installation of the Olympus engines produced a number of problems which necessitated modifications to the engines themselves, their control systems, and the selective fuel system. A lot of work still remained to be done, too, on the pressurisation and radar systems, and it was not until the spring of 1954 that *VX777* was able to start a comprehensive programme of systems trials. Then came the blow: on July 27 1954, while carrying out trials at the Royal Aircraft Establishment, *VX777* was severely damaged in a heavy landing at Farnborough. The accident came only days after the prototype Handley Page Victor, *WB771*, crashed at Cranfield with the loss of its crew when the tailplane and elevators broke away during a high-speed, low-level run.

The mishap to *VX777* caused severe setbacks in the Vulcan trials programme, particularly in development work on the Olympus engine, which in its Vulcan context would now have to start all over again virtually from scratch. This was particularly unfortunate, for a higher-powered version, the Olympus 101, was flying in the Canberra test-bed, and plans were well advanced to install the uprated powerplant in *VX777* when trials were completed with the earlier Mk 100. Meanwhile, the test programme continued as best it could with the first prototype Vulcan, *VX770*, which was able to carry out some of the planned high-altitude trials by being pushed to its limits. Before this, however, *VX770*'s programme included air brake checks, trimming tests, manoeuvreability and handling trials with one or more engines out and the power controls off.

When the high-speed, high-altitude trials began, the results confirmed those already obtained—too late—by the Avro 707A, *WD280*. Quite severe buffeting was experienced at speeds of between 0.80M and 0.85M, which was well below the threshold that could be attained by Olympus-engined Vulcans. A solution clearly had to be found; the only alternative was for the Vulcan to operate at anything up to 20,000 ft below its planned level, which was out of the question. The Avro team already knew the cause of the buffeting, which was particularly marked when the Vulcan was manoeuvred at high Mach values, for it had been established during research flying with the Avro 707A. Airflow was separating from the upper surfaces of the outer wing sections, leading to what is termed a compressibility stall. In the early 1950s, with transonic wing design just beginning to emerge from its infancy, this phenomenon was common to almost all high-speed aircraft, but the penalty was particularly severe in a high-speed bomber design, as it imposed limitations on range, altitude and over-the-target evasive manoeuvres.

VX777 was the first Vulcan to have the visual bomb-aiming blister under the nose. It was also used to test the Phase Two Wing, as shown in this photograph.

XA889 was the first production Vulcan B 1 and was used for Olympus engine development. Note vortex generators on the upper wing surfaces.

Avro had tried all sorts of devices on the 707A, including wing fences and vortex generators, in an attempt to smooth out the boundary layer flow over the wing upper surface at high speed, but none of these had succeeded in eliminating the buffeting entirely. To produce the necessary increase in lift coefficient and push the buffet threshold out of reach of the performance which would be attained by the Olympus-powered Vulcans, it was apparent that the whole leading edge of the outer wing would have to be redesigned. The leading edge of the original, straight Vulcan wing was swept at a constant angle of 52 degrees. The solution reached by the Avro designers, with the help of specialists from the Wing Tunnel Section of Farnborough, was to decrease the angle of sweep by 10 degrees at mid span and then bring it back to 52 degrees further outboard, giving it a slight droop at the same time. This effectively increased the chord of the outer wing by 20 per cent, which in turn produced a peak lift coefficient of 1.3 and pushed the compressibility buffet beyond the speeds and altitudes which would be encountered by the Olympus Vulcan. A pilot could now carry out manoeuvres under fairly high 'g' at speed and height without the risk of sudden buffeting. The new 'kinked' leading edge was tested on the Type 707A, *WD280*, in 1954, and was found to work perfectly well. The knowledge, however, had been acquired too late to save the expensive scrapping of 16 Vulcan leading edges, which were already on the jigs, and the rebuilding of the jigs themselves.

The new leading edge was also developed too late to be incorporated on the first production Vulcan B 1, *XA889*, which was rolled out at Woodford in January 1955. It featured a new glass-fibre nose radome and was finished silver overall. Powered initially by 10,000 lb thrust Olympus 100 engines, it flew for the first time on February 4 1955. A few days later the second prototype Vulcan, *VX777*, also rejoined the test programme, having been rebuilt after its crash at Farnborough; this aircraft too was powered by Olympus 100s, and later in the year it was fitted with the new wing leading edge.

XA891, the third production B 1, was the Olympus 200 development aircraft. It crashed in Yorkshire on July 24 1959, the crew escaping unhurt.

Production Olympus 101 engines were installed in *VX777* in March 1955, after which the aircraft went to Boscombe Down to embark on an intensive series of trials that mainly involved engine handling. These lasted for four months until July, when *VX777* was grounded to receive its new leading edge before embarking on speed and altitude trials.

Late in 1955 the first production Vulcan, *XA889*, was also re-engined with twin-spool Olympus 101s. By this time a second production Vulcan B 1, *XA890*, was also flying; this aircraft, together with *XA889*, was part of the original order for 25 Vulcan B 1s, an additional 37 machines having been ordered on September 30 1954. *XA890* was demonstrated at the 1955 SBAC Show by Roly Falk, who left the crowds in no doubt about the big delta's manoeuvreability by performing a perfect upward roll.

The second prototype Vulcan was the first to begin flight trials with the new extended-chord leading edge, mounted on what was now known as the Phase 2 wing. Preliminary trials began on October 5 1955 and lasted until mid-November, when *VX777* was grounded for the installation of a new auto-stabilisation system. Airborne once again in December, it went on to complete 100 hours of development work in 70 sorties, spread out over six months.

Meanwhile, the Vulcan prototype, *VX770*, had gone to Boscombe Down for trials with the A&AEE. It was followed, in March 1956, by *XA889*, which was the acceptance trials aircraft. Initial CA (Controller of Aircraft) release, which meant that the Vulcan was cleared for entry into RAF service, came on May 29, and *XA889* remained at Boscombe Down undergoing further trials until July, when it was allocated to Olympus engine development at Patchway, Bristol. In March 1957 it flew with the 12,000 lb thrust Olympus Mk 102, and in July 1957 with the 13,400 lb thrust Mk 104.

The second production Vulcan, *XA890*—which was never fitted with the Phase 2 wing—was used for radio and radar trials after its appearance at the 1955 SBAC Show, and was afterwards allocated to the Royal Aircraft Establishment, being first employed on ballistics research at Farnborough and later on Blind Landing experiments at Thurleigh. This was the first Vulcan to feature extended engine nacelles, which were to become standard on all later aircraft. The third production aircraft, *XA891*, which also flew in 1955, was fitted with the Phase 2 wing and was allocated to engine installation development, the work involving fuel clearance trials, tank pressurisation, and nitrogen purging. The next machine in the first B 1 production batch, *XA892*, went to Boscombe Down for armament trials; other Vulcans allocated to the development programme were *XA893*, *XA894* and *XA899*, the latter aircraft going to Thurleigh for auto-pilot clearance. On December 22 1959, while serving with the Blind Landing Experimental Unit, *XA899* became the first four-engined aircraft in the world to carry out a fully automatic landing.

With acceptance trials completed at the various Ministry of Supply establishments, the way was now clear for the RAF to receive its first Vulcan B 1. This was *XA897*, which was delivered to No 230 Operational Conversion Unit at Royal Air Force Waddington, near Lincoln, on July 20 1956. *XA897* was destined to remain at Waddington for only a short time; for reasons which will be explained later, it was returned to Woodford for modifications, and its place at the OCU was taken by *XA895*.

By now, a fair nucleus of RAF air and ground crews had amassed considerable experience in handling the Vulcan, having been attached to Avro and the Ministry establishments. To say that the Vulcan was different from anything the RAF had handled before would be an understatement; in time, the RAF crews would learn that it was just another aeroplane, albeit a very fine one, but its unconventional nature made it a little more difficult to accept as such than, say, the Valiant, which had entered service with No 138 Squadron at Gaydon in January 1955. At first sight, the most impressive thing about the Vulcan was its vast wing area—3,550 sq ft of it—which made the aircraft seem bigger than it really was, an illusion accentuated by its height off the ground. One of the amazing things about first contact with a Vulcan was that one could actually walk underneath it without stooping, unless one was more than 6 ft tall.

Again at first sight, the Vulcan's lengthy undercarriage seemed almost too stalky to support 80 tons of fully-laden aircraft. The nosewheel, with its twin wheels, was situated just aft of the under-fuselage entrance door, and its wheel bay contained the necessary servicing points for hydraulics and brakes. The main undercarriage legs, each with eight wheels grouped in a bogie arrangement, were situated alongside the outer engine ribs, with refuelling and defuelling panels in the wheel wells. The Vulcan's main undercarriage was developed by Dowty, and used an hydraulic system working at 4,000 lb/sq in. Only one shock-absorber was employed in each unit, and the brake piping was concealed inside the hollow main leg. The biggest part of the Dowty bogie was a massive casting produced by Sterling Metals Ltd in Z5Z magnesium alloy. Use of this material kept the weight of the component down to 360 lb; an aluminium alloy casting of the same strength would have weighed 540 lb.

The length of the Vulcan's landing gear permitted advantage to be taken of the high angle of attack possible with a flapless delta both at take-off and landing. In the take-off condition, backward movement of the control column in all tricycle-undercarriage aircraft raises the nose and also causes the centre of gravity to move rearwards; this in turn results in an increase of the nose-up moment, which must be counteracted by returning the control column to neutral or even by moving it farther forward. This characteristic was even more marked on the Vulcan, because of the short elevation moment-arm when in the static position.

One of the most difficult problems which had to be overcome by Dowty in designing the Vulcan's tandem-wheel bogie units was to prevent excessive loading on the front wheels. This could be caused by two factors: the 'slamming' of the front wheels on the runway at touch-down, due to the bogie-beam geometry, and overloading caused by brake torque reaction. The former could cause immediate bursting of the tyres as a result of excessive dynamic overloading, and this in fact happened with Convair's massive B-36 during its early career. The Vulcan's basic undercarriage configuration, however, completely removed this slamming characteristic. The bogie beam was hinged at the front axle to the main leg, which contained no shock-absorber and was free to move inwards, but which could not be pulled out beyond a fixed stop. The main shock-absorber was attached between the rear of the main leg casting and the mid-point of the bogie beam; the rear wheels touched the runway first and rotated the bogie beam around the front axle, which was prevented from moving downwards by the stop mentioned earlier. This rotation of the bogie beam compressed the shock-absorber, and the front wheels contacted the runway with no greater vertical velocity than the aircraft as a whole. As this system required only one shock-absorber, it also reduced the number of working parts to an absolute minimum.

Torque reaction caused by braking presented quite a different problem, being applied for considerably longer periods; it also introduced the risk of severe tyre wear, especially if the wheels were allowed to lock. In the Vulcan, the torque from the front brakes was carried direct to the sliding member of the leg structure, while that from the rear brakes also reacted, through parallel linkage, to the main leg, so that no resultant torque was applied to the bogie beam. The Vulcan's braking system, tyres and wheels were supplied by Dunlop.

For any bogie-equipped aircraft, power steering is essential, and a hydraulic system is provided for that purpose. The nosewheel must also be centred for retraction; on the Vulcan, this was accomplished by a specially-designed jack which could be extended or shortened during castoring or steering, but which was pressure-loaded to a central position by hydraulic pressure before undercarriage retraction took place. The necessary centering force for the Vulcan was obtained with a very small jack, weighing only 2½ lb, which was some 23 lb lighter than a steel spring of comparable performance.

The crew entered the Vulcan's pressure cabin by the under-fuselage hatch position just in front of the nosewheel, an arrangement which caused some misgivings among the three rear crew members, who had no ejection seats and who, being required to make their exit through the hatch in an emergency, felt that there might be problems if the undercarriage was lowered at the time. The hatch itself opened to an angle of about 45 degrees and inside had a ladder, a section of which slid down to hang vertically from the lower edge to make the climb-in easier. Inside the pressure cabin, the two navigators and the air electronics officer sat facing rearwards in bucket seats on a raised platform a little above and behind the door, their instruments positioned in a semi-circle and filling the space above a table running from one side of the fuselage to the other. Their only view of the outside world was through two small portholes, situated high up on either side of the cabin.

Another short ladder led up to the flight deck, with its twin ejection seats. This arrangement appeared somewhat cramped, as though the second seat had been pushed into what looked like a single-seat cockpit as an afterthought, and worming one's way through the narrow gap between the seats was a definite art which required practice to perfect without undue contortions, especially as the throttle console was positioned between the two pilots. The cockpit was equipped with dual control columns of the pistol-grip type on the ends of tubes which slid into the lower part of the blind flying panels. Pilots coming to the Vulcan from other bombers expressed surprise that the control columns were not of the 'traditional' spectacle type, but the fighter-type sticks had one big advantage: they made snatch units unnecessary as part of the ejection system, and if the pilots were forced to eject it was with the comforting knowledge that their legs were unlikely to be parted from them in the process.

The ejection seats were fully automatic Martin Baker Type 3Ks, and the cockpit canopy was jettisoned when the firing-blind handle was pulled—an improvement on the Valiant's escape system, in which the canopy had to be jettisoned first. It should be mentioned here that the lack of ejection seats for the three rear crew in all three V-bombers, Valiant, Vulcan and Victor, gave rise to a lot of criticism in some circles, especially since the Air Staff, in its original Operational Requirement, had asked for the new class of V-bombers to be fitted with a pressure cabin that could be jettisoned in an emergency and equipped with parachutes to form an escape capsule. Such an escape system had in fact been tested in model form by Handley Page in 1948, but the results were far from satisfactory and, as the engineering problems involved were deemed to be insurmountable, the idea was dropped. Not until much later, in 1960, did Martin Baker install an experimental rearwards-facing ejection seat in a specially-modified Valiant; the seat was successfully fired from the static aircraft at Chalgrove airfield in June that year, but by that time Martin Baker were heavily involved in developing new seats for more modern combat aircraft and no further work for seats for the V-Force was undertaken. In fairness, it should be said that the V-Force rear crew themselves never complained about the lack of escape facilities, even when the switch to low-level operations in the 1960s made downwards escape virtually impossible. As one Vulcan navigator put it: 'Even if it had been possible to fit bang seats for the rear crew, it would probably have cost about two million quid to do it. It would have made far more sense if they had shared out the money among the crew members concerned!'

The cockpit layout was good; most of it, in fact, had been designed by Roly Falk. Unlike that of most bombers, the cockpit roof was devoid of any controls or switches, fostering its fighter-type appearance; on the main instrument panel the blind flying instruments were duplicated in front of each pilot, with the engine control panel between. The throttle quadrant was positioned just below the engine control panel, and apart from the throttles it served as a mounting for airbrake switches, parking brake lever and the four fuel contents gauges. The first pilot's console on the port side of the cockpit housed the engine starting, radio, bomb door and power flying control stop panels, while the second pilot's console on the starboard side contained the pressurisation, air-conditioning and de-icing controls. Production Vulcans also had a spring-loaded retractable console housing the fuel system controls and the power control start buttons; when not in use, it was tucked away in a recess under the instrument panel.

The only real problem with the Vulcan's cockpit—and it was a major one—was the view. The canopy covering was completely opaque, broken only by two circular side panels, which meant that the pilots had no vision above or to the rear; they could only just see the wingtips through the panels by leaning as far forward as possible and twisting their heads round. The forward view on the ground was restricted, too, because the cockpit coaming was some way in front of the pilots and the cabin itself was at a consider-able height from the ground; this created a 30-yard blind spot immediately in front of the nose. Other blind spots occurred between the front windscreen panels and the circular side panels. All this created marshalling problems, as the pilot was quite unable to see a marshaller who positioned himself in front of or on the starboard side of the aircraft; there were also problems in checking the full and free operation of the power controls. This had to be confirmed by the crew chief, standing outside the aircraft and plugged into the intercom system, and as an additional check the pilot could refer to a visual indicator, rather like an artificial horizon but with movable indicators to represent the flying control surfaces, which was fitted to the engine control panel. The reason for the lack of cockpit

Above *This view of Vulcan B 1 centre-sections on the production line gives a good idea of the massive and robust nature of the engineering that went into the design.*

Below *Vulcan B 1s, now showing the Phase Two Wing, on the assembly line. XA896, visible in the photograph, was later partly converted to test the BS100 vectored thrust engine.*

transparency was twofold. The first was a question of strength, given the altitudes at which the Vulcan was designed to operate and the possible operating conditions; the second was to give the crew maximum protection from nuclear flash. Once the bomber was on its way to the target there would no longer be any need for the crew to see outside; the windscreen was fitted with anti-flash screens, and the side windows could be completely blacked out with sliding panels.

The Vulcan's electrical system was relatively complex, and air electronics officers coming to the Vulcan from other types needed to do a good deal of homework to master all its intricacies. There were three main systems: 112 volts, provided by four main generators, to supply power for the heavy duty electrical equipment; 28 volts, provided by three rotary transformers, for the secondary systems; and six inverters to energise the AC supplies for equipment such as radio, radar and the flight instruments. The 112-volt supply provided power for main services such as the power controls, pump motors, airbrakes, fuel pumps and radar inverters, and was monitored on a DC control panel to the right of the AEO's position.

The aircraft was fitted with conventional ailerons, elevators and rudder, the elevators being placed inboard of the ailerons on the trailing edge of the wing. All the control surfaces were operated by electro-hydraulic power units, and to guard against the complete loss of a surface through power failure the ailerons and elevators were each divided into two sections, each with its own power unit. The rudder arm was fitted with two power units, one of them a 'standby' designed to ensure complete rudder control if the other failed.

The power controls operated as follows. When the pilot moved the control column, a

The first batch of Vulcan B 1s on the assembly line. The Phase Two Wing had not been incorporated in the design at this early stage.

lever assembly came into play, supplying fluid to one side of a ram in the control unit; this produced movement of the ram connected to the control surface, and the surface movement was relative to that of the control column. When the surface reached the selected position, fluid to the ram was automatically cut off and the surface ceased to move. The movement of the control column was therefore a transmission to a series of hydraulic selector valves in the power units, and there was no risk of aerodynamic loads on the control surfaces being relayed back to the control column. The danger here was that the absence of loading on the control column might lead to a pilot inadvertently over-stressing the aircraft, and to overcome this risk artificial 'feel' was incorporated by means of a boxed compression spring, situated between the control column and the power unit. This spring returned the control column, and therefore the control surface involved, to its original trimmed position after movement, and it could be adjusted through an electric actuator operated by the pilot's trim switch to alleviate stick load during, for example, a prolonged turn.

Changes in indicated airspeed were also fed into the artificial feel system, so that at a high IAS only a small stick movement was necessary to produce high spring compression, so enabling the pilot to sense a heavier loading on the control column. As an insurance against failure of the boxed spring system at high IAS, which would result in the controls becoming very heavy at the low speed necessary for circuit and landing, the pilot could switch the system to its low value by pushing two relief buttons.

If this system was fairly complex, the same was not true of the fuel system, thanks to the brilliantly-devised sequence timers—one on each side of the aircraft—which automatically varied the speed of the fuel tanks' operating pumps in order to keep the cg within careful limits. The timers were electrically-driven cams which rotated and selected the appropriate tanks for a time proportional to the capacity of the tanks, maintaining the right percentage of fuel in each tank throughout the flight. In the event of failure of the timers, the tank pumps could be selected and controlled manually; this was the unenviable job of the co-pilot, although his task was made simpler by a special slide rule on which he could calculate the cg quickly from the fuel gauge readings.

Hydraulic fluid for the operation of the undercarriage, wheel brakes, bomb doors and nosewheel steering mechanism was delivered from a reservoir by three engine-driven pumps, all selector valves being electrically actuated. The bomb doors were operated on the ground by means of an hydraulic power pack, which was electrically operated and which also served to charge the wheel brake accumulators; in addition, it could be used as a standby system in the air should the usual system fail. The air supply for the air conditioning, pressurisation and heating was tapped from each engine; the cabin could be pressurised to give either 8,000 ft or 25,000 ft conditions, up to a maximum of 9 lb/sq in and 3½ lb/sq in respectively, and the cabin was fitted with five controls which enabled any crew member to decompress it. Volume and temperature of the airflow into the cabin could be regulated either automatically or manually by switches on the co-pilot's console; full airframe and engine anti-icing equipment was installed, and hot air was piped into the weapons bay to prevent the icing-up of release and arming mechanisms at high altitude.

The Vulcan's pre-starting check list was lengthy, but reasonably uncomplicated once the crew were thoroughly familiar with the position of all the necessary switches. In an emergency, where ground services were not available, the aircraft's internal batteries could be connected in series for starting up, but normally a 112-volt ground rig was used. In the emergency case, the aircraft batteries would be used to start up one engine, which would then provide the necessary current to start the other three.

With all engines running, the next step was to activate and check the power controls. The crew chief, standing outside the aircraft, played a vital part here, and the pilots cross-checked by referring to the visual indicator in the cockpit. With the final all-clear given by the crew chief, the aircraft was ready to be taxied. Getting the Vulcan moving required quite a lot of power, but once it was in motion sufficient thrust was obtained at idling rpm for transit to the take-off point, the pilot steering the nosewheel by means of a spring-loaded push button on the control column and using the rudder pedals. It was possible to steer the Vulcan by using the toe brakes alone, but this resulted in rather erratic taxiing and produced undue stress on the undercarriage.

The pre-take-off checks were simple; most of them could be carried out by monitoring a cluster of 17 'dolls' eyes' and three red lights on the engine control panel. Once these checks were completed, the aircraft could be lined up on the runway and the engines opened up to full power while both pilots exerted a strong pressure on the toe brakes. The rpm and the jet pipe temperatures were checked, and the brakes released.

Nosewheel steering was used to keep the Vulcan straight during the initial acceleration down the runway until the rudder began to 'bite' at about 60 knots, forward pressure being maintained on the control column to keep the nosewheel on the ground until unstick speed was reached. Slight backward pressure on the stick was sufficient to lift the aircraft off the runway. Unstick speed was in the order of 165 knots, and following retraction of the undercarriage there was a marked increase in acceleration, accompanied by a nose-up change of trim, in the subsequent climb. Optimum rate of climb was obtained at an IAS of 145 knots and was quite impressive, the big delta being quite capable of outclimbing many of the jet fighters in service during the 1950s.

High altitude cruise was at 0.86M, and the Vulcan could reach 0.9M at full power without difficulty in level flight. In a shallow dive, buffeting and noise increased as the limiting Mach number was approached, and here a small device known as an auto-mach trimmer came into action, applying slight up elevator to counteract a nose-down change of trim. Rapid deceleration from a high-speed run was achieved by selecting the high-drag airbrakes.

One remarkable feature of the Vulcan was its rate of descent, which few fighters were able to match. In a maximum-rate descent, the bomber could lose 20,000 ft in 90 seconds flat, recovery to level flight taking only 1,500 ft or so after the pilot started to level out.

In the circuit, speed was reduced to 190 knots on the downwind leg, with throttles idling, high drag airbrake selected and undercarriage down. On final approach, power was once again reduced to a fixed rpm setting, the approach being made at 170 knots. This was about 20 knots above the threshold speed, giving the pilot adequate speed control and forward vision. As the Vulcan had no flaps—the ailerons and elevators taking up almost all the trailing edge of the wing—the airbrakes were used instead. If the threshold was crossed at the correct speed, only a slight backward pressure on the stick was needed to check the aircraft sinking on flare out, and if everything was done properly the touchdown was smooth, assisted by the cushioning effect of the Vulcan's large wing area. The technique for shortening the landing run was to lower the nosewheel immediately and brake continuously, using the nosewheel steering to keep straight. Alternatively, the pilot could stream the brake parachute, which was housed on the starboard side of the tail bullet and which decelerated the aircraft to the same degree as the application of the wheel brakes.

Such, basically, was the aircraft with which the crews who arrived at Waddington to undergo the Vulcan course with No 230 OCU had to familiarise themselves. The pilots of the Handling Squadron at the A&AEE, Boscombe Down, had already expressed their delight with it, and forecast no difficulty in conversion. But even before the OCU course had got properly under way, the Vulcan became the victim of a tragic accident which was to splash its name across the headlines of newspapers throughout the world.

Chapter 3

XA897: triumph and tragedy

On September 9 1956 Vulcan B 1 *XA897*, the aircraft which had been assigned briefly to No 230 OCU before going back to Woodford for modifications, took off from Boscombe Down on the first leg of a prestige flight to New Zealand via Australia, where it was to take part in a display in connexion with Air Force Commemoration Week. It was primarily a diplomatic exercise, but it was also of considerable value in proving the aircraft, and would in fact be the first real long-range flight the Vulcan had so far undertaken. The aircraft captain was Squadron Leader Donald Howard; his VIP co-pilot was the C-in-C Bomber Command, Air Marshal Sir Harry Broadhurst. The other three RAF crew members were all Squadron Leaders, picked for their experience and skill; filling the air electronics officer's post was Albert Gamble, with Edward Eames AFC seated next to him in the navigator's position. The radar navigator's seat was occupied by James Stroud, who in fact was not a navigator at all but a fully-qualified Vulcan pilot; he was taking turns in the co-pilot's seat with Broadhurst as a matter of courtesy. The sixth crew member was Frederick Bassett, the Avro technical services representative who, of course, was a civilian.

The outward flight was trouble-free, the Vulcan stopping over in Aden and Singapore and completing the 3,730-mile sector from Boscombe Down to Aden at an average speed of 545 mph. The whole 11,475-mile flight to Melbourne was accomplished in 47 hours 26 minutes, including stopover times; the actual flight time was 23 hours 9 minutes, which meant that if time on the ground had been reduced to a minimum the aircraft could easily have broken the previous England to Australia record of 35 hours 46 minutes, then held by a Vickers Viscount airliner. The Vulcan reached Melbourne from Singapore on September 11, and was demonstrated by its usual crew while Sir Harry Broadhurst flew to Canberra for talks with Australian Government officials and Service chiefs. The Vulcan's Australian tour later took it to Sydney and Adelaide, from where it departed for Harewood Airport, Christchurch, on September 18, completing the last leg of 1,664 miles in 4 hours 35 minutes.

The return flight was made via Brisbane, Darwin, Singapore, Ceylon and Aden. From there, at 02:50 hours on the morning of October 1, the aircraft departed on the last leg of the 26,000-mile round trip, having demonstrated a number of points, not the least of which was that RAF Bomber Command was now a global strike force to be reckoned with. On his visit to Canberra, Broadhurst had also conveyed the message to ministers that the RAAF's first-line fighter, the Avon Sabre, could not hope to defend Australian territory against an atomic attack delivered by an aircraft like the Vulcan, and neither could any other fighter in the same category. This was not mere salesmanship, designed to persuade the Australians to buy the English Electric Lightning supersonic fighter, which was then flying in its prototype P 1 form; it was also a clear-cut message to any potential aggressor that the RAF was now in a position to strike hard and fast and at long range, with hitherto unparalleled destructive power.

The flight from Aden took 7 hours 10 minutes, with Sir Harry Broadhurst in the co-pilot's seat and taking turns with Howard at the controls. The landing was to be made at London Airport, where a VIP reception committee was waiting to greet the aircraft at the close of its triumphant tour. As the Vulcan cruised high over France, approaching the Channel, Squadron Leader Howard made a radio call to Bomber Command Operations at High Wycombe in Buckinghamshire, and was told that the weather in the London area was $\frac{8}{8}$ cloud at 700 ft, with heavy rain, with $\frac{7}{8}$ cloud at 300 ft and a visibility of 1,100 yards. He was also informed that London Heathrow was equipped with high-intensity lighting, and that normal airline traffic was having no difficulty in operating. However, the decision on whether or not to divert to Waddington, where the weather was much better, was left to Howard; this was usual practice, for the decision in such circumstances is always the aircraft captain's. He decided to land at Heathrow, and Broadhurst did not disagree with him. After all, the weather minima at London Airport were well within the pilot's capabilities; he held a Master Green instrument rating, which meant that he was qualified to descend to the Heathrow break-off height of 150 ft—the break-off height being the height at which a pilot must abandon his approach and initiate an overshoot if he still can not see his way clear to land. It varies from airfield to airfield, depending on obstacles in the area, and also takes into account instrument errors.

The Vulcan was due to land at 10:08 hours GMT. As indicated by Bomber Command Operations, the weather was poor, with mist and rain, although the visibility was slightly better than forecast: between 1,500 and 2,000 yards. Civil airline flights were in fact operating at a reduced rate, using Runway No 1. The Ground Controlled Approach caravans were in position beside Runway 10 Left.

On the ground a reception committee composed of VIPs, families of the crew and media representatives awaited the Vulcan's arrival. The first sign of it was the sound of a brief burst of full power out of the mist at the touchdown end of 10 Left. Watchers standing on the roof of the Queen's building in the airport central area then saw the Vulcan climbing very steeply up from the runway with its undercarriage down. At an angle of about 40 degrees it climbed quietly to about 800 ft, when the cockpit roof blew off and there were two sharp cracks as the pilots ejected in succession. The automatic Mk 3K seats functioned immediately and both men were in stable descent before losing any height. The Vulcan then turned gently to starboard and dived at an angle of 20 to 30 degrees on to the starboard edge of Runway No 4 where it exploded on impact, leaving a 300-yard swathe of wreckage which burnt for nearly an hour. Sir Harry Broadhurst landed on Runway 10 Left and injured both his feet; Squadron Leader Howard touched down on the grass, sustaining a bruised forehead and slight back injuries. The four rear crew members were killed.

An RAF Court of Inquiry was opened the following day, headed by Air Chief Marshal Sir Donald Hardman, Air Member for Supply and Organisation. In addition, on October 26, the Minister of Transport and Civil Aviation requested Dr A.G. Touch, Director of Electronics Research and Development (Ground) at the Ministry of Supply, to carry out an independent investigation into certain aspects of the accident. His terms of reference were, in brief, 'to consider whether, at the time of the accident, there was any failure to operate the GCA correctly at London Airport, and, if so, to consider in what respects and whether, in the light of the circumstances of the accident, any changes are desirable . . .'. Unfortunately, Dr Touch was not able to make use of the evidence assembled by the RAF Court of Inquiry. It is not the RAF's policy to make such evidence public, even in the case of an accident surrounded by as much publicity as this one.

There was no doubt about what had happened. '£1,000,000 JET BOMBER HITS A CABBAGE PATCH,' screamed the *Daily Mirror* headline of October 2 1956. 'A mist-

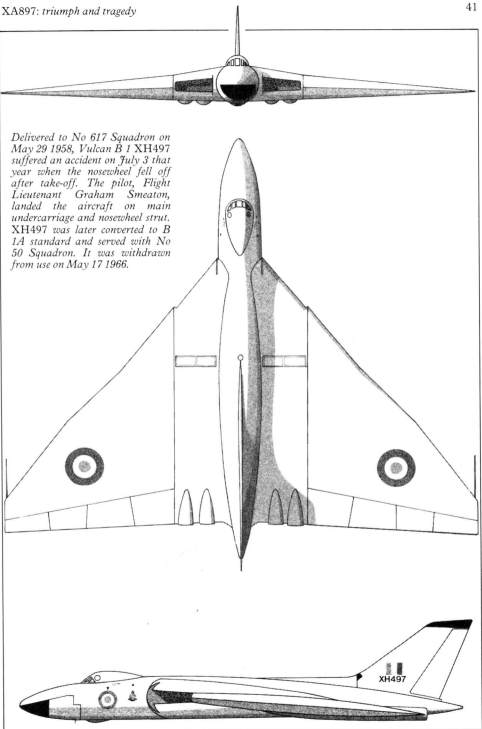

Delivered to No 617 Squadron on May 29 1958, Vulcan B 1 XH497 suffered an accident on July 3 that year when the nosewheel fell off after take-off. The pilot, Flight Lieutenant Graham Smeaton, landed the aircraft on main undercarriage and nosewheel strut. XH497 was later converted to B 1A standard and served with No 50 Squadron. It was withdrawn from use on May 17 1966.

XH497

shrouded cabbage field sealed the fate of the £1,000,000 four-jet Avro Vulcan which crashed and burned out yesterday. The giant bomber, being "talked down" to London Airport by radar through torrential rain and mist, undershot the runway by 600 yards and its landing wheels hit the cabbage field. They were ripped off. Immediately, the pilot put "full power" on the four jet engines and the plane roared into a steep climb. But as it went into the low cloud, the pilot realised it was out of control . . .'.

The Vulcan had indeed struck the ground, and the subsequent technical investigation absolved the aircraft. There had been no technical malfunction of airframe or engines. Why, then, had the tragedy occurred? Under strong pressure from Members of Parliament, Mr Nigel Birch, the Secretary of State for Air, made a statement to the House of Commons on December 20 in which he made references to Dr Touch's report, which had not then been published. Mr Birch said that the aircraft had ample fuel to divert, and that Air Marshal Broadhurst had emphasised to the captain that he should divert if he was dissatisfied with the weather conditions prevailing. The captain decided to make one attempt to land at London Airport. At about 10:04 hours GMT, at a height of about 1,500 ft and about 5 nm from touchdown, and with both altimeters correctly set, the aircraft began its descent under the control of the Talkdown Controller at London Airport. The captain set his break-off height at 300 ft. The GCA talkdown instructions were followed, with some undulation relative to the glide path and some corrections in azimuth, up to a point about three-quarters of a mile from touchdown, when the pilot was informed that he was 80 ft above the glide path. At this point, the weather was at its worst. The pilot received no further information on elevation, and at a point about 1,000 yards from the touchdown point and 700 yards from the threshold of the runway, the aircraft struck the ground. Both main undercarriage units were removed, and the elevator controls were damaged. Subsequently the aircraft rose sharply to a height of 200–300 ft, when it was found to be out of control. The captain then gave the order to abandon the aircraft and himself used the ejector seat. The co-pilot repeated the order and, after trying the controls, also ejected. Within seconds of the order being given the nose and starboard wing of the aircraft dropped and the aircraft crashed to the ground.

The RAF Court of Inquiry, Mr Birch's report continued, found nothing to suggest any technical failure in the aircraft which could have contributed to the accident. They concluded that the captain of the aircraft was justified in deciding to make an attempt to land at London Airport but they considered that, in the circumstances, he made an error of judgement in setting himself a break-off height of 300 ft and also in going below that height. The court drew attention, however, to the fact that though the GCA controller informed the pilot about seven seconds before the aircraft first hit the ground that he was 80 ft above the glide path, he did not subsequently advise him that he was below it; and that after the aircraft had hit the ground he continued his talkdown as if the approach had been normal. The court concluded that, since the aircraft was under GCA control, the failure to warn the captain that he was going below the glide path was the principal cause of the accident.

It was at this point that the minister referred to Dr Touch's report, which is worth looking at in some detail. R/T communications throughout the approach, said Dr Touch, were very good. The Vulcan first touched the ground 1,988 ft from the runway threshold, 250 ft north of the extended centreline, while still under GCA assistance. At impact the aircraft was in a normal approach attitude, with nose up. The rate of descent was not excessive and probably was of the same order as for a normal landing, about 180 ft per minute. The airspeed was 140 to 145 knots. Touch repeated the official weather conditions, but stated that conditions were patchy. At the time of the accident there was mist and slight drizzle in the region of the runway threshold. Horizontal visibility looking

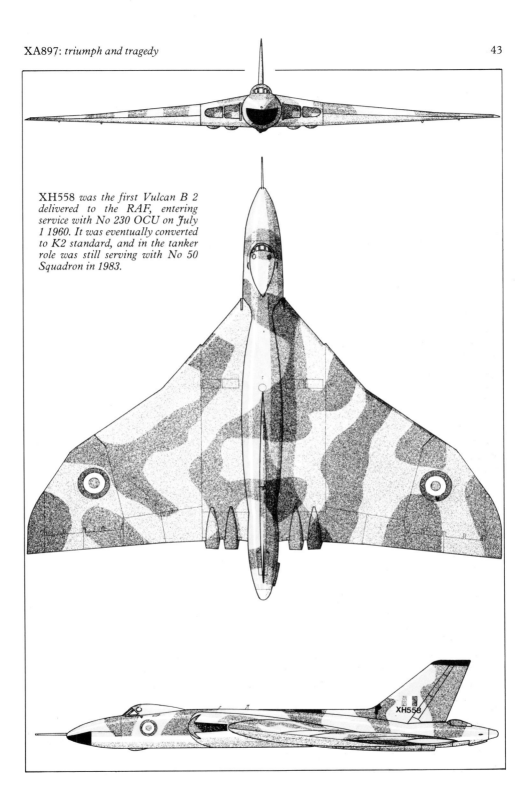

XH558 *was the first Vulcan B 2 delivered to the RAF, entering service with No 230 OCU on July 1 1960. It was eventually converted to K2 standard, and in the tanker role was still serving with No 50 Squadron in 1983.*

outwards along the centreline was about 800 yards. Further back along the approach path, at approximately $1\frac{1}{4}$ nm from touch-down, horizontal visibility at ground level was around 200 yards, but the aircraft was seen at a distance of about 400 yards. In this area it did not appear to have been raining heavily. In Touch's view, '. . . it could be concluded with confidence that errors in setting up the displays, incorrect calibrations, or malfunctioning of any part of the (GCA) equipment did not occur'.

Dr Touch's report reviewed in considerable detail the evidence provided by the GCA record, eye-witnesses, the pilot and co-pilot, the controller and the tracker (a woman air traffic control assistant with experience of some 2,000 GCA approaches). 'The simpler solution,' he stated, 'is that the tracker followed the aircraft echo more or less accurately, but that the controller did not pay sufficient attention to the error-meter after the point "80 ft high". It can be seen from the transcript of the talk-down that after this point, the controller's patter was concerned with range and corrections in azimuth. This shows that he was mainly looking at the azimuth display. It is generally recognised that it is difficult to watch both error-meter and display at the same time.

'On this basis, it is possible to formulate a theory which appears to be a reasonable compromise with the evidence. After "100 ft low" (10 hours 05 minutes 30 seconds) to "on the glide-path" (10 hours 05 minutes $41\frac{1}{2}$ seconds) the rate of descent appears to have been low, of the order of 150 ft/minute, and this was noticed by eye-witnesses. Afterwards, to 10 hours 05 minutes 51 seconds it appears to have increased to at least 300 ft/minute. It is therefore possible that the tracker may have erred slightly on the high side in bisecting the echo. If the latter limit for the time of impact—10 hours 06 minutes 01 seconds—is taken, the tolerances given are possible, and the resulting rate of descent, though high, is acceptable. During the descent, it is not unreasonable to postulate that the tracker lagged behind by 50 ft, especially if a fairly large echo was being used. The error-meter would have reached zero about 5 to 6 seconds prior to impact and the warning light would have come on about 2 seconds before impact. If the tracker switched her light off when she lost the echo just after half a mile, it means postulating that the controller did not observe the meter for a period of 7 to 8 seconds. This is not unreasonable, as he was busy with azimuthal corrections and his last two elevation messages had been spaced ten seconds apart. If he glanced at the meter during the first 5 seconds he would be left with the impression that the aircraft would be returning to the glide-path. The warning light came on too late to be of any value.'

Dr Touch's report went on to accept the GCA record as being correct, subject to normal tracking, observational and timing errors. In his opinion, the only rational explanation for the collision with the ground was that the aircraft entered a steep dive after the point "80 ft high". He stated that, 'The aircraft crossed the centreline roughly at $4\frac{1}{2}$ miles and was always north of it, in spite of three 5-degree corrections. As a result, the controller gave much more attention to azimuth than is normal, and this left him less time for giving elevation and range information. Although the controller did not consider that he was under stress, at least he was being hurried more than he thought. A small sample of talk-downs by other controllers chosen at random show a spread in words spoken per minute of 82 to 126, with an average of 110. On this occasion, the controller averaged 146, obviously reacting to the increased ground speed.

'Legally, the pilot is entitled to receive enough height information by which to fly his aircraft safely and on which to base his decisions. This he did not get. On the other hand, if the flight path previous to the "80 ft high" point is not taken into account, the time interval of the critical phase is so short that no one could blame the controller for not passing further height data. The issue is, therefore, was the last steep descent unexpected, or could it have been foreseen from the previous flight path so clearly that the controller should have concentrated upon the elevation situation? I find this question exceedingly difficult to answer, but on balance . . . I think the verdict should be that the circumstances were such that it should be classed as a true accident and that the controller was not to blame.

'I must conclude that the talk-down in elevation was poor and, because of its negative character, contributed towards creating the final critical stage. The controller is only responsible for passing instructions and information; he is not in control of the aircraft. The ultimate responsibility for the safety of the aircraft and for the decision whether it is safe to descend below the break-off height, rests with the pilot. Consequently, even if the talk-down was poor, it was subject to the overriding judgement of the pilot, and the controller cannot be blamed for subsequent events arising from the poor control . . ..'

Intentionally or not, Dr Touch appeared to be implying that the accident might have been avoided if the pilot, Donald Howard, had taken appropriate action in time. Howard's own comments on the tragedy, together with those of Sir Harry Broadhurst and the controllers involved, were not made public until after the inquest on the accident victims, which was held in Ealing on January 30 1957. They make illuminating reading, for they introduce another possible contributory factor: altimeter error.

At the inquest, the jury returned verdicts of accidental death on Squadron Leader Edward J. Eames, aged 32, navigator; Squadron Leader James G.W. Stroud, aged 29, *second navigator* [author's italics: the description of Stroud as a navigator and not a pilot incensed and embittered not only his bereaved family, but also his colleagues in Bomber Command, and was a poor attempt by officialdom to cover up the fact that he should have been sitting in the seat occupied by Broadhurst during the tricky blind approach]; Squadron Leader Albert E. Gamble, air electronics officer; and Mr Frederick Bassett, of A.V. Roe and Co Ltd.

In his summing-up the coroner, Dr H.G. Broadbridge, suggested there was nothing in the evidence to show criminal negligence on the part of anyone in the aircraft or on the ground; everyone seemed to be doing their duty as they thought right at the time.

Squadron Leader Howard said that before leaving Aden he had received a signal from Bomber Command saying that he was to land at London Airport. Asked by the coroner if he had decided definitely to land there, Squadron Leader Howard replied: 'No. I was going to make an attempt to land, in view of the weather. If I could not, I was going to overshoot and go to Waddington, where it was promised that the weather would be very good. I decided to come down to 300 ft by my altimeter, which represented to me a minimum approach altitude for London Airport of 150 ft over the ground.'

As the Vulcan came in at an approach speed of about 160 mph—'usual for that type of aircraft'—the talkdown from the ground controller was normal, and Squadron Leader Howard said he acted on the information as soon as he received it. Before the talkdown was completed he hit the ground. He now knew—although he did not know at the time— that he was outside the runway when he hit the ground. The last instruction he remembered before hitting it was 'Three-quarters of a mile, 80 ft high'—meaning he was three-quarters of a mile from touchdown and 80 ft above the ideal glide path. He increased the rate of descent.

'I asked the co-pilot, at a range I cannot remember, to look for the high-intensity lighting, which I was going to use to complete the landing. He told me he could see the lights over to starboard. All this time I was looking at instruments, not looking out. I looked for the lights as he told me, and I did not recognise the pattern. They were not what I expected to see. Immediately I had looked I went back on instruments, and he then told me I was very low, and to pull up. I did. At that precise time, the aeroplane just touched the ground and I decided to overshoot. This I tried to do, but as the aircraft accelerated it became obvious that I could not control it any more. It wanted to roll over to the right. I used all the control I had but I could not stop it and I realised I could do no more. My altimeter was showing slightly below 300 ft. I shouted to the crew to get out and when it was apparent that the aircraft was going to roll into the ground decided to eject.'

Asked by Mr L.A. Prickett, representing A.V. Roe and Co Ltd, if he had any idea what happened after hitting the ground to make the aircraft uncontrollable, Squadron Leader Howard said: 'At the time I did not know, and I could not understand why, because the aircraft did not hit the ground hard. But on recollection now, it must have been that the controls were damaged when the aeroplane hit the ground.'

The coroner asked if the altimeter was gravely misleading him. Squadron Leader Howard replied that he believed it was, but he did not know how it could be accounted for, he held a Master Green instrument rating, the highest an RAF pilot could have. He said that there was a known error of 70 ft on his altimeter and he set 80 ft as the height of London Airport above sea level. He agreed that if he had been on the glide-path three-quarters of a mile from touchdown he should have been about 260 ft off the ground. If the altimeter had functioned correctly he would have broken off his attempt to land.

Air Marshal Sir Harry Broadhurst said that he had left it to the judgement of Squadron Leader Howard, as captain, whether he (Howard) tried to land or not. Asked by the coroner whether the talkdown was normal, he replied: 'There was nothing in it to alarm you. It seemed perfectly safe.' Speaking of the lights, he said they appeared as a sort of misty glow on the starboard bow, and he immediately reported them. When the lights began to clear into a pattern he knew they were too low. They hit the ground a glancing blow and he was so convinced that no damage had been done that as the pilot opened his throttles and the aircraft rose he said: 'If we turn slightly left we can still make it.' But the pilot answered, 'No, I am going to overshoot'. Then he said: 'I think we have had it'. He called to the crew to get out, and ejected. Sir Harry tried the controls but got no response, then ejected himself. He said that his and the pilot's altimeters were not coincident on the flight; there was an error of between 50 and 80 ft between the two. Asked if he could account for the additional error in the altimeter, he answered that they had now established phenomena which might account for it.

Mr John Manning, GCA controller, said that the Vulcan was about six miles out when he established contact with it. His screen did not show the aircraft's height above the glide path; that was given to him by a meter operated by his assistant. The aircraft must have come down at a steep angle and touched the ground in a matter of seconds. Mr Manning said that so far as the screen was concerned, the appearance to him of an aircraft on the ground or one passing over safely at a point, say, 150 ft above would be exactly the same. 'From the point 80 ft high the meter showed a descent towards the glide path. I cannot say with accuracy whether it had reached the glide path. I can say it did not go below.'

Miss Ann Collins Maley, the tracker, said that her job was to watch height and range on her instruments, passing the range to the controller verbally and the height by instruments. Replying to the coroner, who suggested that the aircraft must have descended rapidly at some stage, Miss Maley said she did not recollect any rapid descent. When the Vulcan was about two miles away, it seemed to drop about 100 ft below the glide path and she mentioned this to the controller. She agreed that it must have recovered because later it was above the glide path. Squadron Leader Howard was recalled and asked by the coroner whether it would be an abnormal rate of descent to drop 300 ft in 500 yards. He replied that this would be 'fantastic—about 4,000 ft per minute,' and that he would have known if they had been going down at that rate.

Wing Commander C.K. Saxelby, from the A&AEE, Boscombe Down, said it had been found that, when the aircraft came close to the ground, the 70-ft altimeter error could become about 130 ft, added to which there was the 80 ft for London Airport's height above sea level. It was quite possible for there to be a further error of 70 ft caused by friction.

So much for the reports and speculations. The best that could be deduced from them all was that the accident to Vulcan *XA897* was the product of a culmination of errors; no single factor outweighed the others. Perhaps the last word on the matter should come from Sir Harry Broadhurst, one of the two survivors.

'The whole thing is a puzzle to me. It seemed to me an absolutely normal glide approach until the ground appeared in the wrong place. If we had been coming down at an unprecedented rate, we would have hit the ground and the undercarriage would have been forced up into the wings. As it was, we touched so lightly we merely thought the aircraft had burst a tyre or something. We had no idea that the undercarriage had been ripped off. Until then, the captain, obviously very experienced, imagined he was being talked down normally. The fact is, they were still talking him down normally after he had gone up again. Obviously something went wrong. We cannot supply the missing link.'

Broadhurst's 'missing link' was never supplied. But various ham-fisted attempts to pin a disproportionate amount of blame on the aircraft captain, Donald Howard—who later left the RAF and went to the United States, where he died in the 1970s—left a bitter taste in the mouths of many Bomber Command colleagues for years to come.

Chapter 4

The Vulcan enters service

The sudden loss of *XA897*, which was to have been returned to No 230 OCU at the end of its prestige flight, left the OCU with only one aircraft—*XA895*—until January 3 1957, when *XA898* was delivered. This aircraft, in fact, was to spend its entire working life with the OCU, the only Vulcan B 1 to do so, until it was relegated to RAF Halton as an instructional airframe in August 1964.

Three more Vulcan B 1s were added to the OCU's strength before the end of May. The first of these, delivered on March 25, was *XA900*, which was also to spend most of its career with the OCU, apart from a short spell with No 101 Squadron. *XA900* eventually went to RAF Cosford in February 1966 as an instructional airframe and was subsequently preserved (in 1979) for display at the Cosford Aerospace Museum, the last intact example of a Vulcan B 1, albeit in a sorry state of corrosion.

The other two Vulcans, *XA901* and *'902*, were delivered to the OCU on April 4 and May 10 1957 respectively, and on these four aircraft the first OCU course qualified. The groundwork for training the Vulcan crews, and the high qualifications required, had been well established since 1955, when the first crews for the V-Force had begun training on the first of the V-bombers, the Vickers Valiant, at RAF Wittering; since then the Valiant squadrons had amassed two years of operational experience, including bombing operations over Suez in war conditions, so 230 OCU already had the benefit of tested operational procedures to draw upon.

Pilots and co-pilots came to 230 OCU from a tour on Canberras, and were therefore used to flying jets at high altitudes and speeds; once they had got used to the Vulcan's size, and the technical innovations explained in Chapter 2, few of them found any difficulty in coping with the big delta, with its fighter-like cockpit and handling qualities. The first phase of OCU training consisted of four weeks' ground school, during which pilots received instruction on the Vulcan's performance and systems, with emphasis on their particular responsibilities, which included management of the fuel system in the air and so on. Towards the end of the ground school phase, pilots were introduced to the Vulcan flight simulator, which in 1957 was probably the most advanced piece of equipment of its kind in the world. Sixteen hours on the simulator were followed by two weeks of mixed ground school and flying before the final OCU phase, which comprised six weeks of intensive flying. The first instructional flight consisted of two hours' demonstration of the Vulcan's handling at high altitude, followed by roller landings; then came a short cross-country flight followed by a demonstration of the aircraft's emergency systems. The first solo, when the OCU student pilot captained the aircraft for the first time, was usually made on the third exercise. By the end of the course, pilots had accumulated about 50 hours on type, half of this time at night.

Most of the Vulcan Navigator Plotters and Navigators Radar also came from the Canberra squadrons, although some had experience on the Avro Lincoln or B-29 Washington and were thoroughly familiar with the H2SIVA and APQ13 navigational

On July 3 1958, the nosewheel fell off Vulcan B 1 XH497 of 617 Squadron. The rear crew baled out—although one of them was unfortunately killed when his parachute failed to open—and the pilot, Flight Lieutenant Smeaton, landed the aircraft successfully on its mainwheels and nosewheel strut at RAF Scampton.

radar aids. Their workload was high, for there were new systems to be mastered; the Vulcan, for example, was equipped with 'Green Satin', a radar aid which used the Doppler principle to calculate the aircraft's true groundspeed and drift. This information was fed into an analogue computer, which provided a continuous display of the aircraft's position in geographical co-ordinates. The big advantage of 'Green Satin', unlike the earlier 'Gee' fixing system—which relied on three ground stations relaying electronic pulses to receiver equipment in the aircraft and consequently had a range limitation—was that it was completely self-contained. As an added safeguard and check, 'Green Satin' was usually employed in conjunction with astro-navigation, an art in which all V-Force Nav Plotters were highly proficient. They had to be, for if the electronic equipment failed they would have to use 'astro' to navigate the bomber accurately to its target.

The Navigator Radar had an even more exacting task, for he had to master the intricacies of the bomber's nerve-centre, the Navigation and Bombing System (NBS) Mk 1, with its H2S Mk 9A radar and its Navigation and Bombing Computer (NBC) Mk 2. All Radar Navigators for the V-Force had to go through an 18-week course with the Bomber Command Bombing School at RAF Lindholme, near Doncaster. To bring them up to the standard required for entry into the Medium Bomber Force OCUs, the training had to be very intensive indeed; some very experienced men fell by the wayside at Lindholme.

The course began with an introductory phase which provided a background knowledge of computers, radar principles and bombing theory, and then the students plunged straight into the NBS Mk 1, with ground school studies of radar displays and the techniques used in the solution of navigational and bombing equations. Lectures were interspersed with practical exercises carried out in NBS synthetic trainers which were laid out to resemble the installations found in the V-bombers. After ten weeks of ground school, the students entered the flying phase in aircraft equipped with the NBS Mk 1; these were initially Avro Lincolns, later replaced by Hastings T Mk 5 aircraft. As well as the NBS, they also carried 'Green Satin' Doppler equipment (and eventually 'Blue Silk', which was an updated version). Training sorties were of about six hours' duration and were flown on pre-planned routes, specially selected to provide a wide variety of radar scope interpretation problems. The sorties provided two stages of six targets so that with two students alternating between radar and plotting duties, each had six first run attacks as operator, and crew co-operation between the navigators could be practised throughout the sortie, which was controlled by a qualified NBS instructor. Fourteen such air exercises were undertaken by each student before completion of the course, after which he went on to join the OCU.

The third member of the Vulcan's rear crew, the Air Electronics Officer, was a new aircrew category, introduced in 1956 to replace the earlier Signaller. When the Valiant had been introduced in 1955, it had been thought that the transition of existing signallers from types such as the Lincoln would present little problem, and that their task would be much the same—in other words, monitoring the aircraft's electrical systems and operating the W/T and R/T equipment. Most signallers of that era were NCO aircrew and some of

Vulcan B 1s of No 617 Squadron with their air and ground crews at Farnborough in September 1960, where they demonstrated a scramble time of 1 minute 24 seconds.

them were highly experienced, having learned their trade the hard way during the war in Bomber or Coastal Commands, but the complexity of the new V-bombers' electronic systems soon made it plain that no amount of experience could compensate for lack of academic qualification. Working on the theory (perhaps unfairly) that the average NCO signaller would find it hard to cope with the necessary degree of sophistication, the RAF introduced the AEO category, which was aimed at recruiting officer candidates—although NCOs were not debarred from it, provided they attained the required standard. (Curiously enough, although NCO AEOs were eventually phased out of the V-Force, they continued to fly in RAF maritime and transport aircraft, and still do.) All AEOs had to go through the AEO Training School, which was set up at Swanton Morley in 1957. It moved to Hullavington in 1958, and later to Topcliffe.

The AEO course was perhaps the most intensive of all, the students ploughing through electronic theory which was then greatly in excess of what was actually required; flying was carried out in Valetta T 3 or Varsity T Mk 1 aircraft. But there was evidence of shrewd forward-thinking in the comprehensive nature of the course, for electronic refinements—mainly concerned with countermeasures—were on the way which would double the AEO's workload under operational conditions. As it was, an AEO emerging in somewhat dazed condition from his course and joining the OCU might have been forgiven for any feeling of anti-climax when he discovered that the only real counter-measures equipment on the Vulcan was 'Window', bundles of tinfoil designed to confuse enemy radar scanners, which had first been used in the bombing of Hamburg in July 1943.

The countermeasures squadrons of No 100 Group, RAF Bomber Command, had developed electronic warfare to a high degree during the 1939–45 war, and during its closing months 'Mandrels', or screens of aircraft fitted with special jamming equipment, had been a feature of almost every Main Force operation. After the war, however, the development of ECM was allowed to lapse, mainly because the rudimentary nature of the Soviet air defence radar network made it possible for RAF bombers such as the Lincoln to get through to their targets using 'Window' alone. An analysis of wartime bomber losses, however, had revealed the need for new tail-warning radar, and in June 1947 the Air Staff issued a requirement for a Canberra TWR known as 'Orange Putter'. This was followed, just under a year later, by a requirement for similar equipment for the V-Force.

Known as 'Red Garter', the TWR for the first generation of V-bombers would have given both pilot and AEO visual indication of an enemy fighter approaching from astern within 170 degrees in azimuth and 80 degrees in elevation; it would also have given the other crew members an audible warning. The definitive design of all three V-bombers provided space to fit the device's 18-inch scanner in the tail, but trials with 'Red Garter' revealed a number of shortcomings and it was never used. There was still the feeling that, given the air defence state of the art in the Soviet Union during the late 1940s, the V-Bombers could still get through using their superior height and speed in conjunction with 'Window'.

The first winter of the Korean War changed this line of thought dramatically. Along the Yalu River, the Red Chinese, with Soviet help, installed a chain of radar warning stations designed to operate in conjunction with MiG-15 jet interceptors, a combination that soon made that particular bit of sky an unhealthy place for the USAF's B-29 bombers. The Russians were apparently learning fast, and the speed and ceiling of the MiG-15 made it a definite threat to the RAF V-Force, which was then still five years away from becoming operational. By that time, the Russians would doubtless have a new generation of jet interceptors. Almost overnight, the need for effective ECM once again became pressing.

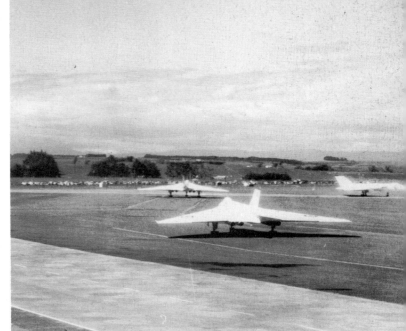

In October-November 1959, four Vulcan B 1s of No 617 Squadron flew to Ohakea, New Zealand, to represent Bomber Command at the official opening of Wellington International Airport. The three aircraft seen in these photographs (the fourth, XH498, having been damaged) went on to complete a round-the-world trip by continuing eastwards across the Pacific to the UK via the United States.

This page and right *While taking part in 617 Squadron's New Zealand tour, the fourth Vulcan, XH498, undershot the runway at Wellington while attempting a landing, sustaining damage to the port undercarriage and fuel tank. The captain managed to overshoot and fly back to Ohakea, where he carried out a successful crash landing.*

Below right XH498 *was repaired at Ohakea and seven months later was flown out by a 617 Squadron crew captained by Flight Lieutenant Bell. It is seen here taking off on its first air test after repair.*

Developing new ECM jammers from wartime designs did not present a problem, but at best such jammers would be stop-gap affairs. No 100 Group had used three principal types of jammer: 'Mandrel', developed at the Wembley laboratories of the General Electric Company and designed to jam the enemy early warning frequency from 88 to 200 megacycles; 'Piperack', developed from 'Mandrel' to cover the 90-110 megacycles frequency used by the German AI radars; and 'Jostle', which emitted a high-pitched wail on 38-42 megacycles VHF and 3-6 megacycles HF, the German fighter control frequencies. It was a noise jammer which Bomber Command needed in the early 1950s; the problem was that such a device could not be fitted to the early generation of V-Bombers because too much space was taken up by the NBS.

To give Bomber Command at least some electronic countermeasures capability, No 199 Squadron—which had been part of No 100 Group during the war—was reformed in July 1951 at the Central Signals Establishment, RAF Watton, equipped with Lincoln and Mosquito NF 36 aircraft and given a radio countermeasures role. In April 1952 it moved from Watton to Hemswell, and by 1956 was flying a mixture of Lincolns and Canberras. Meanwhile, a 'special' Valiant, *WP214*, had been carrying out trials with new ECM equipment at the Bomber Command Development Unit, Finningley, and various other establishments, and in July 1957 No 199 Squadron received the first Valiants to carry the new jammers at Honington. On December 15 1958, 'C' Flight of 199 Squadron moved to Finningley and became No 18 Squadron, which assumed the ECM role in support of the V-Force.

To operate the ECM equipment, each Valiant carried two AEOs. In retrospect, it is doubtful whether the Squadron would have proved very effective under war conditions, for six Valiants could hardly have provided an ECM screen for the whole of the V-Force. In addition, the jamming equipment was subject to severe limitations in that it could cover only a very narrow frequency at a time, and even then the jamming transmissions were only at their best when the aircraft flew port side on to the station that was being jammed. The only real solution was for the spearhead aircraft of the V-Force, the Vulcans and Victors, to carry their own ECM, and this took a considerable time to implement, as we shall see.

In the meantime, the first Vulcan OCU course graduated at Waddington on May 20 1957 and immediately went to form 'A' Flight of No 83 Squadron, the first operational Vulcan unit, at the same station. No 83 received the first of its Vulcans, *XA905*, on July 11 1957, its crews having used aircraft 'borrowed' from the OCU until that date, and the second machine, *XA904*, was delivered on July 16. Two more Vulcans, *XA906* and '907, arrived on August 12 and 29, followed by *XA908* on September 18 and *XA911* on November 1. With these six aircraft 83 Squadron saw out the remainder of 1957, and it was not until February 17 1958 that a seventh B 1 was delivered; this was *XH477*, which was followed by *XH480* on April 22 1958 and *XH503* on December 30.

With its first six aircraft, resplendent in their overall white anti-flash paint, broken only by the RAF roundels and fin flashes, serial numbers, the red cross of the City of Lincoln on their fins and the black antler badge of 83 Squadron emblazoned on their fuselages just aft of the roundel, the unit trained intensively during the latter half of 1957, carrying out a programme which included long-range flights overseas. In October 1957, for example, two of No 83's Vulcans went to Pinecastle Air Force Base in Florida, together with one from 230 OCU and four Valiants of Nos 214 and 138 Squadrons, No 3 Group, to take part in what was to become an annual event for the V-Force: Strategic Air Command's Bombing, Navigation and Reconnaissance Competition. Bomber Command allocated the appropriate code-name of Operation Longshot to the exercise; the competition itself carried the USAF code-name of Iron Horse.

It was a very exacting contest, lasting for six nights; each bomber wing was represented by two aircraft and two crews, each of whom flew on three alternate nights. The route, flown level cruise, covered more than 2,700 nautical miles and included an astro navigation leg of over 800 miles, scored at the end of the sortie by ground radar, and three widely spaced radar bombing attacks, also scored by ground radar. A take-off limit of five minutes and an en route timing tolerance of plus or minus three minutes was imposed; failure to achieve this disqualified a crew, as did failure to achieve a competition total of six scored bomb runs and two scored astro runs.

The two 83 Squadron Vulcans that took part in the competition (the OCU aircraft was held in reserve) flew a slightly longer route than the Valiants, 2,774.5 nautical miles against 2,724.5. There were nine turning points and three target complexes, Kansas City, St Louis and Atlanta, and in the event it was the Valiants which stole the RAF show, with one of 214 Squadron's crews placed 11th out of the 90 competing and the Valiant Wing being placed 27th overall. The Vulcans were further down the list, but it was recognised that their participation had been a 'flag-showing' exercise with considerable training value, for the crews had far less experience on type than their Valiant colleagues and there had been far less time to prepare. The OCU Vulcan, in fact, did not arrive at Pinecastle until October 30, the first morning of the competition, carrying Air Chief Marshal Sir Harry Broadhurst, C-in-C Bomber Command, and the AOC No 3 Group, Air Vice-Marshal K.B.B. Cross. At the close of the competition, Valiants and Vulcans flew home via Goose Bay. It had been a worthwhile and satisfying operation, and one which did much to cement a long-lasting relationship between SAC and the V-Force, although it had been marred by the death of the Bomber Command detachment leader, Group Captain J. Woodroffe, DSO, DFC, who was killed while flying in a B-47 near Pinecastle.

Early in 1958, No 83 Squadron was selected to carry out a series of goodwill tours overseas; some of these were planned and executed on a 'Lone Ranger' basis, and all minor servicing, including the repacking of tail parachutes, had to be done by the crews themselves. On other occasions, ground crews accompanied the Vulcans in Hastings aircraft. On the first such trip, in March 1958, three Vulcans of No 83 Squadron—*XA904*, *'908* and *'911* left Waddington and flew to Wheelus Air Force Base, Tripoli, in 2 hours 45 minutes. From there, after a night stop, the three aircraft crossed the Sahara to Entebbe, Uganda, in 4 hours 55 minutes; navigation over this barren leg presented no problem, for the Vulcans' Doppler systems functioned perfectly and additional frequent checks were made by sun shots and use of the radio compass.

On the day after their arrival at Entebbe, Vulcan *XA904*—piloted by Squadron Leader Don Howard, survivor of the Heathrow crash, with Flight Lieutenant Mountford as his co-pilot—left for Embakasi, Kenya, where it was to be displayed statically as part of the celebrations to mark the opening of Nairobi's new airport. The flying display was to be made by *XA908*, with *'911* as reserve. That evening, a crowd of 30,000 at Embakasi thrilled as the great white delta thundered overhead, having been routed via Mount Kilimanjaro. On the ground, the static display crew looked up enviously; they had spent the entire afternoon answering a barrage of questions and posing for innumerable photographs.

The next day, while *XA904* and *'911* prepared to fly home via El Adem, Libya, *XA908* flew from Embakasi, where it had landed and spent the night, to Salisbury in what was then Southern Rhodesia, covering the 1,075 nautical miles in 2 hours 2 minutes, which was no mean achievement. As an unofficial record was at stake, the aircraft carried out a direct approach and roller landing using the upwind end of the runway, causing no little consternation among the spectators, who had been looking in the opposite direction.

Before landing, the aircraft flew over Salisbury in a huge figure-of-eight, causing traffic jams in the city streets as people watched. After spending the night at RRAF Station New Sarum, the crew of '908 took the Vulcan on a round trip that encompassed Que-Que, Gwelo, Thornhill, Bulawayo, Kariba and Lusaka. Afterwards, *XA908* flew back to Waddington via Embakasi and El Adem, where the crew learned that the other two Vulcans had been diverted homewards via Wheelus because of dust storms over the Libyan base.

A few weeks later, two of 83 Squadron's Vulcans—*XH477* and *XA911*—flew to Buenos Aires as part of a British delegation to mark the Argentine Presidential Inauguration ceremonies, and afterwards went on to Rio de Janeiro for an official visit to Brazil. Air Vice-Marshal G.A. Walker, the AOC No 1 Group, who had also been on the African tour, flew as co-pilot in one of the Vulcans, which were accompanied by a Comet of No 216 Squadron carrying the Right Hon George Ward, MP, Secretary of State for Air.

The Vulcans flew direct from Waddington to Dakar, the West African base in French Equatorial Territory, covering 2,645 statute miles in 5 hours 17 minutes at an average speed of 498 mph. From there they crossed the South Atlantic to Rio, a distance of 3,150 miles, in 5 hours 50 minutes, averaging 540 mph, and the final 1,238-mile leg from Rio to Buenos Aires was completed in 2 hours 5 minutes at an average speed of 594 mph. The two V-Force crews were very well entertained by their Argentine Air Force hosts, and the AAF commander, Brigadier Alfredo Vedoya, was given an hour's demonstration flight in *XH477*, captained by Flight Lieutenant Dudley Lob.

On Inauguration Day, the RAF detachment took part in a 129-aircraft flypast over Government House, the three RAF aircraft flying in a 'vic' with the Comet leading. After passing the saluting base, the Vulcans opened up to full speed and roared upwards to left and right in an impressive display of power that generated spontaneous applause. Later,

Left XH482, *No 617 Squadron's first Vulcan B 1, arriving at Scampton in May 1958.*

Right *Group Captain Finch, former OC RAF Waddington, climbing from a Vulcan at RAAF Richmond after a flight across Australia. This photograph gives a good view of the exit hatch.*

on the last day of the visit to Argentina, *XA911* (Flight Lieutenant P.M. Woodward) made a noisy and effective display before a large crowd at Ezeiza Airport, while *XH477* and the Comet were displayed statically.

Flying on to Brazil, *XH477*—carrying AVM Walker—landed at Galeao Airport in rapidly deteriorating conditions, and Walker wisely went to the control tower to order diversions to Santa Cruz for the other Vulcan and the Comet; the memory of the Heathrow disaster was still too fresh to permit undue risks, and the cloud base at Rio—which was flanked by high hills—was down to 200 ft in heavy rain. The weather, in fact, prevented the Vulcans from carrying out their planned flying display over Rio; it was still pouring rain when the aircraft departed on the long flight to Dakar two days later. From Dakar the Vulcans flew direct to Waddington, following a slightly different route to the outbound one; although the homeward run was 200 miles longer (2,830 statute miles), the aircraft completed it in 5 hours 10 minutes.

The Vulcans' African and South American trips were resounding successes, and typical of the many prestige flights which would be undertaken by Vulcans and other V-Force aircraft during the years to come. Moreover, they enhanced the Vulcan's reputation as a truly global bomber, and by the autumn of 1958 Vulcan crews were departing from the United Kingdom on regular 'Lone Ranger' exercises, bound for various distant points of the compass in the confident knowledge that the aircraft would do all that was expected of it.

Then, on October 24 1958, came another tragedy. Vulcan *XA908* of No 83 Squadron—one of the trio of aircraft which had 'shown the flag' in Africa earlier that year—was flying from Goose Bay in Labrador to Lincoln Air Force Base, Nebraska, as part of a 'Lone Ranger' exercise when it suffered total electrical failure over Dresden, 60 miles north of Detroit, at 35,000 ft. An emergency battery ought to have provided enough power to feed the electrical services for 20 minutes, enabling the aircraft captain to make an emergency descent to Kellog Field, Michigan, but its power in fact lasted for only three minutes, at the end of which time the Vulcan's electrically-operated control surfaces ceased to function and the aircraft went down at a 60-degree angle to crash in a residential area of Detroit. It ploughed through some trees and hit a group of houses, five of which were destroyed; by some miracle only one civilian, an elderly woman, was seriously hurt. Out of *XA908*'s six-man crew, only the co-pilot managed to bale out, but he parachuted into Lake St Clair and drowned because he was not wearing a lifejacket.

Later, it was established that the crash of *XA908* had been caused by a one-in-a-million chance. The main electrical power in the Vulcan B 1 was supplied by four 112-volt DC generators, driven by the engines, and these generators fed the principal electrical services, such as the flying controls, via a single busbar. This was the problem, for although the engines had continued to power the generators, a short-circuit on the busbar had prevented the power from reaching the vital services. This, together with the depleted state of the reserve battery, had added up to disaster. In the wake of this accident, to prevent a similar occurrence, the busbar on all other Vulcan B 1s was split in two.

The accident was doubly tragic, because it came only a month after the loss of another Vulcan and its crew. This was the Vulcan prototype, *VX770*, which crashed on September 20 1958 during a Battle of Britain display at Syerston, Nottinghamshire, following an engine explosion. *VX770*, which at that time was on loan from the Ministry of Supply to Rolls-Royce and based at Hucknall for engine development work, carried a crew of three civilians and an RAF co-pilot, all of whom were killed, together with three airmen on the ground.

Meanwhile, No 83 Squadron—which by now had reached a considerable peak of operational efficiency under the able leadership of its CO, Wing Commander A.D. Frank— had been joined in service by two other Vulcan units. The first was No 101 Squadron, which re-formed at Finningley on October 15 1957, a fortnight after the delivery of its first Vulcan B 1, *XA909*. Previously, it had been the first squadron to operate Canberras, with which type it had seen action over Malaya and Suez before its disbandment on February 1 1957. By the end of April 1958 No 101 had taken delivery of seven more Vulcans: these were *XA910*, *'912* and *'913*, *XH475*, *'476*, *'479* and *'481*. The *XH* series of aircraft, all part of a new batch which had been ordered in 1954, were fitted with uprated Olympus 104 engines of 13,500 lb st.

Vulcan B 1 XA907 of No 83 Squadron in formation with RAAF Sabres and a Canberra during a goodwill visit to Australia.

The third Vulcan B 1 squadron was one of the most celebrated of all wartime bomber units: No 617 Squadron, the 'Dam Busters'. It, too, had operated Canberras in its recent history, and had flown them against Malayan terrorists in 1955, disbanding in December of that year. It now re-formed at its original wartime base, Scampton in Lincolnshire, on May 1 1958, and its first Vulcan, *XH482*, was delivered to Scampton from Woodford on May 5 by Air Commodore J.N.H. 'Charles' Whitworth, who had been station commander at Scampton at the time of the dams raid in 1943. By the second week of November 1958, No 617 had received its complement of eight Vulcan B 1s, the remainder being *XH483*, *'497*, *'498*, *'499*, *'500*, *'501* and *'502*. No 617 Squadron suffered its first Vulcan accident on July 3 1958. The aircraft involved was *XH497*, the third Vulcan to be delivered, and the captain was Flight Lieutenant Graham Smeaton. Following take-off on a training sortie, the nosewheel fell off. Smeaton gained altitude and ordered the rear crew to abandon the aircraft; the exit was made successfully, but unfortunately one of the men was killed when his parachute failed to open. Smeaton, assisted by the co-pilot, landed the aircraft on a foam strip, touching down in the normal attitude on the main undercarriage and then allowing the Vulcan to settle gently on its nosewheel strut. *XH497* was subsequently repaired and continued in service until May 1966. In recognition of his skill, Smeaton was awarded the Queen's Commendation for Valuable Service in the Air.

The year 1959 saw the loss of another B 1, although this was not a squadron aircraft. On July 24, Vulcan *XA891*, the Olympus 200 engine installation development aircraft, experienced engine trouble not long after take-off from Woodford. The aircraft captain, Squadron Leader Jimmy Harrison—Avro's chief test pilot—managed to retain control long enough to fly the rapidly failing machine clear of the densely populated urban areas of Manchester and Leeds and headed for open country in the East Riding of Yorkshire. After transmitting a 'Mayday' call, which was received by RAF Leconfield, Harrison ordered his crew—there were four others in the aircraft, all civilians—to bale out at 14,000 ft over Goole, and then followed suit. The Vulcan went down to explode in a field near High Hunsley; no one on the ground was hurt, and all the crew members were picked up safely. It was the first time that all the crew had escaped from a crashing Vulcan.

What might have been a serious accident was skilfully avoided later in the year, this time by a 617 Squadron pilot. On October 13 1959, a force of four 617 Squadron Vulcans, supported by a Bristol Britannia of No 99 Squadron and under the command of Air Vice-Marshal J.G. Davis, AOC No 1 Group, left Scampton to fly to Ohakea, New Zealand, by way of Akrotiri, Karachi, Butterworth and Darwin. The purpose of the visit, apart from providing training over long-range routes, was to represent Bomber Command at the official opening of New Zealand's Wellington Airport, after which the Vulcans were scheduled to fly home via Fiji, Christmas Island, Honolulu, California, Nebraska and Goose Bay.

The four Vulcans duly arrived at Ohakea on October 19, and five days later one of them, *XH498*, took off for Wellington, where it was to form part of the static display. The pilot, Squadron Leader Tony Smailes, made two attempts to land on Wellington's relatively short runway, but overshot each time. On the third attempt, flying a wider circuit, he seemed fairly set to touch down at the extreme upwind end of the runway, leaving himself plenty of room, but in fact the Vulcan's main undercarriage struck the undershoot area. The impact damaged the port undercarriage, forcing it up into the wing and piercing a fuel tank. The port wing dropped sharply, and only prompt corrective action by Smailes prevented a disaster. As one observer, a RNZAF officer, put it: 'It seemed nothing could save the plane or us. I remember thinking it would be a miracle if the Vulcan didn't overturn and explode, killing us all with burning fuel.'

A full salvo of 21 1,000 bombs drops from a Vulcan to explode in the sea during a practice live bombing sortie.

Smailes, however, applied full power and managed to climb away, with fuel pouring from the damaged tank and the port undercarriage swinging loose. As the Vulcan headed north towards Ohakea RNZAF search and rescue aircraft were placed on standby in the expectation that Smailes would order his crew to bale out. Instead, he executed an emergency landing on a carpet of foam at Ohakea; the aircraft was saved and no one was injured. *XH498* was to remain at Ohakea for the next seven months while repairs were carried out; it eventually returned to the UK in June 1960, and remained in service until it was relegated to instructional airframe duties (serial *7993M*) in the mid-'60s.

Such mishaps, fortunately, were rare: remarkably so, in fact, considering the intensive flying carried out by the three Vulcan squadrons and the OCU as the 1950s drew to a close. Training procedures, which had been subject to a good deal of experiment since 1955, as Bomber Command's medium bomber force worked hard to familiarise itself with its new four-engined jets, were now pretty well formalised, and were the same for all V-Force squadrons.

Vulcan B 1 XH502 of 617 Squadron on a goodwill visit to Taiwan during a Far Eastern tour. Aircraft in the foreground are Chinese Nationalist AF Sabres.

A typical training sortie might involve a $4\frac{1}{2}$-hour cross-country flight around the UK, the crew carrying out simulated radar bombing runs against selected targets. Before such a sortie each crew member would receive an individual briefing, and most of the workload here would fall on the two navigators, with the Nav Radar assembling information on the allocated radar targets and the Nav Plotter collating all relevant route information, including weather details. The co-pilot would be busy, too, calculating such factors as loading, fuel, endurance and weights on take-off and landing, while the air electronics officer would be checking the callsigns and classified codes which were to be used during the sortie. With these preliminaries out of the way, the whole crew would be assembled and briefed by the aircraft captain on the nature and purpose of the sortie.

The Vulcan would then be handed over by the crew chief and the crew would enter the cockpit to begin their pre-flight checks. The checklist was a lengthy one and could take anything up to an hour to complete, although in the case of an aircraft on an alert exercise this would already have been done and everything would be switched on and ready for engine start. The efficiency of the whole procedure depended on the experience of the crew, and V-Force crews were carefully graded into four categories: Unclassified, on first joining their squadron, Combat, Select and Select Star, each category being harder to attain until the final accolade of Select Star was reached by a few, these being the elite crews who could go anywhere at any time, arriving within seconds of their estimate to hit a target with an aiming error of only a few yards.

The real test of expertise was to carry out a successful 'Lone Ranger', usually to El Adem, Cyprus and Nairobi, or a 'Western Ranger' to the United States, flying to Offutt Air Force Base, Omaha, Nebraska, the headquarters of Strategic Air Command, via Goose Bay. One such 'Lone Ranger' was admirably described by an Air Ministry public relations man who made the 9,960-mile trip to Kenya and back in a Vulcan of 101 Squadron.

'The navigator, Flight Lieutenant Colin Forrester, was only 30 seconds late in his calculations at the end of the 2,510-mile flight from Finningley to Akrotiri, in Cyprus. Thereafter he was six seconds early from Akrotiri to Nairobi (3,080 miles), and on time from Nairobi to El Adem and thence on to Waddington. Heights flown were at the relatively low level of 42,000 ft and 44,000 ft.

'The start of this particular Lone Ranger was not auspicious for, on levelling out at 42,000 ft over Guildford, there was a thump and one of the Bristol Olympus engines seized up, a second stopping in sympathy at the same time. Such is the power of these engines, however, that the Vulcan flew quite comfortably on two and almost normally when the third was re-lighted. A return to base, a perfect landing by the captain, Flight Lieutenant Eric Denham, and we were airborne several hours later in another Vulcan, which operated with no trouble at all.

'Carrying a pannier in the bomb bay laden with spare wheels, luggage, spare braking parachutes and extra parts, the aircraft flew smoothly and swiftly to the air force base at Akrotiri in 4½ hours. Once landed, the crew chief, Norman Raney, quickly and efficiently started putting the giant Vulcan 'to bed', aided by the crew—fitting a new tail parachute, folding the used one, fitting the blanks in the air intake ducts, covering the wheels, and supervising refuelling.

'Next morning, after all the checks had been done and the rations put aboard—

XH502 after conversion to B 1A. This aircraft was the last B 1A at Waddington, and was flown to Scampton in January 1968 for ground instructional duties.

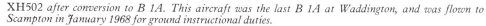

Vulcan B 1A XH481 of 101 Squadron seen at Perth, Australia, after making a UK-Australia non-stop flight in 1961.

sandwiches, chocolate, chewing gum, tinned fruit juice and soup—we were airborne again for the flight to Nairobi, the distance being greater than necessary because Egypt cannot be overflown and there is, therefore, a diversion back to El Adem. The tins of fruit juice were put on the floor, where they are nicely chilled, the outside air temperature at 42,000 ft being minus 50 degrees Centigrade.

'From El Adem there is 2,000 miles of the Libyan desert to cross and the bomber quivered occasionally as it rode the 'cobblestones'—the jet air stream met with at high altitudes. Apart from that, the only diversion is eating or drinking, for the crews are not engaged in split-second exercises on Lone Rangers but on purely long-distance flying, made more boring by the very remoteness that high flying engenders. There is just the bright blue sky and the sun, the bomber's presence on the ground being noted only by a faint hum and a possible flash of light from the cockpit canopy or from the wings painted in white anti-flash paint.

'Embakasi Airport, Nairobi, the final stop on the outward journey, was reached after a total flying time of 10 hours 15 minutes, during which we had covered 5,590 miles . . . The return journey, through El Adem instead of Akrotiri, took a total of 8 hours 30 minutes for 4,370 miles, on both 'legs' the aircraft arriving dead on the estimated time. The only bizarre touch to the trip was the necessity of landing at Waddington to clear Customs, the Vulcan then being flown for 10 minutes across to the home base at Finningley, a mere 40 miles away.'

Western Rangers were welcomed by the V-Force crews, who by the end of 1959 had developed a first-class working relationship with their counterparts in Strategic Air Command, not least because it enabled them to enjoy the generous hospitality of their American hosts. The RAF aircrew quickly absorbed USAF operating procedures and practices, and little basic change from RAF standard procedure was found to be necessary, although flight clearances were far more closely supervised and no aircraft was allowed to take off from a SAC base until the flight plan was cleared by the controlling authority. This clearance would usually be given at the runway marshalling point, and required a full and correct 'read back' of the complete flight plan before take-off was cleared. Fortunately, the Vulcan embodied a modification which permitted the AEO to use the VHF in isolation from the rest of the crew; he therefore handled all clearances, leaving the pilots free to carry out their checks. In Air Defence Identification Zones, position reporting had to be meticulous and punctual, otherwise the aircraft would quickly be intercepted by USAF fighters. Apart from that, as one V-Force navigator noted ruefully, the area in which RAF and SAC practice differed most noticeably was in the quality of the flying rations. Five different USAF flight meal menus were available, ranging from 'bite-size' steak to fried chicken, complete with milk, fruit, chocolate, cigarettes, condiments and tooth pick—a far cry from the standard Bomber Command fare of curly sandwiches, cheese biscuits and lukewarm tomato soup!

As the Vulcan squadrons gradually built up experience, they began to take part in other overseas exercises which, until now, had been the prerogative of the Valiants. These included Exercise Sunflower, which involved a squadron detachment to Malaya of up to a month's duration, local familiarisation flights being followed by air defence exercises with the SEATO air forces; Exercise Sunspot, in which crews would be detached to Luqa, Malta, for visual bombing over the El Adem range in Libya with 100 lb practice or 1,000 lb live HE bombs; and single-aircraft detachments, known as 'Polar Bears', to Norway.

The V-Force's intensive bombing and navigation training reached an annual climax in the RAF Medium Bomber Force Bombing and Navigation Competition. This introduced a considerable element of rivalry, not only between competing crews, but also between the two RAF Bomber Groups involved—No 1 with its Vulcans and No 3 with Valiants (and later Victor B 1s, which participated from 1960). The top squadron received the coveted Laurence Minot Trophy, a 36-inch-high work of art depicting an eagle with outstretched wings mounted on a demi-globe which was supported on an ebony base. The trophy was presented to the Royal Air Force in 1926 by an anonymous donor in memory of Captain Laurence Minot, MC, who was killed in action over Flanders on July 28 1917 while serving with No 57 Squadron, RFC. It was originally awarded for visual bombing and later for H2S bombing, and it became the premier award in the Medium Bomber Force contest in 1957. The Vulcans of 83 Squadron won it in 1957, only six weeks after the Squadron re-equipped, which was no mean achievement, and 617 Squadron won it in 1959, the Valiants of 138 Squadron having captured it in the meantime. The same two squadrons also won the Sassoon Trophy for navigational achievement, and in 1959 No 617 Squadron captured the Armament Officers' Trophy as well, which was awarded for the best NBS bombing score.

The competition was very demanding on all crew members, especially the navigators, who had to show their ability to operate using only limited equipment over a leg of about 800 miles. This meant relying on astro-navigation, the Nav Radar taking celestial shots with a sextant and the Nav Plotter working out headings and ETAs with the information so obtained. The leg terminated over a radar bombing site, the end-of-leg position being determined by a signal sent out from the aircraft. This was plotted by a ground station, and any navigational error calculated accordingly. AEOs were also required to receive coded message groups within a specified time, and all the results achieved were collated to produce individual crew ratings. Each aircraft carried an umpire and the competition lasted for three days—four days, if bad weather intervened.

Then, of course, there were exercises that simulated the 'real thing'. In its early years, the V-Force relied on dispersing its aircraft to airfields all over the United Kingdom to escape the effects of enemy attack on its main bases. There were 36 such dispersal airfields in the late 1950s, later reduced to 26 by 1962. These were Lossiemouth, Kinloss,

Captained by Squadron Leader Ron Dick, this Vulcan of No 9 Squadron—bearing the name Mayflower III*—flew to Hanscom AFB, Massachusetts, bearing messages of greeting from the City Council of Boston Lincs, on the anniversary of the sailing of the original* Mayflower.

Leuchars, Prestwick and Machrihanish in Scotland; Aldergrove in Northern Ireland; Middleton St George (now Tees-side Airport) in Durham; Leeming, Elvington and Leconfield in Yorkshire; Burtonwood near Manchester; Cranwell in Lincolnshire; Shawbury in Shropshire; Valley in Anglesey; Llanbedr and Brawdy in Wales; Bedford; Pershore, near Worcester; Kemble; Filton, near Bristol; Lyneham and Boscombe Down in Wiltshire; Manston, in Kent; Yeovilton; Tarrant Rushton; and finally St Mawgan in Cornwall.

Alert exercises could be called at any time, and V-Force aircrew kept a bag ready packed with all the necessities for an indefinite stay away from their home base. Sometimes, squadrons received prior notice of dispersal, and in this case the exercise was code-named 'Kinsman'; dispersal without notice, on the other hand, was code-named 'Mickey Finn', and could happen at any time of the day or night. (More often than not, it seemed to happen at about two o'clock in the morning.)

Aircrews summoned for an alert exercise would report directly to the Operations Wing to be briefed on the nature of the alert. Crews would first of all be briefed together, and then AEOs and navigators would go off to separate briefings by the Wing Navigation Officer and the Wing AEO. In the meantime, ground crews would be hard at work under the direction of their crew chiefs, fuelling and servicing each aircraft as it came 'on the line'. With the aircrew now in a waiting posture, the ground crews would carry out all checks right up to the engine starting sequence. After a brief ground run the engines would then be shut down once more and the aircraft handed over to the crew, who would enter the cockpit of what was now a 'combat ready' machine. The entrance hatch would be locked in place and, from now on, no one would be permitted inside the cockpit except the crew members.

After an unspecified time, the crews would be brought to Readiness One-Five, and final checks would be completed while they listened for instructions over the 'Bomber Box', the teletalk system linking the aircraft with the Bomber Command Operations Room at High Wycombe, Buckinghamshire. Over the teletalk, crews were able to hear dispersal instructions being issued to other V-Force stations, usually in a set pattern, so they had a good idea when their own turn would come. Meanwhile, the degree of alert was progressively stepped up, with units being brought to Readiness Zero Five.

At Readiness Zero Two the engines were started; it took about 30 seconds to start each one, so all four should have been lit up within two minutes. (Later, a simultaneous starting technique was devised, enabling all four engines to be started at once.) The aircraft would then be scrambled and sent to their dispersal airfields in clutches of four; alternatively, depending on the nature of the alert, they might go straight into a training profile involving a lengthy cross-country flight and simulated radar bombing attacks.

Once on their dispersal airfields, the V-Bombers could be scrambled at a moment's notice, and the crews lived in special caravans close to their aircraft. Air and ground crews might have to live like this for days, waiting for the signal to go, the ground crews carrying out full pre-take-off checks once every 24 hours and the aircrews being progressively updated through successive briefings. When the 'scramble' call came, either by klaxon or a broadcast over the station tannoy, crews would quickly don their flying gear and race for their aircraft. If the scramble was at their home base they would be waiting in the Operations Wing, from where they would dash outside to waiting crew buses in a scramble that looked chaotic, but was in fact very orderly; the AEO would be first into the bus, followed by the two pilots and then the two navigators.

At the dispersal the AEO was first out of the bus and into the aircraft. Throwing himself into his seat on the right-hand side of the rear cockpit, he immediately began tripping the switches which brought in the external power supply needed to start the

Vulcan B 1As of the Waddington Wing at RAAF Richmond.

engines. Once assured by his warning lights that everything was functioning, he yelled 'Externals on!' to the aircraft captain, who had followed him up the ladder and who, by this time, would be squeezing himself into his seat. As soon as he heard the AEO's call the captain would throw the engine starter switch and begin the start-up sequence for the first engine; he would be quickly joined by the co-pilot, who had his own part to play in the starting procedure as the first engine began turning. Fourth man into the cockpit was the Nav Radar, who went straight to his seat on the left-hand side, leaving the last man in, the Nav Plotter, to retract the ladder and close the entrance hatch.

The two busiest men at this time were the pilots, who not only had to start the engines, but also had to strap themselves into their ejection seats, put on their bone-domes and connect their intercom and oxygen leads. Outside the aircraft, the crew chief stood by the external intercom, in touch with the captain, ready to assist with external checks, while ground crew members stood by the chocks and the external power cable, ready to whip them away when the crew chief gave the word. With no engine run-up necessary, the V-Bomber could be taxying inside two minutes, the final checks being made as it moved out to the take-off point. No time was lost in holding short of the runway; the aircraft swung straight into its take-off run from the perimeter track.

It should be stressed at this point that the V-Force, unlike SAC, never maintained an airborne nuclear alert force, and the V-Force was never, as far as is known, required to disperse with nuclear weapons on board. Neither should it be imagined that, if the crisis had come, the whole of the V-Force would have been armed with nuclear weapons; some aircraft would have been tasked to hit their targets with conventional free-falling bombs.

The whole purpose behind the conception of the V-Force was that it should act as a deterrent, and for this purpose nuclear weapons formed a large part of its main arsenal; but there was always the knowledge that, if the V-Force went to war, it would have meant that the deterrent had failed, and the Valiants, Vulcans and Victors would have carried a mixture of loads approximate to their task in the war. Training for conventional bombing was just as intensive, if not more so, than that for nuclear strike.

Nuclear training sorties were made as realistic as possible, with the cockpit blacked out by shields and roller blinds fitted to protect the crew from the nuclear flash that would have resulted from the explosion of their own bomb or any others detonating in the vicinity. The 'standard' British nuclear weapon up to 1960 was still the 10,000 lb MC Mk 1 'Blue Danube', but the V-Force used American weapons too; these were smaller than the Danube, and two of them would fit into a Vulcan's bomb-bay. The stockpile of nuclear weapons for the V-Force was held under conditions of extreme security and secrecy at the wartime airfield of Faldingworth, just inside Scampton's air traffic zone beside the A46 between Lincoln and Market Rasen; No 92 Maintenance Unit was responsible for them, and operated as tight a 'fail-safe' system as possible, with duplication of personnel at all levels. Component parts of the nuclear weapons were shipped separately by road to the V-Force bases, and the only time the parts came together to form a complete weapon was prior to an aircraft being bombed-up. Even then, it was impossible for any single person to arm the weapon; this had to be done by a rigid sequence carried out by three members of a V-bomber's crew.

Such was the secrecy surrounding Faldingworth that, between 1956 and 1980, the airfield was not shown on Ordnance Survey maps and, although it was shown on air navigation charts, it was surrounded by a circle marked with diagonal red stripes, indicating that aircraft were forbidden to fly over it at low level.

By the beginning of 1960, the three Vulcan squadrons of Bomber Command's No 1 Group had assumed the spearhead role of the British nuclear deterrent force, although the Valiant squadrons continued to form its backbone and three squadrons of Handley Page Victor B 1s—Nos 10, 15 and 57—had now been formed to give more modern striking power to No 3 Group. By this time, other Vulcan B 1s had been added to the fleet; on December 30 1958, *XH503* and *XH504* respectively joined No 83 Squadron and 230 OCU, and the OCU also took delivery of *XH505* on March 13 1959, followed by *XH532* on the last day of the month. This aircraft was the 45th and last production B 1, and had been on loan to the Controller (Aircraft) for various trials. Completing the list of B 1 allocations, *XH506* went to 101 Squadron on April 17 1959.

Meanwhile, the future of the British deterrent was being shaped by political events. By the autumn of 1959, the RAF's V-bombers had been joined by 60 Thor intermediate-range ballistic missiles, divided among 20 squadrons of Bomber Command, each with three missiles, at locations all over East Anglia. The Thors were a stop-gap measure and were not part of an independent British deterrent, as they were firmly under American control at all times, but it was expected that they would be replaced early in the 1960s by the British-designed Blue Streak IRBM, which would form the ultimate British deterrent weapon throughout that decade, the V-bombers gradually being phased out in favour of missiles. This was the heart of the notorious Defence White Paper of 1957, which reflected the views of the Defence Minister of that time, Duncan Sandys, who believed that the replacement of manned combat aircraft by missiles was a natural evolutionary step. Those views were wrong, as future events were to prove; yet not even Sandys' most vigorous opponents could have foreseen that one of the aircraft destined for replacement, the Vulcan, would still be at the forefront of the RAF's Order of Battle a quarter of a century later.

Chapter 5

Second generation: the B 2

In September 1952, less than a month after the Vulcan prototype had made its first flight, the news was released by Sir Roy Dobson, Avro's managing director, that the company was developing a delta-wing airliner based on the military version. Known as the Type 722 and unofficially named 'Atlantic', this project had reached a fairly advanced design stage by December 1952; had the aircraft come to fruition it would have been larger than the Vulcan, with a span of 121 ft and a length of 145 ft, and it was estimated that it would have been capable of carrying 113 passengers across the Atlantic at 600 mph.

The Avro Atlantic never progressed beyond the project stage, but work on it provided some valuable pointers to how far the basic Vulcan design might logically be taken. Nevertheless, in the early 1950s, much enthusiastic effort in the Avro design office was being devoted not to stretching the existing Vulcan airframe, but to providing a replacement for it altogether in the shape of a brand new delta-wing bomber capable of supersonic speeds and unprecedentedly high altitudes.

The Avro supersonic bomber project started life with Air Staff Operational Requirement 330, issued in 1954, for a very long range reconnaissance aircraft fitted with the latest electronic systems and capable of operating at speeds and altitudes that would make it immune from attack by either interceptors or ground-to-air missiles. Specification R 156T, which was formulated around the OR, called for a minimum cruise of 2.5M, a minimum range of 5,000 nautical miles, and the ability to reach an altitude of 60,000 ft at a distance of 1,000 nautical miles from base. It was the biggest challenge ever laid before

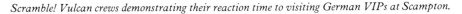

Scramble! Vulcan crews demonstrating their reaction time to visiting German VIPs at Scampton.

Vulcan B 2s of the Waddington Wing in formation with Lightnings.

Two views of a Vulcan B 2 taking off from RAF Scampton.

the British aviation industry, and three designers—Vickers, Handley Page and Avro, who were already working flat out to give the RAF its V-Force—rose to meet it. Detailed submissions went in to the Ministry of Supply in May 1955, and it was the Avro design, the Type 730, which was awarded a prototype contract a few weeks later.

The Avro design envisaged a canard aircraft with unswept flying surfaces, constructed throughout in stainless steel brazed-honeycomb sandwich. Power was to be provided by four Armstrong Siddeley P 159 turbojets, mounted in pairs close to each wingtip. Span was 59.75 ft, length 163.5 ft, and main wing area 2,000 sq ft. The aircraft's reconnaissance system was to be a sideways-looking X-Band radar known as Red Drover, whose 52-ft antenna was built into the side of the 730's fuselage.

The aircraft had conventional ailerons and rudder, longitudinal control being maintained by the all-moving canard nose-plane, which was also fitted with trailing edge elevators. The flying control surfaces were served by a quadruplicated electro-hydraulic power unit designed by Boulton Paul and combined with an electrical 'fly-by-wire' automatic control system designed by Louis Newmark Ltd. The undercarriage, designed by Dowty, consisted of a single-centre-fuselage main unit with four wheels, a twin-wheel nose unit and outriggers on the engine nacelles. For take-off weights above 158,000 lb, up to a maximum of 220,000 lb, four additional wheels could be fitted on the main undercarriage axles outboard of the main wheels; these extra wheels would be jettisoned after take-off.

The 730 was to have carried a crew of three—a pilot and two navigators—housed in a pressurised cabin just aft of the foreplane; the navigators sat side by side, facing aft, and all three crew members had lightweight ejection seats. In the prototype aircraft, the pilot was to have sat under an offset cockpit canopy on a raised seat in the starboard side of the nose, but in the production version this would have been deleted, the pilot being completely buried in the fuselage and seeing outside only through a retractable, electrically-operated periscope. As the aircraft would have been automatically controlled and stabilised in flight, it was planned that the pilot should carry out the management of some engineering systems such as pressurisation, refrigeration and fuel—in other words, he would be free to do the job that had to be done by the co-pilot in the Vulcan, and the two navigators would also be at liberty to get on with their primary tasks.

The 730 was to have been equipped with rocket-assisted take-off gear, provision being made for two jettisonable 15,000 lb thrust Armstrong Siddeley rocket packs to be mounted on either side of the fuselage aft of the main undercarriage. The aircraft's estimated take-off distance to clear 50 ft was 2,230 yds, estimated initial climb rate 12,300 ft/min, cruising speed 2.6M, ceiling in mid-range 66,400 ft, and still-air range 4,740 nautical miles. Landing run from 50 ft, with a 24 ft braking parachute streamed, would be 1,150 yds.

Avro received an Instruction to Proceed in September 1955, and the company worked out a time scale which envisaged the flight of the first prototype in November 1959 and the first production aircraft in December 1961. Ten prototypes were to be built in all, and some of these would incorporate modifications that would turn the original reconnaissance 730 into a pure bomber, a true replacement for the Vulcan and Victor. A step in this direction was taken in October 1955, when the original Air Staff OR 330 was amended to give the Type 730 a bombing capability; the Ministry of Supply issued a revised specification, RB 156D, and Avro incorporated a weapons bay into their design as a result, although it was expected that in its operational form the 730 would carry a 50 ft 'stand-off' bomb with a thermonuclear warhead.

Just as the finalised Avro 698 had emerged as a vastly different design from the original, so the modified Type 730 differed greatly from its earlier concept. The original four P 159

Vulcan B 2 XL426 of No 83 Squadron streaming its braking parachute at Scampton.

engines were replaced by eight Armstrong Siddeley P 176 engines housed in rectangular nacelles; the length was reduced to 159 ft and the span increased to 65.61 ft, while the fuselage diameter grew by two feet.

The development programme which was gradually being built up around the 730 was more thorough and comprehensive than any other in British aviation history. It had to be, for almost everything about the 730 was revolutionary. To simulate the temperature which would be encountered by the 730's skin at 2.7M—about 277 degrees C—a heat-test building was constructed, capable of accommodating a full-size airframe. Two scale flying models were to be built, one going to Armstrong Whitworth for aerodynamic trials and the other to Bristol Siddeley for engine development. The pilot's periscope system was ready to be installed for trials in an Avro Ashton aircraft, and work on the first Type 730 test fuselage was well advanced at Chadderton.

Then came 1957, and the Duncan Sandys Defence White Paper. Overnight, OR 330 was cancelled in favour of further development of Blue Streak, the British IRBM—itself destined to be short-lived, at least as a military missile. As author Derek Wood put it ruefully in his book *Project Cancelled*, 'The 730 was broken up, and the world's first Mach 2 + bomber ended its days cut into giant circular bins for depositing metal refuse in the factory . . .'.

There was a postscript to the Avro 730 story. On April 14 1962 a research aircraft called the Bristol 188 made its first flight, powered by two reheated Gyron Junior engines. It had started life as one of the two scaled-down 730 research models, and it gave an indication of what the full-size 730 would have looked like, except that the canard foreplane arrangement had been replaced by a more conventional 'T' type tailplane mounted on top of the fin. In its modified form, the 188 was to have been used for flight research into the effects of kinetic heating at Mach 2 plus, but its fuel consumption was such that no really long flights at high speed were possible and it was eventually abandoned, after about £20 million had been spent on it.

The demise of the Avro 730 project meant, in all probability, that the Vulcan and Victor would be the last truly strategic bombing aircraft to serve with the Royal Air Force, and with nothing to follow on from them it was clear that their useful lives would somehow have to be stretched as far as possible, until their deterrent role was finally taken over by strategic nuclear missiles. In the case of the Vulcan, as already stated, there was still ample room for development and uprating, and in 1955 Roy Evans, Avro's new chief designer, had initiated some redesign of the basic Mk 1 airframe to allow greater lift and manoeuvreability at the heights to which the Vulcan would be pushed following the installation of more powerful Olympus engines. The key was to increase the wing area, so that wing loading would not increase with greater all-up weights, so Evans and his team took the existing Phase 2 wing and redesigned it, increasing its span from 99 ft to 111 ft and the wing area from 3,446 sq ft to 3,965 sq ft. Married to the powerful Olympus 200 series of engines, this new wing planform gave a substantial boost to the Vulcan's performance at altitude and actually increased the aircraft's range by up to 600 miles, as well as improving its operational ceiling; on March 4 1959, Vulcan *XH533*, fitted with what was now known as the Phase 2C wing, climbed to 61,500 ft.

The Phase 2C wing design was approved by the Ministry of Supply in October 1955, and design of a second-generation Vulcan, the B 2, was started immediately. In March 1956 a contract was issued for the conversion of *VX777*, the second prototype B 1, as the prototype Mk 2. A production order for the B 2 was placed in June 1956, when it was decided to halt B 1 production with *XH532* and to complete the remaining B 1s—the last 17 from the September 1954 contract and eight from the March 1955 contract—to B 2 standard, making a total of 49 B 2s on order at that time.

Vulcan B 2 XM574. *This aircraft originally served with No 27 Squadron, Scampton Wing.*

Conversion work on *VX777* began in August 1956, the aircraft being fitted with 12,000 lb st Olympus 102 engines as well as the Phase 2C wing. Among other variations, the latter incorporated a greatly reduced thickness/chord ratio on the outer panels, and full-span elevons replaced the elevators and ailerons of the Mk 1. *VX777* eventually flew in its new configuration on August 31 1957 and appeared at that year's SBAC display before launching into its programme of aerodynamic trials; these continued until 1960, when *VX777* was withdrawn and used for runway experiments at Farnborough before being broken up there in July 1963.

While *VX777* underwent its programme of aerodynamic trials, other Vulcan B 1s were allocated to different aspects of the development programme. In the spring of 1958, *XA891* was fitted with the new 16,000 lb st Olympus 200 engines, a procedure that involved re-organizing some of the aircraft's electrical systems, and was demonstrated at Farnborough that year; it continued to serve as the Olympus test-bed until its crash in Yorkshire on July 24 1959.

Another B 1, *XA893*, was used to test the revised electrical systems for the B 2. Whereas the B 1 had been fitted with 112-volt DC equipment, the B 2 used a constant-frequency 200-volt AC system, which was less bulky and generally more efficient. Although the combination of the new engines and the electrics still made a tight fit, there was no need to squeeze everything up, as had proven necessary in the trials aircraft, *XA891*. The electrical systems Vulcan, *XA893*, went on to complete its programme successfully and was eventually broken up at Boscombe Down, its nose section afterwards being delivered to No 71 MU for display purposes.

Vulcan B 2 XL320 served with both the Scampton Wing and No 230 OCU during its working life. It was sold for scrap in August 1981.

Vulcan B 2 XM649 *served initially with No 9 Squadron, then with the Coningsby and Waddington Wings. It was sold for scrap in December 1982.*

All the aerodynamic and systems changes that characterized the Vulcan B 2 were finally brought together in the first pre-production aircraft, *XH533*, which flew for the first time at Woodford on August 19 1958. This aircraft embodied the Phase 2C wing, Olympus 200 engines with their enlarged air intakes and 'toed-out' jet pipes, a strengthened undercarriage with a shortened nose leg, the new AC electrical system, and an auxiliary power unit. *XH533* was publicly displayed at the 1959 SBAC Show, together with *VX777* and *XA903*, the latter carrying a Blue Steel development round (see Chapter 6).

It was just as well that the decision had been made to fit the new generation of Vulcans with the AC electrical system, with its greatly boosted power, for when the B 2 development programme was well under way Avro were suddenly issued with an instruction to fit new ECM equipment into their aircraft. So were Handley Page, although in the case of the Victor the necessary modifications were relatively uncomplicated, as most of the necessary gear could be fitted into the existing area of the rear fuselage.

With the Vulcan it was a different story because it meant that the whole of the rear fuselage below the fin had to be redesigned to accommodate the new equipment. The latter included a tail warning radar known as Red Steer, developed by the Telecommunications Research Establishment at Malvern from an AI13 set, which had been standard equipment in the Meteor NF 11/NF 14 night fighter; there was also a warning receiver to alert the AEO when enemy AI or ground radars were 'locked on' to the bomber, and noise jammers to deal with the frequencies which controlled the known Soviet early warning, missile direction and fighter control radars. Strategic Air Command's ECM kit was more sophisticated, but also a great deal more expensive, and what would fit into a B-52 would certainly not fit into a Vulcan; in any case, the RAF's argument was that the key to successful ECM was to prevent the enemy fighter from attaining visual contact with the bomber he was meant to destroy, which in turn meant blocking the radar and VHF frequencies used to guide him to his target—and noise jamming was as good as, if not better than, a lot of other more costly methods.

There is no doubt that the V-Force would have had to make provision for more advanced ECM gear in 1959 if the Soviet system of fighter control had not been so rigid. There were close parallels between the Russian system and the German air defence system at the end of the war, which was hardly surprising, for the Soviet network had been set up with the aid of German technicians and much of the equipment it used was developed from German designs. Like the German system of 1944-5, the Soviet system relied on an overlapping chain of early warning stations, each subdivided into fighter control sectors and, also like the Germans, the Russians used only a limited number of VHF channels to control their fighters. The four Soviet channels in use during 1959–60 were well monitored, and all of them could be jammed by a single piece of equipment known as Green Palm, which, like the wartime 'Jostle' used by 100 Group, sent out a high-pitched wail.

The Soviet fighters of the late '50s also carried a device, developed from the German 'Naxos-Z' of 1944, which enabled them to home on to the transmissions from blind bombing radars such as H2S, so the H2S Mk 9A carried by the Vulcan and other V-bombers incorporated a modification known as 'Fishpool', which enabled the Nav Radar to detect enemy fighters below and, to some degree, on either side of the aircraft.

To accommodate the new ECM gear, then, the Vulcan Mk 2 sprouted a new tail cone, increasing the overall length by 2 ft 10 in, and a flat aerial plate was fitted between the two starboard jet pipes. The rear fuselage bulge first appeared on the second B 2, *XH534*, which flew in 1959 and spent seven years on trials work with the A&AEE before being eventually delivered to 230 OCU in December 1966.

The next five B 2s were also development aircraft. The third production B 2, *XH535*, was operated by the Ministry of Aviation, mainly from Boscombe Down, and it was while flying from its Wiltshire base on May 11 1964 that it was destroyed in a flying accident. After a two-hour flight, the captain, Mr O.J. Hawkins, was carrying out a high rate of descent approach to Boscombe Down at low speed when the aircraft went into a spin. The tail parachute was streamed and the Vulcan recovered temporarily, but entered a spin again and dived into the ground near Andover. Hawkins, who was a Hawker Siddeley test pilot, and his co-pilot, Flight Lieutenant R.L. Beeston, ejected safely, but the four rear crew (Flight Lieutenants Dingley and Young, Flying Officer Chilton and Master AEO Signaller Christian) were killed.

The fourth B 2, *XH536*, was also to suffer a tragic end, although in this case the aircraft was destroyed while in service with No 12 Squadron, after its time with the Controller (Aircraft) and the Ministry of Aviation. On February 11 1966, the aircraft flew into high ground 20 miles north-east of Swansea and the crew of five was killed.

The other three development B 2s, *XH537*, *'538* and *'539*, were all used on trials work with either the Skybolt or Blue Steel missiles, as described in the next chapter, and all except *'539* were subsequently delivered to the RAF. In the meantime, *XH534* had undergone official CA release trials at Boscombe Down during the early months of 1960; the B 2 was given CA clearance as a result in May that year, and on July 1 1960 *XH558* became the first Vulcan B 2 to join No 230 OCU at Waddington, to be followed by *XH559* in August, *XH560* in October, *XH561* in November and *XH562* in December.

When the first Vulcan B 2 was delivered there were still 34 B 1s in RAF service, distributed between Nos 83, 101 and 617 Squadrons and the OCU, and it had already been decided to fit the best of these—29 aircraft in all—with the Mk 2 ECM kit, which meant withdrawing each B 1 from service so that the conversion work could be carried out, mainly by Armstrong Whitworth. The first B 1 to be so converted was *XH505*, in August 1960, and the aircraft was returned to No 617 Squadron, complete with new rear fuselage and ECM plate aerial, with the designation B 1A.

The B 1A conversion programme was not without its problems. Not the least of these was the B 1's DC electrical system, which could not be completely modified to AC, and so the ECM equipment had to be supplied by a specially-installed engine-driven alternator. Nevertheless, Armstrong Whitworth and various sub-contractors managed to complete the whole B 1/1A conversion in 32 months, the last B 1A conversion, *XH503*, being returned to Waddington on March 6 1963.

The introduction of the B 2 into service meant some considerable re-organisation of the Vulcan force, and it was decided to concentrate all the B 1s and 1As at Waddington in three squadrons. The first of these was No 44 (Rhodesia) Squadron, which re-formed on August 10 1960; it had previously been a Canberra unit at Honington until its disbandment in July 1957, and it now came to life again by taking over No 83 Squadron's eight Vulcan B 1s and personnel. In January 1961 the squadron received its first B 1A conversion from Armstrong Whitworth; this was *XA904*, and its career was to be cut short on the night of February 28 1961, when it was badly damaged in a crash landing at Waddington. It ended its days as an instructional airframe.

In June 1961, No 44 was joined at Waddington by No 101 Squadron, which came down from its Yorkshire base at Finningley with five B 1s and two B 1As; No 230 OCU, whose 'A' Flight was equipped with Vulcan B 1s and 'B' Flight with B 2s, moved up to Finningley and relinquished one of its B 1s, *XA895*, to the Bomber Command Development unit there. *XA895*, in fact, had been the first Vulcan to test the new tail cone for the B 2, at Boscombe Down in 1958.

The third of the Waddington B 1/1A squadrons was No 50, which re-formed on August 1 1961 with aircraft relinquished by 617 Squadron (*XH482*, *'483*, *'497*, *'498*, *'499*, *'500* and *'502*). Meanwhile, the first B 2 course had graduated at the OCU, the crews being allocated to No 83 Squadron, which used borrowed aircraft for the time being. The squadron moved to Scampton in October 1960, and there, on December 23, took delivery of its first B 2, *XH563*. This was followed, on January 13 1961, by *XJ780*, then by *XJ781* (February 22 1961), *XJ782* (March 1 1961) and *XJ783* (March 10 1961).

On April 1 1961, No 27 Squadron re-formed at Scampton alongside No 83. This was a former Canberra unit, having disbanded in December 1957. Its first Vulcan B 2 was *XJ823*, delivered on April 20 1961; this aircraft was followed by *XJ824* (May 15 1961), *XH555* (July 14 1961), *XJ825* (July 27 1961) and *XH556* (September 26 1961).

The third of the Scampton B 2 squadrons was No 617, which had turned its Vulcan B 1s over to the newly re-formed 50 Squadron. No 617's first B 2 was *XL318*, delivered on September 1 1961, and this was followed by *XL319* (October 20 1961), *XL320*

(December 1 1961), *XL321* (January 10 1962), *XL359* (February 1 1962), *XL360* (March 1 1962) and *XL361* (March 14 1962).

The tempo of Vulcan B 2 deliveries was now increasing, and early in 1962 another Lincolnshire airfield, RAF Coningsby, was made ready to receive a second B 2 Wing. The first of the Coningsby squadrons was No 9, which had been one of the first squadrons to equip with Canberras and which had disbanded at Coningsby on July 13 1961. It now re-formed on March 1 1962 and took delivery of its first Vulcan B 2, *XL386*, on May 11, followed by *XL388* on June 13 and *XL390* on July 19. The second Coningsby squadron, No 12, had also been a Canberra unit, disbanding at the same time as No 9; it was re-formed on July 1 1962 and received its first B 2—*XH560*, a former OCU aircraft— on September 25.

Another former OCU Vulcan B 2, *XH562*, was the first to be taken on charge by the third Coningsby squadron, No 35, which had disbanded as a Canberra unit at Upwood, Huntingdon, in September 1961. It re-formed as part of the V-Force on December 1 1962, and the B 2s allocated to it came in the main from the Scampton squadrons, which were beginning to receive new aircraft modified to carry the Blue Steel missile. *XJ823*, for example, came from No 27 Squadron, while *XL321* came from No 617 after a brief spell with the OCU.

The three Scampton squadrons were by this time very experienced on the B 2, and had taken part in several exercises designed to test the aircraft and procedures under simulated war conditions. The most realistic of these took place in October 1961, when the Americans invited Bomber Command to participate in Exercise Skyshield, designed to test the efficiency of the North American Air Defense Command, with its early warning radar chains backed up by squadrons of long-range interceptors and ground-to-air missiles. The ultra-modern nature of America's radar screen had, in fact, caused a few heart-stopping moments at Colorado Springs, NORAD's operations centre, a year earlier, when tracking stations on the Distant Early Warning Line in Greenland had picked up

A member of XL388's crew explains the workings of the Vulcan to some USAF ground crew.

Vulcan B 2 XL388 was a regular visitor to the United States on 'Western Ranger' sorties. It is seen here, with an 83 Squadron crew, at the usual terminus of such flights: Offutt Air Force Base, Nebraska.

what appeared to be a massive missile attack coming in from the Soviet Union. In fact, the powerful radars had been bouncing echoes off the moon, coming up over the horizon a quarter of a million miles away.

Eight Vulcan B 2s—four from No 27 Squadron and four from No 83 Squadron—were detailed to take part in Skyshield, which involved a series of 'saturation' attacks on the American air defences by USAF bombers acting as hostiles. The four 83 Squadron aircraft went to Lossiemouth in Scotland to attack with the northern wave, while the No 27 Squadron Vulcans were detached to Kindley Air Force Base, Bermuda, to make their attack from the south. All ECM systems were to be used in the bid to break through the tight screen of USAF (and, in the northern case, RCAF) interceptors—F-101 Voodoos, F-102 Delta Daggers and Avro Canada CF-100s.

The simulated attacks took place on October 14, the Vulcans in each case preceded by USAF bombers. The northern wave was led by B-47 Stratojets, flying at low level with their jammers full on; next came B-52 Stratofortresses, flying between 35,000 and 42,000 ft, with ECM-equipped Martin RB-57s carrying out diversions; and finally, at 56,000 ft, the four No 83 Squadron Vulcans, coming in singly with an interval of several minutes between each aircraft. Predictably, the fighter defences concentrated on the B-47s and B-52s, and by the time the Vulcans penetrated North American airspace the defenders did not have sufficient fuel to climb to 56,000 ft and take them on. The lead Vulcan reported picking up a transmission from an F-101's fire control radar, but the other three detected nothing hostile at all and all four aircraft came through to land at Stephenville, Newfoundland.

The southern attack followed much the same pattern, except that in this case the four No 27 Squadron Vulcans made their penetration on a broad front, instead of in stream. Fifty miles from the coast, with fighters being launched to intercept from bases all along the eastern seaboard, the southernmost Vulcan suddenly turned north, leaving the other three to run the gauntlet of the interceptors and, at the same time, to provide a jamming screen to shield the lone aircraft. The northbound Vulcan flew parallel to the coast, then turned in to land at Plattsburgh AFB, New York, its approach completely undetected. The other three Vulcans reported intercepts, but took appropriate evasive action to get away; the ceiling of the Vulcan was greater than that of either the F-101 or F-102, and at 56,000 ft the big delta could out-turn and out-climb anything, at least in 1961. (As one RAF Lightning pilot put it: 'We like intercepting Vulcans. They fight back. The b.....s just go into a tight upward spiral under full power, and they're as hard as hell to catch.' Vulcan crews, for their part, were quite adamant that they could 'hack' a single interceptor of the Lightning's calibre, while admitting that they might have a problem in dealing with two at the same time.)

The results of Exercise Skyshield were perhaps no fair indication of how the Vulcan would have fared in a real war situation, for in the European context it was unlikely that the V-Force would have had the benefit of a jamming screen thrown out by preceding USAF bombers to assist its progress. An article by American writer Richard C. Peet, in the USAF's Air Force and Space Digest magazine, summed up the war role of the V-Force as follows:

'We have become accustomed to thinking in terms of SAC alone in the retaliatory role. We overlook the fact that, in the event of actual nuclear hostilities, the first manned strike on Soviet defences will likely be spearheaded by someone else. Preceding SAC and its B-52s, and perhaps even blasting a path for it, will be the V-bomber force of the RAF . . . .'

Details of the targets assigned to the V-Force in the early 1960s remain secret, but it is likely that fighter airfields, radar complexes and SAM missile sites in northern Siberia featured high on the target list. Attacks on these by the V-Force, added to the disruption already created by ICBM strikes, would have torn great gaps in the already overstretched Soviet air defence system covering the Arctic regions across which the main SAC assault would come. Other targets would probably have included major Soviet naval complexes such as those at Murmansk and Archangel'sk, where an important part of Russia's ocean-going submarine fleet was based. Within the constraints of their combat radius of 1,500 nautical miles or so, the V-bombers would have been carefully routed to achieve maximum surprise on the way to their targets, and also to give them a chance of survival on the way out. Post-strike, part of the force would have been able to return to bases in the UK, for some of these would have survived; in the early 1960s the USSR had neither missiles nor strategic bombers in sufficient numbers to saturate bases in both Britain and North America, despite Premier Khrushchev's threat in 1960 that 'If war came, that well-known aircraft carrier, Britain, would go down on the first day'. But if return to Britain proved out of the question, a number of other options remained open: diversion to bases in Iceland or Greenland, for example, or—depending on what fuel remained after negotiating the enemy defences, and the position of the target—to fly south to a NATO base in the Mediterranean.

By 1962, although the Blue Steel missile was not yet in service, the V-Force possessed a formidable arsenal of free-falling nuclear weapons and would have proved quite capable of devastating the Soviet Union's industrial economy as an independent force, if such a need had ever arisen. The Vulcan and Victor had sufficient range to penetrate to most industrial targets west of the Ural Mountains, within an arc stretching from Novaya Zemlya to the Caspian Sea—an arc that included the Soviet Union's life blood, the oil of the great Caucasus fields—and, under optimum conditions, would still have had sufficient fuel to gain friendly bases in the south, say in Iran.

The megaton-range weapons for the second generation of V-bombers had been developed in the 1950s with American help, following a Statement on Defence issued by the British Government in February 1955 to the effect that Britain was to proceed with the development and production of British thermonuclear weapons. By May 1957, an experimental British megaton-range assembly was ready for testing, and on May 15 that year this was dropped over the Christmas Island test range by Valiant *XD818* of No 49 Squadron, captained by Wing Commander K.G. Hubbard. The explosion produced a yield of about one megaton, and three more tests—all involving warheads in the megaton range—were carried out from Christmas Island before the end of 1957. The operational British warhead evolved from these trials was given a colourful code-name which is still classified and similar codes were applied to subsequent warheads, both British and American, which were thereafter married to the thermonuclear devices employed by the V-Force.

With the use of a megaton-range weapon, there could be no question of overflying the target in a straight line, even at a speed of 0.9M and an altitude of 56,000 ft. Weapon release was therefore followed by an immediate maximum-rate turn through 180 degrees and evasion under full power. These tactics were valid as long as Bomber Command might expect potential targets to be defended only by radar-directed high-altitude interceptors, but by the end of 1960 major Soviet target complexes were defended by batteries of V750VK (SA-2 'Guideline') surface-to-air missiles, with their slant range of 25 miles and ceiling of 60,000 ft. The solution was to equip the V-Force with a weapon that could be released well clear of the target, outside the defensive missile screen; that weapon was Blue Steel, but it did not enter service until February 1963, and for more than two years the V-bombers, despite updated jamming devices, were vulnerable.

It was during this period that the V-Force was called to the highest state of alert in all its ten years of maintaining Britain's nuclear deterrent. It happened during the Cuban

Missile Crisis of October 1962, when the Russians sought to introduce IRBMs into Cuba (because, as is now known, a second-generation ICBM on which their hopes were pinned was a failure, and they were seeking to plug what they considered to be a dangerous gap). During this crisis period the squadrons of the V-Force were brought up to a high degree of readiness: civilians employed on the V-Force bases were sent home, the bases themselves sealed off from the outside and their perimeters secured by armed patrols, while the aircraft were armed—not necessarily with nuclear weapons—and stood combat-ready for a period of three days. At no time during that period, however, was any part of the V-Force ordered to disperse, although Air Marshal Sir Kenneth Cross, the C-in-C Bomber Command, thought it advisable.

Much of the groundwork beneath the V-Force's operational procedures in the early 1960s, including the operational testing of new systems, was laid by the Bomber Command Development Unit, which was formed at Wittering in May 1954 and equipped initially with Camberras. These were later joined by a flight of Valiants from No 138 Squadron, but as time went by, with the increasing tempo of V-bomber trials, the utilisation of aircraft presented a problem, as there were understandable conflicts between training, operational and trials requirements. In June 1959, therefore, a BCDU Trials Flight was established, with three 'permanent' Valiants and some Canberras.

There was further re-organisation after March 1960, when the BCDU moved to Finningley and was expanded into sections that included Trials Organisation, Navigation and Bombing Trials, Electronic Countermeasures Trials, Technical Trials and Research and Analysis. The bulk of the flying was done by the BCDU's established aircraft and aircrews, although the nature of some flight trials demanded the participation of one or several squadron V-bombers, as for example in Intensive Flying Trials, or radio, radar and ECM compatibility trials.

Four Vulcans, three of them B 1s and the other a B 2, are on record as having been attached to the BCDU at various times, mostly on ECM trials work. The first was *XA895*, which was used to test the ECM tail cone, and this was followed by *XA907* and *XH500*, the first aircraft to be converted to B 1A standard. The B 2 was *XL391*, which carried out low-level trials at the end of 1963, and in doing so ushered in a new era of V-Force operational procedures.

Chapter 6

Vulcan and Blue Steel

In 1954, with the first of the RAF's V-bombers, the Valiant, still a year away from entering service, the Royal Aircraft Establishment and A.V. Roe began studies of 'stand-off' bombing as a possible means of extending the combat radius and increasing the survival prospects of the new generation of bombers.

Most of the development work on the missile, which was eventually to receive the name Blue Steel, was done in the laboratory, but in 1955 a number of problems arose in finalising the missile's design, and these could only be solved by carrying out free flight trials. In addition, there was seen to be a need to build up a flight trials organisation which, when eventually presented with the operational Blue Steel, would be able to conduct proving trials efficiently and safely. For these reasons, it was planned that two series of air-launched free flight test vehicle trials should precede trials of the operational weapon system.

In March 1956, A.V. Roe received a development contract from the Ministry of Supply, while Armstrong Siddeley were contracted for the propulsion motors, Elliotts, under RAE design authority, for the inertial navigation system, and de Havilland engines for the power supply turbines and also for some of the motors which were to be used in the early test vehicles. The Armament Department of the RAE was to be responsible for the armament system; all other equipment and the airframe were to be A.V. Roe's responsibility, as was the overall co-ordination of the programme.

The first series of trials, which took place in 1957, used $\frac{2}{5}$ scale models of Blue Steel which were launched from Valiant *WP204*. The aircraft was based at the Avro Weapons Research Division, Woodford, and drops were made over the Aberporth range. The scale models used a solid-fuel rocket motor firing through twin blast pipes, and carried a 24-channel telemetry set. Aerodynamic controls were the same as on the full scale missile and the test vehicle was steered on its programme path by an autopilot. The missile was carried inside the Valiant's bomb bay so as to avoid, at this early stage, the various problems that would be encountered by external carriage, and was dropped in the same way as a ballistic bomb. The autopilot then took over and the motor fired a few seconds after launch; the missile then accelerated to moderate supersonic speed, performing various programmed test manoeuvres on the way. Some of the flights lasted several minutes and were normally terminated by operation of the destruct system. The preliminary trials were mainly complete by the end of 1958, although a few more scale models were launched in 1959 from the Valiant and also from Vulcan *XA903*, to give selected RAF V-Force crews some experience in launching techniques prior to the testing of the full-size missile.

The second series of trials involved full-scale missiles, which were intended to be constructed of stainless steel and as similar as possible, structurally, to the operational Blue Steel, although they were to be powered by de Havilland Double Spectre engines instead of the Armstrong Siddeley Stentor of the operational version. The trials had

Vulcan B 2s of the Coningsby Wing—Nos 9, 12, and 35 Squadrons—formate over the Lincolnshire countryside in a flypast to mark the Station being granted the Freedom of Boston, its parent town, in 1963.

various objectives. For example, very little information was available at that time on the environment of high supersonic speed flight; Blue Steel's ballistic trajectory would be very different from that of any other type of missile so far investigated by the British industry, and its effect on the missile's internal equipment had to be carefully studied. Moreover, conditions inside the missile during prolonged carriage at high altitude could only be established by trials, and this was also true of how the missile would behave on release from the parent aircraft. A simple release system was planned, but trials might show that something more complex was needed. The interface between the equipment carried in the aircraft and that in the missile was something which needed very close examination; in fact, the successful 'mating' of missile and carrier aircraft was to give problems throughout Blue Steel's operational life.

The plan was to construct the full-scale models in stainless steel, like the operational Blue Steel, but because of manufacturing difficulties it was decided to use aluminium alloy instead. The first two second-series models, both inert dummies, were dropped in 1958, and were followed by a number of powered models, launched in 1959 and 1960 at Aberporth and Woomera, Australia. Trials with full-scale, stainless steel Blue Steel test vehicles began at Woomera in the summer of 1960, using Vulcan *XA903*; these were now fitted with Stentor engines in place of the Double Spectre, and in fact resembled the operational missile much more closely than had originally been planned, making up to some extent for previous delays in the test programme caused by the manufacturing difficulties. Their main function was the in-flight proving of the internal systems, and a large number of captive flights were made to prove the accuracy and reliability of the inertial navigation system, as well as to develop the reliability of the weapon system during prolonged carriage and also to prove certain aspects of the armament system.

The main decisions about Blue Steel's aerodynamics were taken in 1955, when it was decided that the missile should have a canard configuration, which gave a favourable centre of pressure change at increasing Mach numbers, and a small 60-degree delta wing, which gave favourable performance both at transonic speed and at the low supersonic speed at which the missile would pull up into a climb. To some extent, the wing span was determined by the geometry of the carrier aircraft, but the real criterion was that the missile should not lose excessive height after release before starting to climb. The missile's foreplane, whose span was half that of the main wing, was all-moving in the pitching plane, an arrangement preferred to a flap control, which would have had a higher trim drag. The missile was also fitted with two fins; these were similar in plan form to the wing and foreplane, except that the lower fin was larger than the upper, partly to simplify installation in the parent aircraft, and partly to increase stability, for the effectiveness of the bottom fin was greater than that of the top fin while the missile was at positive incidence.

The remainder of Blue Steel's aerodynamic design was decided over the next two years, and was supported by an extensive programme of wind tunnel tests. In addition, a series of free flight trials was made, using $\frac{1}{8}$ scale models; these were ground launched using tandem solid rocket boosters of two types, so that the subsequent decelerating glides could cover either the supersonic or the transonic speed range. The configuration was slightly different from the operational design as it was based on early project studies, and also the

Line-up of Vulcan B 2s of 617 Squadron, with Victors at the far end of the flight line. XL319, *nearest the camera, is now in the North East Aircraft Museum, Sunderland.*

model base was modified to include pyrotechnic flares for visual tracking.

Blue Steel's guidance and control system consisted of three parts: the inertial navigator, supplied by Elliotts, the flight rules computer and the autopilot, both supplied by A.V. Roe. The navigator computed the present position of the missile; the flight rules computer (FRC) determined the flight plan, and the autopilot commanded the control movements necessary to obtain the desired flight path. The present position computer in the navigator measured the acceleration in the horizontal plane in two directions aligned with the vertical points of the compass, and by integration obtained the velocity components and the position. During the captive phase of the flight, Blue Steel's navigation system was coupled with that of the aircraft, providing additional information to the crew on their position and also, by comparing data from fixed points along the route, allowing corrections to be fed into the missile to align the horizontal table carrying the accelerometers. The navigator also incorporated a homing computer which took information about the missile's present position and velocity and computed the steering signals necessary to bring it to its target.

The flight rules computer took information from both the present position computer and homing computer, and used it to decide when the missile was to climb or cruise, how the power was to be used, and for other decisions that went into determining the flight plan. During the final stage, its function was to connect the steering signals provided by the homing computer to the autopilot so that the missile steered accurately to the target; in the earlier stages, however, it regulated these demands to obtain a better performance and a tactically better flight plan. The autopilot was of the normal kind, with gyroscopes and accelerometers as sensing instruments, electronic computing circuits and a hydraulic power phase to drive the control surfaces.

To train aircrews in the operation of Blue Steel navigation and monitoring systems a special Trainer version of the missile was built. This was geometrically similar to the operational weapon and was attached to the bomber in the usual way, but it was without rocket engine, propellant or armament system and was not released in flight. It was equipped with the complete inertial navigator, but the FRC and the autopilot were represented by a switching simulator. This also provided indications to the cabin monitoring instruments and could also insert artificial faults during flight. It proved to be a highly valuable training aid, giving a realistic representation of the navigator behaviour during long carriage flights.

The decision to use an inertial navigation system in Blue Steel, taken in 1954, was a bold one, and showed considerable forward thinking on the part of the weapon's designers. The inertial navigator meant that the missile was entirely self-contained, needing no assistance from an external source after launch; it neither transmitted nor received radar or radio signals, which meant that it could not be jammed en route to the target.

The Bristol Siddeley Stentor rocket motor that powered the operational Blue Steel used kerosene as fuel, with hydrogen peroxide as the oxidant. It had two combustion chambers, both of which fired while the missile was being boosted to supersonic speed. The larger chamber was then cut off by command from the flight rules computer; the smaller continued to run at full thrust for most of the climb and was then throttled back to cruise level by the FRC. The propulsion system comprised a kerosene tank and a peroxide tank, both of which had free surface nitrogen pressurisation to feed the kerosene pump and the two peroxide pumps; these were driven by a steam turbine which ran on peroxide decomposed by a catalyst.

The pumps fed the propellants under pressure to each of the combustion chambers, and the system was self-sustaining while the pumps were supplying peroxide to the turbine, but it was necessary to provide a separate peroxide supply from a start tank to start the

Handling the Blue Steel missile on the ground was a complex operation requiring the use of several kinds of associated equipment, as shown in these photographs.

This picture of Blue Steels lined up in their maintenance hangar shows how they were kept under almost antiseptic conditions—although in this case, some of the 'spit and polish' may have been due to an impending AOC's inspection.

turbine running. This was fed to the turbine when the start tank was pressurised by the opening of the nitrogen control valve, which was actuated by a signal from the FRC. A changeover valve ensured that as soon as the outlet pressure of the large chamber peroxide pump rose above the start line pressure, the start line was isolated and peroxide was fed from the pump to the turbine, the system then being self-sustaining. When the small chamber was running alone its thrust could be varied by a throttle, which controlled the supply of peroxide to the turbine. The correct ratio of kerosene and peroxide was maintained by a mixture ratio controller, and a nitrogen purge system was provided which operated when the engine started and also on shut-down, to ensure that all the kerosene was cleared from the burners as a safety precaution. The propulsion system generally gave very little trouble during flight testing, although with early test vehicles motor stoppages were experienced immediately after the main chamber was cut off; this was caused by fuel 'sloshing', which uncovered the propellant outlet pipe. It was cured by fitting baffles in the peroxide tank, and the operational missile experienced no troubles of this nature.

Blue Steel's auxiliary power system presented a number of headaches in the early days, because of the need for power both while the missile was being carried by the parent aircraft and also in free flight. The missile's power had to come from the aircraft during carriage, and batteries were deemed unsuitable during the free flight phase because of the comparatively long flight time. There was no question of drawing power from the propulsion system, because this did not operate throughout the flight. It was therefore decided to use hydraulic pressure as the main source of power, the oil pressure coming from an electrically-driven pressure pump in the aircraft bomb-bay during carriage and from a steam-turbine driven pressure pump in the missile during free flight. The only connections this system required between the aircraft and missile were two self-sealing pull-off hydraulic couplings for high pressure and low pressure oil respectively. The changeover from aircraft to missile system was effected by having the oil supply from the aircraft at about 2,000 lb/sq in and that from the missile at 4,000 lb/sq in, together with the judicious use of non-return valves—the missile supply being started up a few minutes before launch.

The hydraulic supply produced in this way was used to power the control surfaces and fin folding mechanism, and also to provide all the missile's electrical power by driving an alternator. Stainless steel piping was used throughout the hydraulic system; other features included the operation and interlocking of the automatic fin-folding with the under-carriage retraction of the parent aircraft, and the automatic locking of the foreplane for a few seconds after launch to avoid the danger of accidental pitch-up and possible collision with the carrier aircraft.

One major problem that had to be overcome was that much of Blue Steel's internal equipment did not take kindly to extremes of temperature; some of it, in fact, had to be held within quite close temperature limits. Nevertheless, the missile had to be carried, sometimes for many hours, below the aircraft fuselage at ambient temperatures down to perhaps –70 degrees C; on the other hand, in free flight the outer skin heated up rapidly, and further excess heat could be produced by the equipment itself, some of which had to be running for several hours before launch. This temperature control problem was dealt with in three ways: first, by double-skinning much of the missile in order to slow down the ingress of heat in free flight and the loss of heat during carriage; second, by piping a supply of warm air into the missile from a heat exchanger during carriage, the flow of air being regulated by temperature sensors at various points in the missile; and third, by the use of liquid freon, produced by a refrigeration system installed partly in the aircraft and partly in the missile, and piped into those items of equipment which were both heat-producing and temperature-sensitive.

Another problem was that Blue Steel was designed to be used by both Vulcan and Victor, two aircraft whose geometry and systems engineering differed considerably. The missile had to be compatible with both, and special Blue Steel equipment had to be devised and carried in each aircraft. Its incorporation required a great deal of detail design, very little of which was common to the two aircraft. The interface between the missile and aircraft was complex and included the aircraft structure, fairings, release mechanism, hydraulic power supplies, electrical control, warm air and refrigerant supplies, monitoring the data transfer and lanyard operating units; there were three of the latter, each with 157 contacts, and to ensure that all of them separated cleanly on release at the same instant they were buttons that touched, rather than pins.

The aircraft also required special controls for the missile navigational system, as well as monitoring indications that the various systems were functioning properly, and fitting these into crew compartments which were already well filled with other equipment presented no small problem. Trials aircraft, in addition, had to carry even more monitoring equipment.

Most of the early captive trials of Blue Steel and the shorter of the free flight trials were done at Aberporth, using aircraft based at Woodford. Three Vulcans were involved: as well as *XA903* and *XH539*, which carried out launch trials, *XH538* was used to prove a variety of systems. The first firing tests of Blue Steel at Woomera took place early in 1961 from Vulcan B 2 *XH539*. Most of the missiles involved in these trials were transported to

Australia by air, either in transport aircraft or on the V-bombers, but a few went by sea. All the missiles went through a thorough ground test cycle before flight.

A considerable number of captive trials were done to assess the accuracy of the navigation system and also to prove the aircraft-missile systems involved in the hydraulics, warm air supply and refrigeration. For the navigator trials, the missile was carried through a flight plan which was fully representative of a launching trial right up to the point of release at the range head; there, instead of releasing the missile, the electrical connections only to the navigator were disconnected and the aircraft with the captive missile flew on to the normal target area. Blue Steels used in free-flight trials were fitted with a destructive system, for use if the missile strayed outside the range boundaries or if the tracking system lost sight of it.

A parachute recovery system was developed early in the Blue Steel trials programme, but considerable difficulties were experienced during the deployment stages and the complete system was not working until near the end of the model trials programme. Parachute recovery of full scale missiles was not attempted because the early trials were over the sea at Aberporth, and many of the later ones, which were representative of the operational role, required the missile to be flown to impact. In this case, very little of the missile was recoverable, as it exploded and disintegrated, but when a fault condition developed in flight and the missile was broken up by command from the ground, large sections of it were often recovered with only superficial damage. Valuable information could be obtained from the examination of such wreckage. In one case, the small propulsion chamber failed some way down the trajectory, and the missile was eventually

Vulcan B 2 XL321 *of 617 Squadron with Blue Steel.* XL321 *is now at RAF Catterick, where it is used for crash rescue training.*

blown up by a ground command. It was subsequently found that the drive shaft from the gear box in the hydrogen peroxide pump which fed the small chamber was broken, and that this had occurred during flight. Tests showed that the materials and manufacture were not at fault, but that the supporting roller bearing on the forward end of the gear box had seized in flight, causing the pump drive shaft to shear.

Over 80 different kinds of special equipment were developed for the in-service handling of Blue Steel and its various sub-assemblies. Such equipment included the airfield transporter trolley, designed to carry the missile from its preparation building to the parent aircraft. The missile was filled with propellant while on this transporter, which was fitted with missile propulsion system monitoring equipment to ensure that the kerosene and peroxide were under constant surveillance. Another example was the low-loader, from which the missile was actually loaded on to the aircraft; two different designs were prepared, one operating mechanically and the other hydraulically. The latter was ultimately chosen for Service use, as it had height adaptors to cope with the different ground clearances of Victor and Vulcan.

Special check-out equipment had to be provided to the RAF both for overall test of the missile and for testing sub-assemblies. Development of this check-out equipment lagged somewhat behind that of the missile because its design could not start until the corresponding missile equipment had been designed in some detail. So that the missile trials should not be held up by lack of equipment, early test vehicles were checked out by laboratory personnel using equipment such as oscilloscopes and signal generators and whatever 'lash-ups' were necessary; later test vehicles and early operational-type missiles,

Vulcan B 2 XL361 of 617 Squadron streams its braking parachute. In December 1981, this aircraft was badly damaged at Goose Bay, Labrador, while en route from Canada to the UK, and was abandoned.

on the other hand, had 'custom-built' tests sets to check out all the main missile sub-assemblies.

Later operational-type missiles were checked out by special equipment supplied to the RAF and known as TSOM (Test Set, Overall, Missile), abbreviated to TOM by the personnel who used it. TOM's diagnostic powers were limited to deciding which, if any, of the main missile systems was at fault, this information being presented generally to 'go' or 'no-go' lights. If a fault was diagnosed in any unit, the unit could then be removed completely and checked by the use of unit test equipment. Missiles in storage were subjected to periodic TOM tests, and of course were tested before being 'mated' with an aircraft. During the missile loading operation, a large water-filled bath was placed close to the aircraft so that anyone who became contaminated by hydrogen peroxide, which could cause serious injury if it came into contact with bare skin, could be immersed immediately.

The first squadron to equip with Blue Steel was No 617 at Scampton, in the late summer of 1962. By the beginning of October the Squadron had achieved an emergency operational capability with the weapon, and would doubtless have used it then had the Cuban missile crisis flared into war, but it was not declared fully operational until February 1963, somewhat later than planned. As the modified Vulcan B 2s were returned to Scampton, complete aircrews were sent to Lindholme to attend the Blue Steel Course at the Bomber Command Bombing School. Pilots and air electronics officers remained only for the first five days of the course, during which time they received instruction on the complete weapon system and on the handling techniques applicable to those systems under their immediate control; navigators, on the other hand, stayed at Lindholme for a full month, covering the functional aspects of the weapon with particular emphasis on the operational procedure involved in setting up, carrying and launching the missile. The first part of the course dealt with the inertial navigation system and the second part comprised a detailed study of the weapon's 'plumbing'. Practical training was carried out on NBS synthetic Blue Steel trainers, and consisted of various exercises based on operational profiles. Subsequently, students came to the Blue Steel Course from the Vulcan (and, later, Victor) OCU, and went on to their operational squadrons afterwards.

No flying was done by the Blue Steel students at Lindholme; intensive flying with Blue Steel training rounds started once the crew returned to their squadron. Operational Blue Steels were not carried on training exercises, being reserved for aircraft on Quick Reaction Alert, and only a few Bomber Command crews were ever to have the chance of firing a live missile over the Woomera range. Those who did were impressed, as one Vulcan captain reported:

'It was quite a sensation. Nothing happened for what seemed like quite a long time after weapon release, and then suddenly it appeared right in front of the nose, trailing smoke and flames and going incredibly fast, straight up. It was a bit unnerving, I suppose because it was completely unlike anything one had experienced before.'

Under operational conditions, of course, the aircraft would have steep-turned away immediately after weapon release, which was at a height of 50,000 ft. There was a complex fail-safe system, involving separate actions by the aircraft captain, the AEO and both the navigators, which had to be gone through before the missile could be launched. The main combustion chamber then powered Blue Steel up to 70,000 ft and accelerated it to 2.5M, at which point the main chamber shut down and the smaller chamber took over, sustaining the flight until, about four minutes after launch, the missile was bunted into a long dive on to its target, 100 nautical miles from the launch point. At this range it was accurate to within half a mile, which was quite acceptable in view of the fact that it carried a megaton-range thermonuclear warhead.

The above is a typical Blue Steel flight profile, but there were other variations. It could,

This page and overleaf *End of a Vulcan: On April 6 1967, Vulcan B 2 XL385, carrying a Blue Steel training round, was completely destroyed by fire at RAF Scampton. Five crew and one air cadet passenger escaped unhurt.*

for example, be launched from either high or low level, and its trajectory could be varied to give it a range of up to 200 nautical miles at a maximum speed of 1.6M, followed by a subsonic (0.8M) dive on to its target. With this profile, a Blue Steel launched over Lincolnshire could have flown as far as Edinburgh, which makes one realise how viable the 35 ft long, 13 ft span missile really was. (In fact, it is quite astonishing that, whereas details of free-falling thermonuclear weapons were kept a closely-guarded secret, a mass of information on Blue Steel was released *in 1963*, the year it became operational—and this was the very weapon that would have given the V-Force a real chance of survival!)

Later in 1963, No 617 Squadron's two sister units at Scampton, Nos 27 and 83 Squadrons, also equipped with Blue Steel, and the weapon's Service deployment was completed when two of No 3 Group's Victor B 2 squadrons, Nos 139 and 100, followed suit at Wittering from the summer of 1963.

The Blue Steel squadrons formed the spearhead of Bomber Command's Quick Reaction Alert force, and were to do so for a further five years. QRA had been inaugurated in February 1962, and the original procedure involved one aircraft from each V-Force squadron being maintained in an armed condition. Later, Operational Readiness Platforms were constructed at the ends of runways, the aircraft on readiness being parked combat-ready on short strips angled into the runway to facilitate rapid take-off. Scramble time was further reduced when, in 1962, an RAF engineer officer developed a mass rapid start technique, enabling all four engines of a V-bomber to be started simultaneously. With mass rapid start, four Vulcans on QRA could be airborne within 90 seconds of starting to roll.

The introduction of Blue Steel into operational service had an interesting side effect. Because the aircraft/missile navigational system relied on very accurate position fixing on the run-up to weapon release, the navigational charts used by Bomber Command had to be updated and, if necessary, modified to rule out any slight errors. Before Blue Steel became operational, therefore, large areas of the earth's surface were photographically mapped by the Valiant B(PR) 1s of No 543 Strategic Reconnaissance Squadron, based at Wyton in Huntingdonshire; two of these aircraft were capable of photo-mapping the whole of the Mediterranean in a single sortie.

Blue Steel had a lot of development potential, which unfortunately was never realised; had it been otherwise, the RAF might have had a 'cruise missile' in the mid-1960s. The original Blue Steel could fly at 70,000 ft, boost itself to 110,000 ft in a very short flight profile, or, with very minor changes in its systems, fly at 1,000 ft; in other words, it was a highly adaptable weapon, and its designers went to considerable pains to extend its operational capability. In 1957, in parallel with the development of the original Blue Steel, Avro proposed several variants of the basic missile, one of which was a low-level version powered by a 4,000 lb st Viper turbojet fed by a ventral intake; the missile had an estimated range of 600 miles at 500 ft, and a cruising speed of 0.9M.

In a bid to extend the high altitude range of the existing Blue Steel, Avro also proposed the Blue Steel Mk 1*, which would have had a kiloton-range warhead, a more compact guidance system and two solid fuel booster rockets in addition to the main rocket motor. This version, which would have carried more fuel, had an estimated range of 400 miles. Other projected variants included the Blue Steel Mk 1B, which also had extra fuel and a higher Mach number; the Mk 1C with extra boosters; the Mk 1D with externally-mounted HTP tanks; the Mk 1*E using hydrazene fuel; and the Mk 1S with external drop tanks.

The real viable development, however, was the Blue Steel Mk 2, which was developed in response to Ministry of Supply Specification 1159 for a long-range stand-off missile to supersede the Mk 1. The fuselage configuration of the Mk 2 was much the same as that of the Mk 1, but the Stentor rocket motor was replaced by four Bristol Siddeley ramjets at the wingtips and two solid fuel rocket boosters mounted dorsally. The design speed of the Mk 2 was 3.0M, with a range of up to 800 miles at 70,000 ft, and the inertial navigator was replaced by a Doppler system. A total of £825,000 was spent on the development of Blue Steel Mk 2 before the project was cancelled in December 1959.

At this time, it was still considered that the Hawker Siddeley Blue Streak IRBM would become the ultimate British deterrent weapon, and agreement had already been reached for the supply of 60 Thor missiles by the USA to bridge the gap until Blue Streak became operational. The Thors, however, were vulnerable to attack: they were liquid-fuelled and consequently took a considerable time to prepare for launching. They would only have been viable if Bomber Command had received several hours' prior warning of an enemy attack, instead of the few minutes that were expected. Blue Streak suffered from exactly the same drawback, and was consequently the target of much criticism, particularly from the Royal Navy, which was pressing for a combination of nuclear submarines and Polaris missiles, and also from the Air Staff, who justifiably believed that the combination of V-bomber and long-range stand-off missiles added up to a more flexible system than any fixed-site, unhardened IRBMs.

In April 1960, Blue Streak was finally cancelled as a military missile on the grounds that it was too vulnerable, too costly, and was experiencing many problems with its liquid fuel system. The Prime Minister, Harold Macmillan, was discussing the possibility of buying Polaris from the United States, but no decision was yet on the horizon; in the meantime, Britain had no strategic missiles apart from the vulnerable Thor, and it would be three years before Blue Steel was operational.

There was, however, another option, and one that might give the British airborne deterrent credibility for years to come, long after Blue Steel had outlived its usefulness. Its name was Skybolt.

Chapter 7

Vulcan and Skybolt

On December 21 1959 a new air-to-ground stand-off missile entered service with the US Strategic Air Command. Designed and built by North American, and designated GAM-77 (later AGM-28), it was called the Hound Dog, and formed the missile portion of the Weapon System 131-B installed in the B-52G bomber. Hound Dog, which was to equip 29 SAC Wings by the summer of 1963, was 42 ft 6 ins long and was powered by a Pratt & Whitney J52 turbojet. Like its British counterpart, Blue Steel, it had a small delta wing and a canard-type delta foreplane; also like Blue Steel, it was inertially guided. There the similarity ended. A B-52 could carry two Hound Dogs, each of which had a 4-megaton warhead. The missile could be programmed to attack at either high or low level; it could change course and altitude, and also make dog-leg or feint runs. It cruised at 2.0M at 52,000 ft, and its range was over 600 miles.

Like Blue Steel, Hound Dog was a third-generation weapon; a logical next step after free-falling kiloton-range and megaton-range weapons. Yet it was never designed to be anything more than an interim weapon system for, even before it was tested, the USAF had launched a design competition for an air-launched strategic missile system in the true sense: a system whereby the launch aircraft would carry the weapon to its release point, after which it would behave like a ground-launched IRBM and follow a spatial trajectory before its warhead impacted on the target, over 1,000 miles away. Fifteen American aerospace companies entered the running in the race to develop an air-launched ballistic missile, and it was the Douglas Aircraft Corporation which, on May 26 1959, was awarded a design study contract and named as prime contractor for the new weapon system, which carried the original designation WS-138A. In February 1960 Douglas received a further contract which called for the building of several research and development test vehicles; the missile was now designated XGAM-87A, and the name Skybolt was given to it. Other companies involved in the project were Aerojet-General, who were made responsible for the missile's hypersonic (9.0M) two-stage solid-fuel propulsion system, General Electric, whose responsibility was the design of the re-entry vehicle carrying the warhead, and the Nortronics Division of the Northrop Aircraft Corporation, who were to design the weapon's stellar-monitored inertial guidance system, consisting of an astro-inertial system and star-tracker linked to a ballistic missile computer.

The 38 ft long Skybolt, which had a range of 1,150 miles—Douglas having decided to sacrifice range, weight and warhead size so that up to four individually-targeted missiles could be carried under the wings of the Boeing B-52H or the Convair B-58—was properly termed an airborne strategic delivery system, and came within the IRBM category. It was the first (and, so far, the only) air-launched missile in the world to do so, and would have altered the whole concept of strategic nuclear warfare. It was small wonder, then, that in 1959 the RAF began to show a serious interest in acquiring Skybolt as an eventual replacement for Blue Steel, in order to extend the life of the British airborne deterrent into the 1970s.

Vulcan B 2 XH537 carrying two dummy Skybolt rounds on underwing pylons.

In March 1960, as the result of a meeting between Harold Macmillan and President Dwight D. Eisenhower at Camp David, a Memorandum of Agreement was reached under which Skybolt would be supplied to the RAF. The missile was still a long way off being tested, but it was envisaged that if all went well it would become operational with SAC about the end of 1963. It would now be carried only by the B-52H Stratofortress, the B-58B version of Convair's Hustler having been cancelled in the meantime. The Anglo-American agreement was ratified in May 1960 by British Defence Minister Harold Watkinson and US Secretary of Defense Thomas Gates, and it was decided that Britain would buy an initial batch of 100 Skybolts.

Although Avro, with their considerable experience in Blue Steel development, were selected as the main contractor for the British Skybolt system, and although the Vulcan B 2 was designated as the primary carrier, Hawker Siddeley, Vickers and Handley Page all submitted their own proposals. Hawker Siddeley, who were then projecting a maritime version of the Trident airliner to replace Coastal Command's Shackletons (a need that was ultimately to be filled by the Nimrod), proposed a variant capable of carrying four Skybolts, while Vickers put up a similar idea in connection with their VC 10. Handley Page, in attempting to convert the Victor B 2 into a Skybolt platform for three missiles, found insurmountable difficulties right from the beginning in the low ground clearance of their design, and even though the company, under the dynamic leadership of Sir

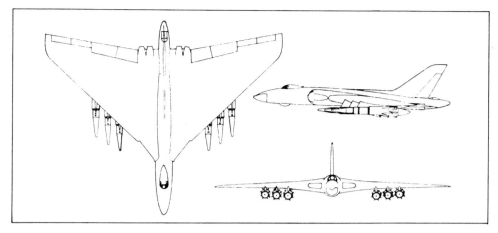

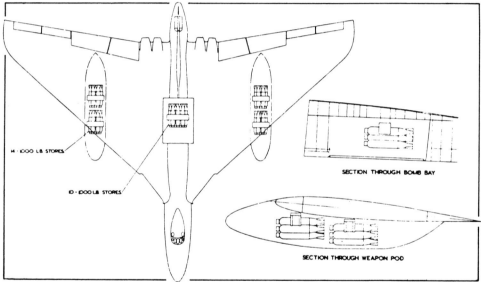

Top *The Vulcan Phase 6, with increased wing area and uprated engines, was projected to carry two, four or six Skybolt missiles.* **Above** *In its conventional mode, the Vulcan Phase 6 would have been able to carry 38 1,000 lb bombs.*

Frederick, worked hard to convince the government that the Victor could be adapted to carry two, four or even six Skybolts on underwing hardpoints, there was no way in which the technical problems could be overcome.

Although the Trident and VC 10 contenders were not yet out of the running, it was decided that the Vulcan B 2, carrying two Skybolts initially but with a possibility of extending this capability to four or six missiles per aircraft, would pioneer Skybolt's introduction into service with Bomber Command. Vulcan B 2s then on the production line were to be modified with underwing hardpoints and the electrical systems necessary to mate the Skybolt with its parent aircraft, while aircraft already built were to be converted in batches, retrospectively. New-build Mk 2s, beginning with the 40th aircraft, would emerge with a strengthened wing structure, Skybolt attachment points outboard of the undercarriage, and 20,000 lb s t Olympus 301 engines.

The Vulcan allocated to Bristol Siddeley for trials with the Olympus 300 series engines was *XH557*, the first to leave the Woodford assembly line with the new large engine intakes that characterised the Olympus 201/301 fit. With a mixed Service and civilian crew *XH557* flew from Boscombe Down to Filton on September 16 1960, and its landing there almost ended in disaster. Approaching from the west in rain and low cloud, the Vulcan touched down too far along the main runway; the pilot streamed the brake parachute, but this failed to deploy and he applied full power to go round again. As the Vulcan rotated the parachute suddenly deployed fully and the subsequent high drag retarded the aircraft's lift-off, with the result that its main undercarriage ripped through the boundary fence where the overshoot area adjoined the A38 road and also damaged some lamp standards. As the Vulcan started to climb under full power, its jet exhaust uprooted petrol pumps and shattered windows at a nearby garage. Fortunately, there were no serious casualties, although one civilian was treated for shock.

XH557 climbed up through the overcast, and its undercarriage was inspected by another aircraft before the pilot diverted to St Mawgan in Cornwall, where he made a safe landing. The aircraft returned to Filton later that month, and after two Olympus 21A test engines had been fitted in the port engine bays it went to Woodford for Company handling assessment; it then flew to Patchway, where trials were carried out with 21As and Mk 301s. After 221 test flights, some at low level, *XH557* went back to Woodford for refurbishing in July 1964 and was delivered to the Coningsby Wing in the following year. After lengthy service, this famous B 2 was eventually sold for scrap in December 1982.

In January 1961, Vulcan *XH563* of No 83 Squadron flew to the Douglas factory at Santa Monica, California, to carry out electrical compatibility tests, and then went on for further trials to the Wright Air Development Division at Wright Patterson AFB, Ohio, before returning to squadron service. (This aircraft, incidentally, was eventually converted to SR 2 standard for service with No 27 Squadron, and was preserved as 'gate guardian' outside the operations centre at RAF Scampton.) In July 1961, AEI were awarded the main UK contract for production of the Vulcan/Skybolt electrical and interface equipment, which included an analogue digital computer.

Meanwhile, on January 12 1961, a B-52G had made a six-hour aerodynamic proving flight carrying four dummy Skybolts. No problems were experienced, and in June the first production model B-52H began a series of aerodynamic flight compatibility tests. These were followed, in the autumn, by the first weapon release trials, when B-52F serial *57-038* dropped a series of inert Skybolt rounds.

In the United Kingdom, a British warhead was being developed for Skybolt, and in November 1961 Vulcan *XH537*, a Ministry of Aviation development aircraft, flew from the Weapons Research Division at Woodford with two dummy Skybolts on underwing pylons. On December 1 this aircraft made the first dummy Skybolt drop (by a Vulcan) over the West Freugh Range, Scotland; this was followed by three more drops, all with dummy rounds, by *XH537* and *XH538*. The latter, which made its first Skybolt drop on December 9, had also been heavily involved in Blue Steel trials. All dummy Skybolt drops were made from 45,000 ft at a speed of 0.84M.

By this time, Avro and Douglas had established an excellent working relationship with one another, and co-operation was placed on an even sounder footing when, in 1962, a British Joint Trials Force—eventually to total some 200 personnel—was created in the United States at Eglin AFB, Florida, under the command of Wing Commander Charles Ness. Eglin was the home of the USAF Air Proving Ground Centre, which in 1962 was commanded by Major General Roberts, and responsibility for all Skybolt trials rested here.

The first live launch of a Skybolt missile took place from a B-52F on April 19 1962, and was a disappointment: although the first stage booster worked perfectly well, the second stage failed to ignite. In a second live launch, on June 29, it was the first stage booster which failed to ignite properly, and the missile had to be destroyed by the range safety officer. A third launch, on September 13, seemed more promising; both stages fired successfully on this occasion, but then the missile suddenly veered off course and had to be destroyed. Both stages also fired on the fourth launch, which was made on September 25, but the second stage burned for only 15 seconds, with the result that, although Skybolt flew well, it fell a long way short of its planned range of 900 miles on this particular trial.

By this time, the whole Skybolt development programme had come under review by US Secretary of Defense Robert McNamara, who was having serious doubts about it. The original idea behind Skybolt was that it would form one point of a triangle of three US deterrent missiles, the other two being Minuteman and Polaris. McNamara's growing opinion, in view of the latest information on the numbers of operational ballistic missiles the Russians had at their disposal, was that Polaris and Minuteman were sufficient to counter any threat, and that therefore Skybolt was unnecessary. Moreover, the Skybolt programme had cost $500 million by the end of 1962, and all the USAF had to show for this escalating expenditure was failure. On November 7 1962 McNamara recommended to President John F. Kennedy that Skybolt be cancelled.

There is little doubt that McNamara was right, from the American point of view. The submarine-borne Polaris was already operational, and Minuteman, which had been successfully test fired, was about to become so. The decision to cancel Skybolt was made purely on technical and cost-effectiveness grounds, and not, as some British circles were at pains to establish, because President Kennedy had no real liking for the British and no longer wished Britain to have her own independent deterrent. This idea was nonsense; in 1962 Britain already had a deterrent, or was about to have one in the operational sense, in the form of Blue Steel. The trouble was that the cancellation of Skybolt meant that there was nothing to come after Blue Steel.

On December 19 1962 Prime Minister Harold Macmillan and President Kennedy met at Nassau, in the Bahamas, to discuss the whole Skybolt question. Even at this stage, plans were being made to carry out live Skybolt firings from a Vulcan early in 1963, and other projects designed to increase the operational effectiveness of the system in RAF service were still being considered. Because the operational Skybolt would give such a massive boost to Bomber Command's deterrent power, enabling the Vulcans of the V-Force to strike deep into the heart of the Soviet Union, the Air Staff thought it quite likely that, in the event of a build-up to war, the Russians would give higher priority to pre-emptive strikes on RAF bomber airfields. In 1961, therefore, the Air Staff made a close study of what they termed a 'Continuous Airborne Deterrent', involving aircraft with long endurance and carrying four or six Skybolts being in the air on a relay system 24 hours a day. To achieve this successfully, an aircraft with a greater endurance than the existing Mk 2 Vulcan would be needed, and late in 1961 the British Aircraft Corporation, into which Vickers had been absorbed, put forward a proposal for a 4,000-mile range VC 10 carrying four Skybolts. The RAF had just placed an order for five VC 10s for RAF Transport Command in September, with the prospect of more to follow, so BAC considered it had a fighting chance of securing a contract for a Skybolt-equipped variant.

Avro, which had become part of the Hawker Siddeley Group, countered with their own proposal, which was presented to the Air Staff on December 19 1961. This involved the Vulcan Phase 6, which was to be powered by uprated Olympus 23 engines and given a larger wing with a straightened leading edge to accommodate them, as well as the extra

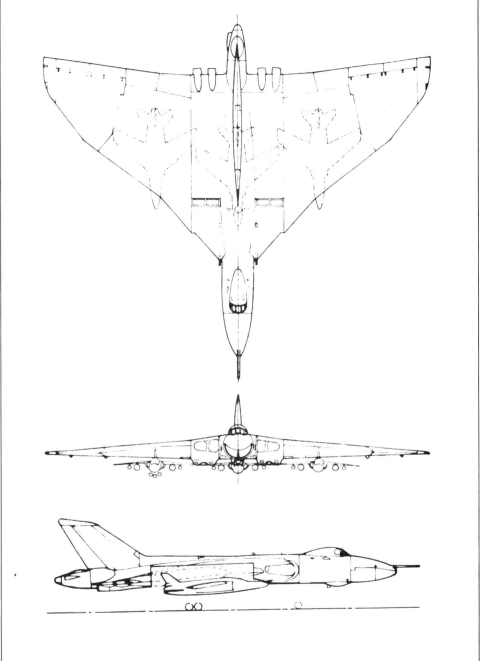

After the demise of Skybolt, it was briefly considered using the Vulcan B 2 as a carrier aircraft for three Gnats, each carrying a kiloton-range nuclear weapon.

fuel required; the fin area was also to be increased. All-up weight of the aircraft, with six Skybolts on underwing attachments, would be more than 350,000 pounds. A crew of six would be carried, seated in pairs one behind the other and all having ejection seats, with rest bunks at the rear of the cabin for those off duty. The extra crew, and modified seating arrangement, meant that the Phase 6's nose had to be extended by 10 ft 9 ins. Total endurance of the Phase 6 was to be seven hours, and average annual utilisation of each aircraft was estimated at 2,900 hours.

With only two Skybolts, endurance of the Phase 6 could be increased to 12 hours, dropping to ten hours with four missiles. This meant, in effect, that if Bomber Command launched a Vulcan Phase 6 every two hours, with various combinations of missiles and varying range requirements, 48 Vulcans Phase 6 could keep 84 Skybolts in the air around the clock at an annual operating cost of £55 million. Considering that the maximum range of a Vulcan Phase 6 carrying a full load of six Skybolts would have been in the order of 5,000 nautical miles, this airborne alert force would have formed a very credible deterrent indeed, and would of course have been backed up by existing Skybolt-equipped Vulcan B 2s. As a bonus, Hawker Siddeley also offered a conventional version of the Phase 6 which could carry no less than 38 1,000 lb bombs, ten in the main weapons bay and 14 under each wing in pods.

Another project studied by Hawker Siddeley at about that time, but one which carried far less credibility than the Phase 6, involved a vertical take-off version of the Vulcan with ten B 59 lift engines fitted in the bomb bay. These would, in theory at least, have enabled the Vulcan to take off vertically in a matter of seconds if its base were threatened with attack, forward propulsion being supplied by its normal Olympus engines. Weapons would have been carried on underwing hard points. The weight penalty, however, would have proven enormous, and the project was dropped after some initial design study work had been carried out.

Mating Skybolt with the Vulcan had produced very few problems, and tests with dummy missiles had shown that the Vulcan was a very stable launch platform; the combination, in fact, seemed to be an ideal one, and in many respects the Vulcan was far better suited to Skybolt than was the B-52. Yet the hard fact remained that when Kennedy and Macmillan met at Nassau in December 1962, Skybolt had been test-fired five times and had failed on every occasion.

Kennedy and Defense Secretary McNamara therefore felt perfectly justified in cancelling further development; they had been on the verge of doing so throughout 1962, and the test failures were the final nails in Skybolt's coffin. Macmillan and his advisers should have been alert to the hardening American attitude; the USAF had voiced its fears that Skybolt would be cancelled often enough during the preceding months, when USAF and RAF personnel involved in the project met for their frequent conferences. To say that the Americans had not considered the British standpoint over Skybolt, however, would be wrong, for the British involvement had kept the project going for much longer than was really necessary in Washington's eyes. What the Americans—that is to say, Kennedy and McNamara—had failed to do was to appreciate the British reaction when Harold Macmillan was informed of the final decision at Nassau. Moreover, the President did nothing to ease the atmosphere of tension and distrust on the British side when he mentioned that he was committed to the policy of a European multilateral nuclear force under NATO control, which would replace the British and French independent nuclear forces; it served only to bolster the British opinion that the cancellation of Skybolt was a political move designed to achieve this aim.

President Kennedy, amazed by the British reaction which he now, at last, began to appreciate fully, realised that the time had come to make concessions. His first act was to offer Britain the whole Skybolt programme, which was promptly deemed out of the question because of the cost involved—although, as has been pointed out more than once, it would probably have worked out cheaper than the nuclear submarine/Polaris combination. Kennedy then offered to bear half the Skybolt development cost, which was extremely generous, for it meant that he would have had to justify in Congress the expenditure of a lot of US taxpayers' money on a weapon system which would be of no benefit to the United States, but this offer too was rejected. The case for the RAF was put forward eloquently by the Assistant Chief of Air Staff, Air Vice-Marshal Christopher Hartley, but in the end it made no difference. Macmillan opted for the submarine-borne Polaris, on terms as favourable as he could get, having also rejected an offer of Hound Dog as an alternative missile system for the V-Force.

Skybolt, which had cost Britain £27 million, was dead, and so was the future of the British airborne nuclear deterrent. The irony was that, while the Nassau talks were in progress, the B-52F trials aircraft took off from Eglin AFB on December 19 and launched a Skybolt over the Eastern Test Range; the missile worked perfectly and reached its target area, 1,000 miles downrange in the Atlantic.

It was officially stated in February 1963 that four or five 7,000-ton nuclear submarines, each capable of carrying 16 Polaris missiles, were to be ordered for the Royal Navy to take over and maintain the British nuclear deterrent. However, it would be the late 1960s before the first of these craft became operational, and in the meantime the deterrent still remained in the hands of RAF Bomber Command. At the tip of Bomber Command's nuclear spearhead were the three squadrons of Vulcans and two of Victors, armed with Blue Steel, and after the demise of Skybolt—with the resurrection of a Mk 2 version of Blue Steel out of the question—various proposals were put forward to extend the combat radius of the V-Force and enable it to maintain the deterrent after Blue Steel Mk 1.

One such proposal was put forward by Rolls-Royce, and involved a stand-off weapon powered by a turbojet, in the same way as Hound Dog. The missile, designed to be carried by the Vulcan and also the TSR-2 (which was destined to be cancelled in turn in 1965) would have cruised at 1.8M and would have had a range of 1,000 miles, with an estimated accuracy of one or two miles at that distance. With cost in mind the whole thing was to use existing equipment as far as possible, including a variant of the Elliott inertial navigator designed for Blue Steel.

The Rolls-Royce proposal never got beyond the project stage, and neither did another, put forward by Hawker Siddeley, which was considerably more fanciful. This involved hanging three Gnats under a Vulcan B 2, one partly recessed in the bomb bay and the other two on the Skybolt hardpoints under the wings; the Gnats were to carry kiloton-range weapons and four long-range fuel tanks apiece. The Vulcan would release them at anything up to 1,000 miles from their targets, and assuming that these were attained successfully the Gnat pilots were then faced with the choice of baling out or using whatever fuel remained in a bid to reach friendly territory. The whole idea was reminiscent of wartime kamikaze tactics and was quietly dropped, but the principle must have been filed away somewhere, because during a series of air defence exercises in 1971–2 Gnats, flying in close formation with Vulcans, were used to simulate Soviet bombers with stand-off weapons attacking targets on the east coast of the British Isles.

There was a curious postscript to the Skybolt story, but it took 20 years before it was written. During the Falklands operation, Vulcans armed with anti-radar missiles were to be used against Argentinian installations, as we shall see in detail later—and it was the wing hardpoints designed to uplift Skybolt which carried those weapons into action.

Chapter 8

Maintaining the deterrent

In February 1963, the Air Officer Commanding-in-Chief, Bomber Command (Air Marshal Sir Kenneth Cross) held a Press conference at RAF Scampton to introduce Blue Steel, and stated that it would remain valid as a weapon for 'quite a number of years'. Its importance lay in the fact that it gave the V-Force a continued operational viability into the mid-1960s in the face of increasingly efficient Soviet fighter and SAM defences; in fact, it was to remain operational until 1970, several months after the RAF's nuclear deterrent role had been handed over to the Royal Navy.

This was the time when the V-Force was at its greatest numerical strength. By the end of June 1964 there were 159 V-bombers in service, 70 of them Vulcans, and later that year, when all five Blue Steel squadrons were fully operational, the Force was also at the peak of its offensive power. There were at that time 43 Valiants, 69 Vulcans (45 of them B 2s, 24 armed with Blue Steel) and 32 Victors, of which 16 carried Blue Steel.

Below *Vulcan B 2 of the Waddington Wing at RCAF Goose Bay.*

Opposite *Vulcan B 2 of the Waddington Wing approaches and lands at Tengah, Singapore, on an 'Exercise Sunflower' deployment.*

By this time, the first of the V-bombers, the Valiant, had ceased to be part of the deterrent force. In 1960–1 three Valiant squadrons, Nos 49, 148 and 207, had been assigned to the Supreme Allied Commander, Europe (SACEUR), and two others, Nos 90 and 214, had been turned over to the flight refuelling role. From 1963, Bomber Command's Vulcans and Victors were given a flight refuelling capability, the fuel being delivered via a nose-mounted probe which was first tested on *XH478*. Aircraft, beginning with the Blue Steel-equipped Vulcan squadrons of the Scampton Wing, were withdrawn from service singly so that the necessary modifications could be carried out by Flight Refuelling Ltd.

The years after 1963 also saw major changes in the V-Force's operational procedures, the greatest such change being an emphasis on the low-level delivery of weapons in order to prolong the Force's viability with both Blue Steel and free-fall weapons, and both technical developments and training were directed towards this end. The switch to low-level operations marked the eventual end of the Valiant's career, for the stresses imposed by this type of work led to the development of cracks in the aircraft's rear spar, with the result that the type was withdrawn from service from the beginning of 1965.

The Vulcan, on the other hand, was robust enough to withstand the rigours of prolonged low-level operations, and adapted itself to its new role without difficulty—although there was a corresponding increase in crew workload, for there was no room for error in crew co-operation in the blacked-out cockpit of an aircraft thundering along at 1,000 ft or lower. The start of low-level operations in 1964 also led to an increase in overseas sorties, as low-level training in the UK was restricted by the density of urban areas and air traffic.

The main responsibility for handling aircraft on overseas low-level training fell on the Royal Air Force Bomber Command Detachment at Goose Bay, Labrador, which had been responsible for servicing and despatching Vulcans and other V-Force aircraft on their Western Ranger flights to and from Offutt AFB, near Omaha. An agreement was set up between the British and Canadian Governments under which crews of the Medium and Tactical Bomber Force were detached to RCAF Goose Bay every week throughout the year. During their stay, each crew flew three out of four special low-level routes, covering some of the wildest territory in Labrador and some of the hardest, from the radar-fixing point of view, in the world. In fact, it approximated very closely to the type of country across which the V-Force might have to penetrate in attacks on the Arctic regions of the Soviet Union.

When low-level training started, the RAF detachment at Goose Bay was under the command of Squadron Leader Victor McNabney, GM, who had a staff of about 70 officers and airmen. The RAF's centre of operations was No 1 hangar, which was large enough to hold two Vulcans or Victors and was heated in the winter—a vital factor, for winter at Goose often meant temperatures of minus 38 degrees F combined with icy winds gusting up to 80 mph.

When a Vulcan arrived at Goose Bay it was met by a servicing team of nine men; this team would be responsible for looking after the aircraft throughout its eight-day stay, working in conjunction with the machine's crew chief. Crews were sent to Labrador only after having accumulated experience on the UK low-level routes, and most found that with this preliminary training they could handle a low-level route over strange country—even country where the only features were natural ones that varied in shape according to the time of year—with complete success. The main problems they encountered were turbulence, of which there was a lot, and heat in summer. The average annual temperature at Goose was 32 degrees F, but it could rise to 100 degrees in the height of summer, and the blacked-out confines of a Vulcan cockpit could become very hot indeed.

RCAF Goose Bay, with its 11,000 ft runway, was separated from the nearest civilisation by over 700 miles of bush country. Sited on the 53rd Parallel, it was surrounded by rugged terrain of rocky soil, the vegetation consisting mainly of evergreen spruce. Hills pushed up out of the flat landscape at heights of between 1,000 and 3,000 ft within a 100-mile radius; 80 miles to the east the Mealy Mountains rose to 3,750 ft, while 400 miles to the north the mountains of the Torngat Range reached 5,500 ft.

In 1964 terrain-following radar for the Vulcans was still a thing of the future, so careful route planning was essential. After that, track-keeping was done entirely by radar, the navigators maintaining a constant radar fix on the aircraft's position and leap-frogging from pre-planned fix to pre-planned fix. Mapping and 'cut-off' of signals on the radar screen gave warning of approaching high ground; a word to the pilots and the aircraft would be eased up over the contours, the aircraft captain keeping a careful check on height with reference to the information fed to him by the Nav Radar. The co-pilot's task was to manage the fuel and, when conditions permitted, keep an additional check on the Vulcan's position by map-reading. Training flights were made in Visual Meteorological Conditions, but every effort was made to ensure that the operations approximated as closely as possible to the real thing; the black-out curtain would be down behind the two pilots and the shutters in place over the windows in the side of the rear cockpit. At a later date, when terrain-following radar was introduced, the blinds would also be down over the cockpit windscreen and the sortie would be flown with the whole cockpit blacked out.

V-Force at Goose Bay: two Vulcans and a Victor under a snow-laden sky.

Left *The keen rivalry between two V-Force squadrons, Nos 9 and 617, was epitomised by the 'Tirpitz Bulkhead'. Both squadrons claim to have sunk the battleship* Tirpitz *in 1944 with their 'Tallboy' Lancasters, and the bulkhead, a trophy from the ship, has shuttled back and forth between their respective crew rooms ever since. On this occasion it was 'rescued' from 617 by 9 Squadron, whose CO at that time, Wing Commander Ron Dick, is seen shaking hands with fellow conspirator Flight Lieutenant Peter Armstrong.*

Right *The Vulcan's low-level role is well illustrated in this shot of a Scampton Wing B 2.*

Below *Vulcan B 2* XH562 *served originally with 230 OCU and subsequently with No 35 Squadron.*

Above *Striking photograph of Vulcan B 2 XM595 of 617 Squadron being readied for a night sortie from Scampton.*
Below *A misty touch-down for Vulcan B 2 XM656 of the Waddington Wing at Goose Bay, Labrador.*

While the Blue Steel-equipped Vulcan squadrons at Scampton (whose modified aircraft, incidentally, now bore the designation B 2A) worked hard to perfect low-level launch techniques for their missiles, the B 2 squadrons at Cottesmore and the B 1A squadrons at Waddington concentrated on low-altitude delivery techniques with their free-falling bombs. The Vulcans, in keeping with their new low-level role, also lost their light paint-work, which was replaced by light grey/dark green camouflage. Another, sadder loss in 1964 was the gradual disappearance of squadron badges from individual aircraft; this was the result of the introduction of a centralised servicing scheme throughout the Medium Bomber Force, which meant that individual aircraft were 'pooled' and, after servicing, could be allocated to any of the units within their Wing. There was one concession: all the aircraft of the Waddington Wing retained their City of Lincoln fin badge.

Low-level operations raised, once again, the vexed question of ejection seats for the rear crew, which had been debated on and off since the London Airport disaster of 1956. In 1960 a Valiant had been modified by Martin-Baker to take a rearward-facing ejection seat in the crew compartment; three dummy ejections were made from this aircraft, at ground level, 200 ft/250 knots and 200 ft/300 knots, and these were followed, on July 1 1960, by a successful live ejection at 1,000 ft and 250 knots, the 'guinea pig' being W.T. Hay. The success of these trials encouraged Martin-Baker, entirely without official backing, to fit three rearward-facing ejection seats into the fuselage of a Vulcan B 1, if Bomber Command would be willing to let them have one on loan.

The design worked out by Martin-Baker was quite ingenious. First of all, one of the pilots would operate a lever to jettison a hatch over the head of the Nav Plotter, who sat in the middle of the rear trio; this action would also operate a cartridge which would automatically fold the rear crew table and pull tight all three sets of shoulder harness, straightening the backs of the crew to avoid spinal damage. A separate ejection control, also operated by the pilots, would first of all 'bang out' the Plotter; once he was clear the Nav Radar's seat would have been automatically positioned under the central hatch and he would have gone out in turn, followed by the AEO. The whole sequence took less than three seconds, and featured a built-in mechanism that prevented the pilots from ejecting until the last rear crew member had gone.

No Vulcan was ever allocated to Martin-Baker for airborne trials, but a series of tests was carried out on the ground with the aid of rocket-powered sleds and in the air using Valiant *WP199* at speeds of up to 450 knots, and these proved that rearward-facing seats would be able to clear the Vulcan fin by $5\frac{1}{2}$ ft. But rear ejection seats were never adopted, and the main reason was that the idea was tested at too late a stage in the V-bombers' development. Despite Martin-Baker's laudable initiative, the cost and the technical problems involved in fitting the B 2 generation of bombers then on the production line, and in retrospectively fitting the Vulcan B 1As, would have been prohibitive. The best that could be done was to equip the rear crew seats with assister cushions, which were inflated by compressed air and literally pushed the crew out of their seats towards the escape hatch.

As though to underline the escape problems that might be encountered when the V-Force went low-level, the very beginning of low-level training was marred by a fatal accident when Vulcan B 1A *XH477* of No 50 Squadron—one of the aircraft which had taken part in the prestige tour of South America in 1958—crashed in Scotland on a low-level sortie from Waddington on June 12 1963. All five crew were killed.

The year 1964 saw the progressive phasing-out of the Vulcan B 1/1A, beginning with the aircraft on 230 OCU's inventory. The first to be relinquished was *XA896*, which flew to Hucknall in June for conversion as test-bed for the Bristol Siddeley BS100 vectored-thrust engine, which was to have powered the Hawker Siddeley P1154 V/STOL Mach 2

Above *Vulcan B 2 of the Scampton Wing, detached on a 'Sunspot' exercise, overshooting at RAF Luqa, Malta.*

Above right *Vulcan B 2 XL361 of Scampton Wing shows off its underside while on deployment in Cyprus. Note bomb-bay recess to accommodate Blue Steel.*

strike fighter. However, conversion work was only partly completed when the P1154 project was cancelled, and *XA896* was later broken up. The OCU's other four B 1s went to Halton, Cosford, Cranwell and Newton for use as instructional airframes during the next 18 months, so that by the end of 1965 the OCU was equipped entirely with B 2s.

Of the other B 1s and 1As, *XA905* of the Waddington Wing went to RAF Newton as an instructional airframe, *XA906* of 44 Squadron was withdrawn in March 1967 and sold for scrap in November 1968, and *XA907* was withdrawn in November 1966 and scrapped in May 1968. *XA908* had already been lost in the Detroit crash of 1958, but its sister aircraft, *XA909*, had gone on to serve with the Waddington Wing after conversion to B 1A, but it was also ill-starred. On July 16 1964, while serving in No 101 Squadron, the aircraft

suffered an engine explosion over Anglesey, North Wales. The pilot, Flight Lieutenant M.H. Smith, from Salisbury, Rhodesia, sent out a Mayday and a Gnat trainer was sent up from RAF Valley to assess the damage. A short while later, Smith began to lose control, but managed to steer the aircraft away from populated areas before it went down to crash in a field near Gwalchmai. Smith and the other four crew members abandoned the aircraft successfully.

XA910 of 44 Squadron went as an instructional airframe in 1964, but scrapping was the fate of *XA911*, which had been used in the making of a Ministry information film about the V-Force entitled *Delta 83*. Also scrapped were *XA912* and *XA913*, while *XH475* became an instructional airframe from November 1967. *XH476* was withdrawn in May 1967 and scrapped in January 1969, while *XH477*, as mentioned earlier, crashed on a low-level exercise in Scotland in 1963.

XH478, the aircraft which had been used to test the Vulcan's nose-mounted flight refuelling probe, eventually went to Akrotiri, Cyprus, for ground training as *MC8047M*. In November 1973, it was briefly 'impressed' into Royal Navy service by No 809

Squadron, Fleet Air Arm, who emblazoned its wings with the legend 'Fly Navy' and its tail with the No 809 Squadron crest! The next B 1A, *XH479*, went to Halton as an instructional airframe, while the last 15 aircraft (*XH480–483*, *XH497–506*, and *XH532*, the last production B 1) were all broken up for scrap with the exception of *XH481* and *XH483* which went to Cottesmore and Manston for fire-fighting practice, *XH498* and *'499*, which became instructional airframes, *XH502*, which was flown to Scampton for ground instructional duties before returning to Waddington for fire-fighting practice, *XH504*, which went to Cottesmore, and *XH505*, which was allocated to Finningley for the same purpose. All three squadrons of the Waddington Wing re-equipped with B 2s.

Several Vulcan B 1s, none of them ex-squadron aircraft, were assigned to engine development work. The first was the original prototype, *VX770*, which was delivered to Rolls-Royce at Langar in August 1956 and was fitted with four 15,000 lb st Conway RCo5 engines, with which it began trials—including a visit to Malta, where tropical tests were carried out—on August 9 1957. It had completed about 800 flying hours when it broke up and crashed during a 'Battle of Britain' air display at Syerston on 20 September 1958, all its crew being killed. Its place was taken by *XA902*, which had been damaged in a landing accident with No 230 OCU in February 1958 and subsequently repaired; it was now fitted with Conway 11 engines, with which it carried out a two-year test programme before being temporarily withdrawn and fitted with Rolls-Royce Speys in the inboard engine bays. It flew in this configuration between October 1961 and the middle of 1962,

A sight that thrilled millions of spectators world-wide over the years: a Vulcan B 2 crams on power at an air display.

playing a valuable part in the Spey test programme, until it was withdrawn from use.

The first production B 1, *XA889*, was allocated to the Olympus 100 engine development programme, as was *XA891*. The latter, as we have seen already, crashed in Yorkshire in 1959, but *XA889* served for a decade more and was not withdrawn from use until 1971.

The fifth Vulcan B 1 allocated for engine development was *XA894*, which, after service with the A&AEE at Boscombe Down, went to Patchway in July 1960 and was converted as a test-bed for the Bristol Olympus 22R, which was to power the BAC TSR-2 tactical strike and reconnaissance aircraft. The engine, fuelled from two tanks in the bomb bay, was mounted in a nacelle beneath *XA894*'s fuselage. First flight with the 22R was made on February 23 1962, and the aircraft appeared at that year's SBAC Show with the more powerful Olympus 22R-1, which was fitted with a high performance reheat system. Unfortunately, during a full reheat ground run on December 3, the LP shaft of the 22R-1 failed and the engine disintegrated, spewing out metal fragments which ruptured both the bomb bay and main fuel tanks. Such was the force of the break-up that the LP turbine disc was hurled for half a mile in bounds of 150 yards, narrowly missing the Bristol 188 research aircraft. *XA894* burst into flames and was completely destroyed; the crew made a very rapid exit and escaped unhurt, and there were no casualties to personnel on the ground.

The most famous Vulcan engine test-bed of all was undoubtedly *XA903*, the former Blue Steel trials aircraft and 15th production B 1, which went to Patchway in January

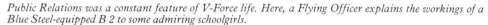

Public Relations was a constant feature of V-Force life. Here, a Flying Officer explains the workings of a Blue Steel-equipped B 2 to some admiring schoolgirls.

1964 for a major overhaul and modifications prior to the installation of the prototype Bristol Siddeley 593, the engine that was to power the Anglo-French Concorde SST. A lot of preparatory work was necessary, including the removal of the internal fuselage hardpoints left over from the Blue Steel trials, a complete repaint (in the original white anti-flash scheme), the fitting of fuel tanks, water tanks (for icing trials) and engine-associated avionics in the bomb bay, the removal of the visual bomb-aiming blister under the nose, and the installation of a mass of monitoring equipment in the rear crew compartment, which made conditions there even more claustrophobic than usual.

The combination of *XA903* and Olympus 593 flew for the first time on September 9 1966, with Rolls-Royce (Bristol Engine Division) Chief Test Pilot Tom Frost as captain, and on the following day the aircraft was demonstrated at the SBAC Show. After Farnborough the trials programme got under way, tests having first been made to ensure that the crew could get out safely and clear the underslung engine if anything went wrong in the air. The tests involved releasing a pair of parachute-equipped dummies from the escape hatch at a speed of 170 knots IAS.

XA903 went on to test all the Olympus 593 variants, including the 593-610 which was fitted to production Concordes. There was only one lengthy break in the programme, following an incident in February 1970 when, in the course of noise measurement trials at Filton, a hydraulic line fractured, causing severe loss of pressure in the undercarriage system. The captain diverted to Boscombe Down, only to find it closed, so he went on to Fairford and touched down safely despite the failure of the braking parachute to deploy and the resulting heavy braking causing one of the units to catch fire. *XA903* did not fly again until August, and went on to complete the Olympus 593 programme on July 21 1971. At that time it had made 219 test flights, during which the test engine had been run for 248 hours.

In August 1971, *XA903* went to Marshalls of Cambridge for more conversion work in connection with its next project, which was the testing of the Rolls Royce/Turbo-Union RB 199-34R, developed to power the Panavia MRCA—or Tornado, as it would eventually be known. Conversion was completed in January 1972 and the aircraft flew for the first time with its under-fuselage RB 199 on April 19 1973, captained by test pilot Harry Pollit. The engine nacelle represented a Tornado starboard half-fuselage, with the appropriate air intake; also built into it was a weapons bay to accommodate two 27 mm Mauser cannon and 150 rounds of ammunition.

The RB 199 was run in flight for the first time on July 26 1973, and reheat was used for the first time in April 1974. The first phase of the test programme, using developed versions of the engine, continued into 1976, and also during that year the two-gun Mauser installation was butt-tested at Boscombe Down. This was followed by airborne single-gun firings over the Aberporth range, with Harry Pollit at the controls; it was the first and only occasion on which a cannon had been mounted on and fired from a Vulcan.

Flight testing of the RB 199 went on into 1978, and *XA903* took the RB 199 Mk 101, the production version, through its trials until August 18 1978, when the Vulcan made its last flight as a test-bed. At that time it had made 125 flights in the RB 199 development programme, during which the engine had been run for 203 hours.

XA903 was now the last airworthy Vulcan B 1, and during the latter part of its career as a test-bed it had suffered from a growing spares problem. RAF Maintenance Units no longer held spare parts appropriate to the B 1, so it had become necessary, on occasions, to rob spares from instructional airframes in order to keep '*903* flying. In 1977 the aircraft was completely re-wired, following the discovery that the DC system wiring had deteriorated badly; this had never before been carried out on a Vulcan, for the aircraft's wiring had been designed as long as the airframe life. The end of *XA903*'s long and active

Most pictures of V-Force aircrew were posed: this one was not. The crew of XM650 of Waddington Wing had just climbed from their Vulcan after taking part in the navigation competition phase of 'Giant Voice', December 1971. Left to right: Paul Hammond (co-pilot), Gus Gillies (nav plotter—on ladder), Roger Stone (nav radar), Les Aylott (captain) and Roger Bagnall (AEO). They had flown a 6 hour 25 minute sortie.

career came on February 22 1979, when it was flown to RAE Farnborough—the airfield from which it had carried out so much test work in the late 1950s—to be used as a crash rescue training airframe. As this chapter is being written, at the end of August 1983, there are no plans to preserve the last of the working Vulcan B 1s. Yet if any aircraft deserves preservation, it is surely this one.

Returning to the mid-1960s and the Vulcan's operational role with Bomber Command, the last Vulcan B 2, *XM657*, was delivered to No 35 Squadron in December 1964, and in that month the Coningsby Wing (Nos 9, 12 and 35 Squadrons) moved to Cottesmore, in Rutland. The Waddington Wing (Nos 44, 50 and 101 Squadrons) still had its B 1As, and for a time it was considered replacing the SACEUR-assigned Valiant force, which was retired in January 1965 because of fatigue problems, with these Vulcans, but this was not implemented.

QRA was maintained, and now the QRA force had the full benefit of the early warning radar system at Fylingdales, in Yorkshire, which had been in sustained operation since January 1964. Nevertheless, although the V-Force's primary function remained QRA, with its mixture of megaton-range stand-off and free-fall weapons, it also exercised a formidable deterrent capability with conventional weapons, as it showed during the

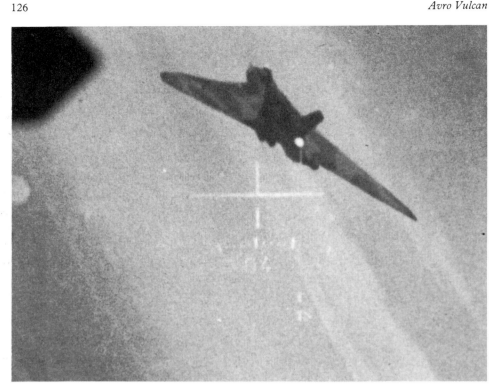

Vulcans in action: These shots of a B 2 of the Waddington Wing were taken by a RAAF Mirage fighter during a deployment to Malaysia.

period of confrontation with Indonesia during 1963–5. The 1957 defence agreement between Britain and Malaya was extended in 1963 to cover all the territories of Malaysia, formed on September 16 that year by the former 11 Malay states, Singapore, Sarawak and Sabah. Under this agreement, Britain undertook to help Malaysia, on request, to meet any attack or threat of attack on her territory. In return, Britain was to be allowed to maintain forces and bases in Malaysia for this purpose and to enable her to play her part in Commonwealth defence and the preservation of peace in south-east Asia. The treaty was in fact invoked by Malaysia after Indonesian 'confrontation' developed from interim propaganda into open attacks across the borders of Sabah and Sarawak and armed landings in Malaya and Singapore.

Although the brunt of the air operations against Indonesian infiltrators was borne by Far East Air Force's 'resident' units, such as No 20 Squadron's Hunter FGA 9s and 45 Squadron's Canberra B Mk 15s, a detachment of the V-Force was maintained throughout the period of confrontation either at Tengah or Butterworth. Vulcan detachments were usually drawn from the Waddington Wing, transits to the Far East being made either by the Middle East CENTO route or the Westabout Reinforcement Route, which would be used to deploy aircraft to the Far East if the CENTO route were ever denied by political considerations or enemy action. Despite some reports to the contrary, V-Force aircraft deployed to the Far East were tasked exclusively for the conventional bombing role, and were never armed with nuclear weapons. The Vulcans (and Victors) were never called upon to go into action, but had this been necessary their contribution would have been considerable: potential targets during the confrontation period were well within unrefuelled range of a Vulcan carrying a full load of 21 1,000 lb bombs.

'Sunflower' detachments to the Far East, usually with eight aircraft flying in two waves,

greatly relieved the monotony of routine V-Force operations. The Westabout Reinforcement Route entailed night stops at Goose Bay, Offutt AFB, McLellan AFB (Sacramento),
Hickam AFB (Honolulu), Wake Island and Anderson AFB on Guam, and a typical
Vulcan detachment would consist of 66 officers, 151 NCOs and airmen and 45,000 lb of
spares and ground equipment, the latter airlifted in Hastings and Britannia aircraft (later
VC 10s and Hercules). During Sunflower detachments, the transport squadrons involved
would be engaged in their own exercises, designed to cut down times on the
reinforcement route. Vulcan detachments, for example, would be preceded by a Transport
Command aircraft which would deposit Transit Servicing Parties at McLellan, Hickam,
Wake and Anderson; these parties were to assist Vulcans staging through these airfields,
and were afterwards recovered by a follow-up transport aircraft which would fly them
through to Tengah.

Deployment via the Westabout Route usually took about a week, with the crews enjoying
a day off at Honolulu and Guam, although in a real emergency the deployment could have
been achieved far more quickly, with tanker aircraft positioned along the route to cut out
some of the stages. On arrival at Tengah the Vulcans were very quickly re-established;
ground crews were organised into two shifts and four Vulcans would be detailed for
flying, with two in reserve and two on servicing. The highlight of a 'Sunflower' exercise
was a visit, usually by four aircraft, to Darwin for some very realistic war training with the
RAAF Mirages. The value of northern Australia was that the Vulcans were far less
constrained by air traffic requirements and were even able to use their jamming
equipment on a far less restricted basis. From mid-1967, Vulcans were usually
accompanied on detachments to Darwin by Lightnings of No 74 Squadron, which was
then based at Tengah; the Lightnings exercised alongside the Mirages in carrying out
interceptions on the V-bombers. There were no holds barred in these exercises, as one
incident serves to illustrate. A detachment of No 44 Squadron Vulcans went to Darwin,
which on this particular occasion was also their target, and the first series of 'attacks'
produced disappointing results, with very few of the Vulcans getting through the screen
of Mirages and Lightnings. It was soon realised that the RAAF had been doing some
clever detective work: by logging and analysing the movements of the RAF squadron's
aircraft, they had succeeded in working out the whole of the approach route and the air
times on target, giving the Mirages and Lightnings a considerable (and not very ethical)
advantage. Retaliation of some sort was clearly in order, so a certain RAF wing commander,
who had better be nameless, decided that it would be only fair to cheat a little in return by
providing the Australian air traffic control, who had been quietly passing on information
to the defenders, false flight plans. The result was that the Vulcans came in from an
entirely unexpected direction, taking the fighter defences completely by surprise, and
they came in with ECM going full blast, using chaff and jammers they were not supposed
to use. All the Vulcans got through, but the jamming threw the air traffic control system
into complete chaos and almost caused a diplomatic incident. The consensus of opinion
among the 'V' crews, as they enjoyed a subsequent 'binge' with some very subdued
fighter jockeys, was that they remained completely unrepentant of any embarrassment
they had caused. For once, squadron morale was through the roof.

V-Force morale, it must be admitted, gave some cause for concern during the years of
QRA, especially among the Blue Steel squadrons, which were not detached overseas and
whose crews consequently spent years in the same location. In the mid-1960s, too, there
did not seem to be much on the horizon, especially following the cancellation of the
TSR-2 by Harold Wilson's Labour Government. Admittedly, it was not just in the V-
Force that morale was low during this period; it was low throughout the Royal Air Force.
But it was Bomber Command, or more specifically the Vulcan crews of No 1 Group, who

High over Australia, a Mirage climbs to intercept a Waddington Wing B 2 taking part in an air defence exercise in 1969.

brought the general feeling home to the authorities at a notorious dining-in night, held at Waddington in October 1965, to mark the 25th anniversary of the Group's re-formation—the authorities in question being the Chief of Air Staff, Air Chief Marshal Sir Charles Elworthy, and the C-in-C Bomber Command. The various representatives of the 1 Group squadrons were brought to Waddington by coaches which, naturally, called in at several hostelries en route, so that when the time came for the after-dinner address by the CAS the participants were not slow to air their grievances. Every officer in the V-Force subsequently received a bill for the resultant damage to furniture and fittings—including the officers on the 3 Group Victor squadrons, who had not participated in the dining-in and who therefore felt some justifiable animosity. The '1 Group Dining-In Night' has passed into legend, and 20 years later everyone involved has a good laugh about it, but it was serious enough at the time in that it reflected a growing mood of depression which was quite uncharacteristic of the Service, even in times of adversity.

There were four Vulcan losses between the summer of 1965 and January 1968, two of them involving fatalities. The first was B 2 *XM576* of the Scampton Wing, which—with a No 83 Squadron crew—drifted to the left of the runway at Scampton during an asymmetric approach on May 25 1965 and crashed while attempting to overshoot; there were no casualties, but the aircraft was damaged beyond repair. Then, on February 11 1966, *XH536* of the Coningsby Wing flew into high ground 20 miles north-east of Swansea during a low-level navigation exercise over Wales, killing all five crew members. A few days later, on February 18, the undercarriage of *XH556* of No 230 OCU collapsed

during an engine start at Finningley; the aircraft sustained Category V damage and was stricken off charge the following day.

The fourth loss resulted in the death of four rear crew, three of whom might have been saved had the aircraft been fitted with rear ejection seats. It happened on January 30 1968, when B 2 *XM604*, captained by Flight Lieutenant Peter Tait, took off from Cottesmore on a routine high-level sortie. Soon after take-off the bomb-bay temperature was found to be increasing, so Tait decided to abandon the sortie and return to base with the intention of burning off fuel in the circuit. He made one circuit, then the co-pilot made another on the ILS, and on the overshoot Tait took over control and initiated a left turn to avoid an unseen contact ahead. At this point there was a sudden explosion followed by vibration so intense that Tait found it impossible to read his instruments. (It was later established that a fire in the No 2 engine had led to turbine disc separation; the disc had entered the bomb-bay, severely damaging the flying controls.) The Vulcan's port wing started to drop; Tait took corrective action but was unable to level the wings, so he ordered the rear crew to get out. With the help of the co-pilot, he continued his efforts to level the wings by using trim, rudder and throttles in an attempt to gain a few precious extra seconds for the men in the back, but these actions had no effect and he ordered the co-pilot to eject. Tait had heard the rear crew acknowledge his order to abandon the aircraft, but was unable to see if they had managed to get out because the blackout curtain was down behind him. He had done everything he could. The Vulcan was now in a steep dive to port, and when he pulled the handle of his own ejection seat it was with the almost certain knowledge that it was too late to save himself; the Vulcan's nose-down attitude was such that he ought to have ejected straight into the ground. It was only a miracle that saved him. As his seat's drogue parachute started to deploy, the seat and Tait passed between some high-tension cables; these were fouled by the drogue, which caused a short, and the cables acted like arrester wires, braking the seat sharply and causing it to swing like a pendulum beneath them. It struck the ground fairly hard but in an upright position, enabling Tait to release himself and walk away, shaken but otherwise unhurt. Unfortunately, all four rear crew were killed, although the co-pilot, Flying Officer M. Gillett, escaped.

This crash resurrected the lack of rear crew ejection seats and caused a major outcry in the British Press. In the words of a *Daily Mirror* correspondent: 'What, precisely, do the men in the back of V-bombers feel when they know that their pilot and co-pilot can eject themselves to safety, whereas they themselves need at least eight seconds to scramble out if the aircraft is about to crash? I expect no answers . . ..'

There were no real answers, but it should be remembered that out of 71 aircrew killed in 16 V-bomber crashes between 1955 and 1968 (of which seven involved Vulcans) 21 pilots and co-pilots also lost their lives, and some of them might have got out. So did they deliberately stay with the crashing aircraft, knowing that the rear crew had little or no chance of escaping? I put this question to Air Commodore Ron Dick, a former commanding officer of No 9 Squadron, who told me:

'Pilots would, naturally, make every effort to control the aircraft for as long as they could in an effort to get the rear crew out. You can imagine the scene: the pilot is trying to control the aircraft and at the same time peering over his shoulder to see what's happening in the back, knowing that it must be absolute bedlam in there. By the time he even thinks about ejecting, it is probably too late. I think maybe that's how the majority of V-bomber pilots were killed.'

Left *During the same exercise, a B 2 makes a low-level attack on Darwin harbour, June 1969. The Vulcan would probably have been shot down, but it had completed its simulated weapons release and was climbing away when intercepted.*

Of the seven Vulcan losses mentioned above, two occurred as a result of flying into high ground during low-level navigation exercises, and to reduce the risk of future accidents of this kind priority was given to the development of a terrain-following radar for installation in the Vulcan; in 1966, *XM606* of the Cottesmore Wing was sent to Cyprus to carry out comparative low-level TFR trials with a Victor, both aircraft being temporarily on loan to the Ministry of Aviation. Nevertheless, it was some time before TFR became a standard feature on the Vulcan, and although it was valuable in that it reduced the risk involved in low-level operations it was not a fully automatic system and its use involved a high workload on the part of both pilots, who were required to cross-check its information with that provided by the Nav Radar. The TFR had originally been developed by Ferranti for the ill-fated TSR-2, and it was subsequently adapted for use by the V-bombers.

In the spring of 1968, as usual, the efficiency of the V-Force was brought to the test in the annual Bombing, Navigation and Communications Competition, which involved one crew from each V-Force squadron flying a five-hour navigation sortie and four crews from each squadron flying sorties which involved simulated attacks on targets from high and low level. The 1968 event was perhaps more significant than usual, for it was the last time that the competition was held under the authority of Bomber Command. At 00:01 hours on Tuesday April 30 1968, Bomber and Fighter Commands merged to form Royal Air Force Strike Command, with Air Chief Marshal Sir Wallace Kyle as AOC-in-C.

All aircraft of the V-Force, together with the Victor tanker force, now came under the control of No 1 (Bomber) Group, with its HQ at Bawtry, Yorkshire. The Vulcan and Victor B 2s still formed the new Command's offensive front line, and in the conventional

role the Vulcan was now equipped with 1,000 lb free-falling retarded bombs to enable attacks to be carried out from low level.

Inevitably, the re-organisation sent winds of change rippling down through the Command. From June 1968 QRA was now maintained exclusively by the Vulcan squadrons, for the two Victor Blue Steel squadrons relinquished their QRA role, No 100 disbanding on October 1 and No 139 on December 31. Before that, on December 31 1967, No 12 Squadron had disbanded at Cottesmore; its aircraft went to Waddington, where Nos 44, 50 and 101 Squadrons completed the exchange of their Vulcan B 1As for B 2s in January 1968. No 12 later re-formed on October 1 1969 at Honington with Buccaneer S2Bs, which it employed mainly in the maritime strike role.

In January 1969, the two remaining squadrons of the Cottesmore Wing, Nos 9 and 35, left for Akrotiri, Cyprus, where they were to form the Near East Air Force Bomber Wing, replacing a Canberra Wing (see next chapter). The remaining Vulcan squadrons maintained QRA in the United Kingdom until June 30 1969, when the strategic nuclear deterrent role was finally handed over to the Royal Navy. On July 3, the Minister of Defence, Mr Denis Healey, paid a muted tribute in a Parliamentary written answer to 'the way in which the officers and men concerned at all levels in the Royal Air Force have discharged their arduous responsibilities over the last 12 years'. A more comprehensive tribute was paid by the Chief of the Air Staff, Air Chief Marshal Sir John Grandy (a

Vulcan B 2 XL427, fitted with a Blue Steel training round, on detachment to Honolulu during a round-the-world flight.

Left XA903 *pictured at Farnbrorough after its last flight. Left to right: Ian Conradie (co-pilot), Rolls-Royce test pilot; Graham Andrews (captain), Rolls-Royce chief test pilot; Bill Wherrell, Aircraft Department, RAE Farnborough; Mike Parkinson (flight engineer); and Paul Rash (flight test engineer) (RAE).*

Below left *Vulcan B 1 XA903 was Blue Steel trials aircraft, and afterwards served for many years on engine development work. It is seen here landing at RAE Farnborough with a prototype RB199 engine underslung (RAE).*

former AOC-in-C Bomber Command), who signalled the then AOC-in-C Strike Command, Air Chief Marshal Sir Denis Spotswood, to say that it was appropriate to remember that the task of QRA had meant 'maintaining, at all times throughout seven years, the highest state of readiness which the Royal Air Force had known in peacetime. The way in which QRA has been performed and the reaction of the force to the operational demands of our plans and those of SACEUR has been an unsurpassed demonstration of professional skill, dedication and tenacity. The long hours of arduous duty in cockpits, crew rooms, dispersal, hangars and operations rooms have brought the reward of knowing that a vital task has been successfully completed.'

The 'vital task' now rested within the great black hulls of the Royal Navy's Polaris submarines, cruising on station beneath the Arctic ice-pack and elsewhere. As far as the RAF was concerned, the ending of QRA also meant the culmination of planning which had begun with the conception of the V-bombers in 1946, and which had resulted in a strong, original and highly developed British airborne contribution to the Western strategic nuclear deterrent forces. It did not, however, mean an end to the operational use of the Vulcan; all remaining squadrons now assumed the conventional bombing role with free-fall weapons, although they could still be tasked for strategic nuclear operations if the situation demanded it, and it was now planned that the Vulcan force would serve until 1980.

There were now seven Vulcan squadrons in all—three at Waddington, two at Scampton and two at Akrotiri. On August 31 1969, No 83 Squadron, the first to equip with the Vulcan, had disbanded at Scampton. It was truly the end of an era.

Chapter 9

NEAF Bomber Wing

No 35 Squadron was the first to establish itself at RAF Akrotiri, Cyprus, on January 15 1969, and was followed by No 9 Squadron on February 26. The two squadrons, which formed the Near East Air Force Bomber Wing, gave a massive boost to the RAF's striking power in the Mediterranean. NEAF's responsibilities were both national and international. Its principle tasks were to contribute to the force levels of NATO and to provide support for the Central Treaty Organisation, whose member nations were the United Kingdom, Iran, Pakistan and Turkey, with the United States as an associate. The presence of a strong offensive element within NEAF became a matter of great importance when the RAF's last base on the mainland of Africa—El Adem, Libya—closed in March 1970, for it was correctly anticipated that Soviet influence in that area would greatly increase in the future.

Below and opposite *Vulcan B 2s of the Near East Air Force Bomber Wing (Nos 9 and 35 Squadrons), Akrotiri, Cyprus.*

This page *Vulcan B 2s of the Near East Air Force Bomber Wing (Nos 9 and 35 Squadrons), Akrotiri, Cyprus.*

The 9 Squadron Bat, presented to Wing Commander Ron Dick in Christchurch, New Zealand.

At that time, NEAF's commitments to NATO were fulfilled by the RAF squadrons based on Malta, while the Cyprus squadrons were responsible for maintaining the CENTO commitment. NEAF's policy was one of flexible response; although the resident units could cope with all normal commitments, there was always provision to bring in reinforcements from the United Kingdom if increased pressure demanded it.

No forces were actually allocated to CENTO, which had no international command structure on the lines developed within NATO; the function of the two Vulcan squadrons was to provide a tactical bombing spearhead for CENTO if such was required, but the aircraft would have remained firmly under RAF control. Because of the diversity of their task, the Vulcans carried out very varied training profiles, with aircraft detaching westwards to the United Kingdom and eastwards to Singapore, although the long-range sorties were usually undertaken by No 35 Squadron, with No 9 Squadron's area of operations restricted to the Middle East. This could make life somewhat tedious for the No 9 Squadron crews, as a former CO, Wing Commander (later Air Commodore) Ron Dick explains:

'We very seldom got any of the exotic trips, and in 1972 I was looking for a series of long-range trips for the squadron so that they could get out of the rut of flying up and down over the Mediterranean. We had some very good New Zealand contacts, because some former Squadron officers were New Zealanders; they included Flight Lieutenant Harry Denton—now a sheep farmer—who, on January 1 1945, had been the captain of a No 9 Squadron Lancaster in which the wireless operator, Flight Sergeant George Thompson, had won a posthumous Victoria Cross during a daylight attack on the Dortmund-Ems Canal.

Wing Commander Ron Dick and his crew approach Ohakea with an escort of RNZAF Skyhawks.

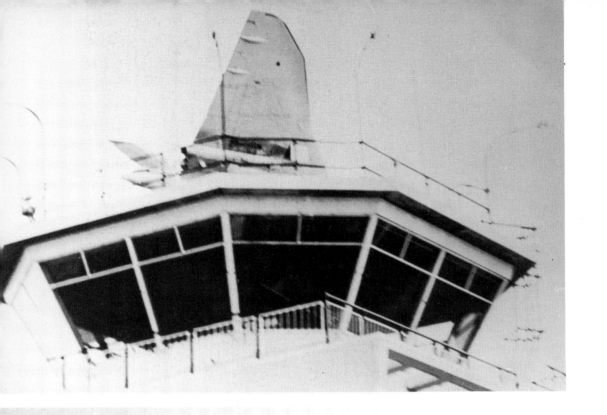

During their stay in New Zealand, Wing Commander Ron Dick demonstrated the Vulcan over every major town and city. It is seen here giving a display over Ohakea—and probably causing a few anxious moments for the air traffic control staff!

Chief Tech Pearsey, the Vulcan's crew chief, appears somewhat bewildered on discovering that the RNZAF had appropriated 'his' aircraft with some neat paintwork during the night...

'Harry Denton had been over to visit us when the VC crew held a reunion after 25 years; it was a very emotional occasion, and Harry happened to mention what a shame it was that No 9 Squadron nowadays never seemed to take a Vulcan to New Zealand. So I set to work on the idea, and on building up some associations in New Zealand, and the thing that really convinced me that the project would be worthwhile was that an old lady—86 at the time—who had been married to a No 9 Squadron officer of the 1920s era, had a trophy in the form of a bat, the Squadron crest, which had been presented to her late husband by his CO when he left the RAF to join Imperial Airways. It was actually one of the models made by Station Workshops at a time when the design of the badge was being finalised, so it was of considerable historic interest.

'After the former officer died in 1971, his widow wrote to our man in Wellington and asked if the squadron would like the memento back. I received a signal as a result, asking me to confirm that we were indeed based in Cyprus and to supply the address to which the bat should be sent. I sent back an immediate signal, saying for goodness sake don't send it—we'll send an aircraft to collect it.

'I was just in time. Our RAF colleague in Wellington already had the bat in a box and was about to despatch it on the first stage of its journey, via a Hercules to Singapore, when my signal reached him. I subsequently made out a case for a No 9 Squadron aircraft flying to New Zealand to take part in the 1972 air show at Hamilton, and off we went.'

The eventual destination of the Vulcan was RNZAF Station Ohakea, the terminus of many past V-Force long-range navigational exercises. Captained by Ron Dick, the aircraft made the journey via Masirah, Gan, Tengah, Darwin and RAAF Richmond, Sydney. At Darwin the Vulcan encountered torrential rain, the aircraft entering cloud at 200 ft after take-off, and the entire crossing of the Australian continent was made over dense cloud. Wing Commander Dick and his crew made the crossing from Richmond to Ohakea in 2 hours 45 minutes at high speed, high level cruise. During their eight-day stay in New Zealand they demonstrated the aircraft at the Hamilton air display and over every major

Still bearing its RNZAF insignia, Wing Commander Dick's Vulcan lands at Singapore on the homeward journey. The aircraft had suffered cracked windscreens on the high-altitude flight over Indonesia.

town and city in both North and South Islands, and in the course of their tour they landed at Christchurch for the highlight of their visit, the presentation of the trophy. The occasion was attended by much Press and TV coverage, and today the silver bat adorns the Squadron's table on guest nights.

The Vulcan returned to Cyprus via its outward route, but on the home run a snag was encountered over Indonesia when the windscreen heating failed at high level, causing the windscreens to crack. The aircraft had been away from its ground support for some considerable time, and a combination of other, smaller snags caused a lengthy delay at Tengah while these were rectified. Nevertheless, both from the navigational and public relations point of view, it had been a very worthwhile and rewarding exercise. Both squadron commanders in the Near East Bomber Wing worked hard to get their aircraft into as many interesting and constructive places as possible to vary the more routine sorties, which might involve a four-hour, 2,000-mile trip round the Mediterranean with the aircraft carrying out low-level simulated attacks and fighter affiliation exercises, or practice bombing and flare-dropping by day or night over Episkopi Bay, where there was a local range. In planning overseas sorties, the squadrons always had an eye to improving navigational efficiency over long ranges, although sometimes there were other reasons.

'In 1971,' says Ron Dick, 'it was suggested to us that we had had little or no contact with the Ethiopian Air Force since the RAF had pulled out of Aden in 1967, and that it might be a good thing to re-establish relations. I went on the first trip together with Wing

Wing Commander Dick and his crew back in Singapore. Left to right: Flight Lieutenant John Clark (nav plotter), Chief Technicians Pearsey and Clarke (crew chiefs), Flight Lieutenant Bob Sinclair (nav radar), Flight Lieutenant Adrian Summer (co-pilot), Wing Commander Ron Dick (captain) and Flight Lieutenant Maurice Stocks (AEO, kneeling).

Commander John Sewell, who was then OC Bomber Wing. We could not fly along the Nile route, because at that time Egyptian air space was closed to combat aircraft—although I believe that transport types were permitted to overfly—so we went the long way round via the CENTO route through Turkey and Iran, refuelling at Masirah, where we spent the night before flying down the Arabian coast and over Djibouti into Ethiopia. We landed initially at Addis Ababa, where we had a tremendous reception, and then went on to Asmara.

'At both these places there were Cheshire Homes—sanitaria founded by Group Captain Leonard Cheshire, VC—and the people who ran them, quite young girls in their twenties, saw more human catastrophe every day than most people see in a lifetime. Now, No 35 Squadron had already contacted the Cheshire organisation and was contributing to the Addis Ababa home from a distance, sending parcels and so on, and we paid a visit to it while we were there. It dealt mainly with polio victims, mostly children; the girls used to tour the surrounding villages and bring them in for treatment.

'We decided to sponsor the Asmara home, and the best way of doing that was to fly out loads of medical and other supplies the children needed so desperately. We had conferred with the Ethiopian Air Force commander at Asmara Air Base, who had indicated to us that the Middle East Vulcans might be permitted to use the large open spaces of central

Ethiopia for low-level training, so there was our pretext; we said we would go home and think about it, and perhaps pay further visits in the future.

'This we did, and were quite successful in establishing a case for setting up low-level training routes in Ethiopia; unfortunately, before the scheme could get properly under way the Vulcans were pulled out of Cyprus. However, we made good use of the few trips we did for the benefit of the children; we had large panniers in the bomb bays and we would fill these with all sorts of things, from cuddly toys to furniture needed by the hospital. It was a very rewarding exercise indeed, especially at Christmas.'

So, from an instrument of massive destruction, the Vulcan became, albeit briefly, an angel of mercy.

The NEAF Vulcan squadrons suffered one serious accident during their time in Cyprus. It happened on May 25 1973, when *XJ781* was visiting Iran with a No 9 Squadron crew. As the aircraft approached Shiraz the port undercarriage failed to lower. A foam strip was laid and the captain made a good touchdown, but the Vulcan veered off the runway, tearing off the starboard and nose undercarriage legs. The crew, fortunately, escaped with nothing more than a shaking. The aircraft was examined by a RAF technical team, declared to be damaged beyond repair and stricken off charge on May 27.

In the summer of 1974, the northern part of Cyprus was invaded by Turkish forces and the British Sovereign Base Areas were placed on full alert. The Bomber Wing dispersed, the majority of the aircraft going to Malta, and subsequently carried out a wide variety of operational tasks in support of the British forces in Cyprus. These involved, among other things, acting as airborne relay stations, cruising at 40,000 ft over the Mediterranean and re-transmitting signals to points east and west. Vulcans had been called upon to carry out this kind of operation before, at various times; as long ago as 1958, Bomber Command and RAE Farnborough had developed a system whereby speech from the aircraft could be transmitted to Bomber Command HQ at High Wycombe, or to other RAF communications centres, and fed into land-lines direct.

The Turkish invasion precipitated the end of the NEAF Bomber Wing as such. As part of a political move, designed to help defuse an extremely tense situation in the eastern Mediterranean, the two Vulcan squadrons were withdrawn from Cyprus and relocated in the United Kingdom, No 9 Squadron going to Waddington and No 35 to Scampton. The Vulcan force was now entering the last years of its existence, but much still lay ahead of it in the way of achievement.

Chapter 10

Conventional strike force

By the end of 1970, the whole of No 1 Group's Vulcan force had assumed the conventional bombing role as part of the integrated NATO structure. At Scampton, the Vulcans of Nos 27 and 617 Squadrons had relinquished their Blue Steels, stocks of which were cut up for scrap; the aircraft were gradually withdrawn for modifications before being returned to squadron service. The whole force continued to exercise its low-level role, in which the principal armament was now 1,000 lb retarded bombs, and emphasis was placed on night operations to enhance survivability in a hostile environment.

Below *Vulcan B 2s at Nellis AFB. XM603 is now preserved at British Aerospace, Woodford, in its original white finish.*

Opposite *Vulcan B 2As of the Waddington Wing at Nellis AFB for 'Red Flag' exercises. Note passive ECM fin fairing and TFR radomes.*

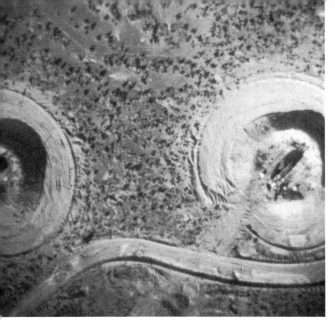

The 'opposition' which had to be overcome by attacking aircraft, including Vulcans, on realistic 'Red Flag' exercises: SAM sites and 'enemy' fighter airfields, populated in this case by time-expired RF-84F Thunderflashes.

Although the Vulcan continued to be a viable aircraft in its low-level tactical bombing role, technical problems tended to accumulate with length of service, and early in 1971 engine explosions—both involving aircraft of the Waddington Wing—caused the loss of one Vulcan and severe damage to another. In the first incident, on January 8 1971, Vulcan *XM610*, with a No 44 Squadron crew captained by Flight Lieutenant G.R. Alcock, was tasked for a low level sortie over Northumberland. Midway through the sortie, Alcock decided to climb away from the low-level area due to deteriorating weather conditions, but as engine power was increased there was a loud explosion and No 1 engine caught fire, followed quickly by No 2 engine. All members of the crew took prompt and proper corrective action and both fires appeared to have been extinguished.

The aircraft continued to climb on its two remaining engines, but at 6,000 ft Flight Lieutenant James Power, the AEO, reported that part of the underside of the port wing was burning fiercely. Flight Lieutenant Alcock flew on above cloud, towards the sprawling conurbation of the Tyne, until the Vulcan was over open ground in southern Northumberland. The cloud had now broken up affording sight of the ground, and at this point Alcock ordered the rear crew to abandon the burning aircraft, which they did successfully. Despite the obvious personal risk, Alcock and his co-pilot, Flying Officer Peter Hoskins, remained with the Vulcan and headed south towards RAF Leeming, the Master Diversion Airfield near Northallerton in Yorkshire, where Alcock considered that there might be a slight chance of landing the crippled aircraft. However, the aircraft became increasingly difficult to control and Alcock realised that it would have to be abandoned. Both pilots remained at the controls for a further 12 minutes in order to clear the densely populated Tyne area and head the Vulcan out to sea. The port wing and rear fuselage were by now well alight and the aircraft might have broken up at any moment; pieces of burning debris were falling from it. In the end the Vulcan became uncontrollable as the fuel tanks started to explode, at which point Alcock ordered Hoskins to eject and then used his own ejection seat. *XM610* crashed in a field in County Durham, narrowly missing the village of Wingate. Alcock's courage and determination earned him

Above *Valcan SR2 XH534 of No 27 Squadron, August 1976. Note unit's 'Dumbo' insignia on fin.*
Below *Vulcan B2 of No 617 Squadron over the North Sea.*

Below *A B2 of the No 35 Squadron, at the Vulcan 'Silver Jubilee Meet' at RAF Scampton.*

Two views of **XM575** *of the Waddington Wing, with 44 Squadron badge on tail.*

Shadow of a Vulcan B 2 passes over another at the end of a line of Phantoms at RAF Coningsby.

an Air Force Cross, while the other crew members (Flight Lieutenants James Power and James Vinales and Flying Officers Rodger Barker and Peter Hoskins) were awarded Queen's Commendations for Valuable Service in the Air.

Fate plays strange and often cruel tricks. On October 14 1975, Garth Alcock was the captain of one of the newer B 2s, *XM645*, on detachment to Malta with a No 9 Squadron crew when the aircraft undershot the runway at RAF Luqa. The port undercarriage was pushed up into the wing, starting a fire as the aircraft bounced back into the air. Alcock managed to retain control and climbed to give the rear crew—who on this occasion were five in number—a chance to get out, but as he did so the fire caused an explosion and the aircraft started to break up. Alcock and his co-pilot ejected as the Vulcan disintegrated around them and escaped with their lives, but the other five crew were killed. A woman civilian was also killed by wreckage falling on the airfield, and two more civilians were injured when the main body of the debris fell on the adjacent village of Zabbar.

Returning to 1971, the second incident involving an engine explosion occurred on February 23 when a Vulcan of No 101 Squadron, captained by Flight Lieutenant Michael Paley, took off from Waddington at dusk on a routine training sortie. When the aircraft was only 200 ft off the ground on the climb-out there was a violent explosion and fire broke out in the wing beneath the number three engine bay. The appropriate emergency drills were promptly carried out, and although parts of the burning wing were falling away and the aircraft's handling qualities had been adversely affected by the damage, Paley completed a copybook circuit of the airfield and an immaculate overweight asymmetric landing. He was awarded a Queen's Commendation.

Despite centralised servicing, the UK-based Vulcan squadrons were now starting to re-apply their badges on the nosewheel doors and entrance hatches of their aircraft, and in

1970 the Vulcans were repainted in a glossy polyurethane finish which was current until the autumn of 1972, when a new low-visibility matt paint scheme was adopted. This was applied over a period of time to individual aircraft as they went for major overhauls to the MUs at St Athan or Bitteswell. There were slight changes in the Vulcan's outline, too; towards the end of 1972, *XM597* of the Waddington Wing underwent trials at Boscombe Down with the Marconi Space and Defence ARI 18228 radar warning receiver, whose antenna was mounted in a fairing on the fin. The 18228 was developed from the earlier 18223, but whereas the latter could only display data on a single threat at any one time, the CRT display of the 18228 could show several at once, indicating bearing, transmission type and other data. *XM597* returned to squadron service with the new fin outline in February 1973, and other Vulcans were similarly modified at a later date. At the same time, improvements were made in the Vulcan's active ECM jamming system, code-named 'Blue Diver'.

Vulcans were still detaching overseas, although perhaps not as frequently as they had done in the 1960s. One of the more striking overseas deployments of the early 1970s was made in January 1972 by four Vulcans of No 44 Squadron, together with 45 officers and 135 airmen from RAF Waddington. The practice deployment involved a round trip of more than 30,000 miles, and was the first major demonstration of British air power by the Medium Bomber Force in the Far East for some time.

The force of four Vulcans, led by Wing Commander Maurice Fenner, left Waddington on Sunday January 23 1972, flying via Lajes in the Azores to Bermuda. From there they staged through the USAF bases at Omaha, Sacramento, Honolulu, Wake Island and Guam before reaching their first main destination at Tengah, Singapore, on January 28, having lost a day by crossing the International Date Line. As usual, following the now well-established procedure, the engineering and other support parties began flying out in Air Support Command VC 10s and Britannias three days before the departure of the Vulcans. They included six Transit Servicing Parties, each with an officer and eight men, who were positioned at the overseas bases through which the Vulcans passed on their

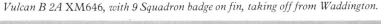

Vulcan B 2A XM646, *with 9 Squadron badge on fin, taking off from Waddington.*

outbound flight. Essential spares were flown out in Hercules transport aircraft.

From Tengah, the squadron carried out low-level training sorties around Malaysia, including some practice live bombing on Song-Song range near Penang Island. During these operations, the Vulcans were 'opposed' by Malaysian-based Mirage fighters of the RAAF, which carried out numerous interceptions. One Vulcan crew flew to Kair Tak, Hong Kong, during the eight-day deployment.

On February 4 the Vulcans left Singapore for RAAF Darwin, preceded by their main support party. For the next 18 days they flew a rigorous training programme of High-Low-High profile sorties in Northern Australia and carried out further conventional weapons training in the form of live bombing attacks on Darwin's Quail Island range. Facilities at Darwin were shared with the Mirage crews of No 76 RAAF Squadron, detached from their base at Williamstown, Newcastle, New South Wales, and one of the high spots of this phase of the detachment was a large-scale air defence exercise in which Mirage aircraft worked in conjunction with other RAAF elements to track and intercept an attacking force of Vulcans.

During their stay in Australia, two Vulcan crews carried out weekend 'Lone Ranger' flights to Williamstown and to RAAF Amberley, near Brisbane. At the close of the detachment, the Vulcans returned to Waddington via Singapore, Gan and Masirah, with a final call at Akrotiri. In total, they had been absent from the UK for five weeks.

March 29 1972 saw the disbandment of No 27 Squadron, which had shared Scampton with No 617 for more than a decade. No 27, however, re-formed on November 1 1973 at Scampton in the maritime radar reconnaissance role with four Vulcan SR 2s, which were B 2s modified for strategic reconnaissance. The aircraft were *XH560*, *XH563*, *XJ780* and *XL361*. The re-formation of No 27 Squadron permitted the disbandment, in May 1974, of No 543 Squadron, whose Victor SR 2s had undertaken the strategic reconnaissance task since 1965 and whose global mapping activities had played an important part in the operational effectiveness of Blue Steel, which depended on accurate knowledge of where the missile was at the time of launch and also of the target's co-ordinates.

In the winter of 1973, therefore, the resident Vulcan units at Scampton were Nos 27 and 617 Squadrons, together with No 230 OCU, which had moved there from Finningley at the end of 1969. In the autumn of 1973 the three squadrons of the Waddington Wing had been temporarily relocated at Scampton and Fairford while the Waddington runways were re-surfaced, but by the beginning of 1974 all three squadrons were once more operational at their home base.

The Vulcans of Strike Command's No 1 Group were still participating in the annual USAF Strategic Air Command Bombing and Navigation Competition. In 1971, for example, the RAF entered three teams with crews drawn from Nos 27 and 101 Squadrons; this contest, code-named 'Giant Voice', was the sixth in which Vulcans had taken part. The four Vulcans involved in the December 1971 competition—which also marked the 25th anniversary of SAC's formation—were *XM600*, *XM602*, *XM650* and *XM654*, each of which carried a black panther's head insignia (the badge of No 1 Group) on the fuselage side and the Union Flag on the fin. The competition was in three parts: 'Giant Voice 1' was a night navigation exercise flown by three Vulcans, 22 B-52s and two FB-111As; 'Giant Voice 2' involved a night navigation exercise by 30 KC-135As; while the Vulcans also participated in 'Giant Voice 3', which was a simulated daylight bombing mission flown by a total of 27 aircraft with high-altitude bomb releases over Greenville, Mississippi and Birmingham, Alabama, followed by a low-altitude mission over the Gulf of Mexico and terminating with four low-level simulated bomb releases over Florida. One of the RAF Vulcan teams came fourth in this part of the contest.

From 1977, Strike Command Vulcans and crews also deployed to the United States to

Vulcan B 2A XL390 of the Scampton Wing leads a Jaguar, Canberra and Buccaneer on a representative flypast to mark the 10th Anniversary of Strike Command, April 1978—which was also the 60th Anniversary of the RAF. Only a few months later, in August 1978, XL390 crashed during display practice near Glenview Naval Air Station, California, killing its crew.

take part in 'Red Flag', the air warfare exercise held under very realistic conditions over the Arizona Desert. For this purpose the Vulcans were sent to Nellis AFB, from where they operated mostly at night and at low level, and despite the fact that the ground was not ideal for terrain-following some good results were achieved, demonstrating that the Vulcan still had the ability to penetrate advanced defence systems.

There were two Vulcan losses in the late 1970s. The first was *XM600* of the Waddington Wing, which was on a routine training sortie on January 17 1977 when a fire broke out in the bomb bay area and spread to the port wing. The captain ordered the crew to abandon the aircraft, which crashed at Spilsby, ten miles north-east of RAF Coningsby in Lincolnshire. One crew member was injured; the remainder landed safely.

The second aircraft was *XL390* of No 617 Squadron, which was on a visit to the United States as part of a force of four Vulcans taking part in the 1978 'Giant Voice' competition. While practising for a display to be given at Glenview Naval Air Station on August 11, *XL390* crashed and exploded, killing its crew.

The Vulcan's operational life had now been extended far beyond the planned date and, as one squadron commander put it, the aircraft was 'way over the hill' by 1979. The progressive rundown of the V-Force started in 1980, and the first Vulcan to go was *XM653* of the Waddington Wing, which was flown from Waddington to St Athan on December 18 that year, to be placed in MU storage before being sold for scrap on July 28 1981. It was followed to St Athan on March 11 1981 by *XH538* from Scampton; this was the aircraft which had contributed so much to the Blue Steel and Skybolt development programme, and its inglorious fate was to be scrapped in turn in August 1981. Also from Scampton, on April 7 1981, went SR 2 *XH534*, which was scrapped in February 1982, and on June 9 1981 *XH554* was flown from Scampton to RAF Catterick for crash rescue training with the RAF Fire Fighting and Safety School. Catterick lies adjacent to the A1 south of Scotch Corner in North Yorkshire, and its runway—now unused except by communications aircraft—is relatively short, so when the Vulcan landed all traffic was halted. The local police need not have worried. The Vulcan's pilot showed the aircraft's short landing qualities to good effect, and it stopped with plenty of tarmac to spare.

XH559, the B 2 which had spent all its working life with No 230 OCU, was flown from Scampton to St Athan in May 1981 to be scrapped, and this was followed, as part of the progressive wind-down of the Scampton Vulcan force, by *XL320* on June 2. Other Vulcan disposals in 1981 were *XL317*, which was flown from Scampton to Akrotiri on December 1 1981 for use with the Akrotiri Engineering Wing as a ground instructional airframe; *XL361*, which sustained Category 3 damage at Goose Bay in December 1981, was classed as not worth repairing and abandoned there; *XL389*, which went to St Athan for scrapping on April 6 1981; *XM599*, to St Athan in June 1981; *XM605*, which was flown from Waddington to Castle Air Force Base, California, by a No 44 Squadron crew on September 8 1981 for permanent display at the RAF Museum there; and *XM608* and *XM609*, both of which were reduced to scrap at St Athan in the spring of 1981.

As far as the units were concerned, No 230 OCU was the first to disband, in the summer of 1981, and this was followed on December 22 that year by No 617 Squadron, whose Vulcan *XL318* flew the unit's last sortie over Derwent Reservoir on the 11th of the month. It was an appropriate occasion, for *XL318* had been the first B 2 taken on charge by the squadron. At the end of February 1982, this aircraft was dismantled and shipped to Hendon by road for display in the Bomber Command Museum there. Happily, No 617's absence from the RAF's Order of Battle was a temporary one; the squadron re-formed on the first day of 1983 as Strike Command's second Tornado GR 1 squadron.

Scampton's other two Vulcan squadrons, Nos 27 and 35, both disbanded in March 1982, No 35 on the first of the month and No 27 on the last day. Like 617, No 27 later re-formed as a Tornado unit, but it was 617's old rival, No 9 Squadron, which had the honour of being the first to operate the RAF's new and potent strike aircraft; disbanding as a Vulcan squadron on May 1 1982, it re-formed on Tornadoes at RAF Honington exactly a month later.

Of the other two Vulcan squadrons, No 101 disbanded on August 5 1982 and was in the process of re-forming as a VC 10 tanker unit as these words are being written a year later. No 44 was the last to go, disbanding on the last day of 1982. Before that, however, momentous events had taken place which, on the very eve of its expiry after a quarter of a century of squadron service, were to give the Vulcan its first and only taste of action, and assure it of an even firmer place in the RAF's hall of fame.

Chapter 11

'Black Buck': a dramatic swansong

The British Government's decision to launch a task force over 8,000 miles of Atlantic Ocean to retake the Falkland Islands in 1982 posed considerable problems for the UK forces earmarked to carry out the operation. Britain has a long history of fighting successful campaigns at great distances from home, but never before, in modern warfare, had her area of operations been so far removed from friendly land-based air power.

Ascension Island, which was quickly to become the major staging post for 'Operation Corporate', as the Falklands operation was known, was 4,000 nautical miles away, far outside the combat radius, even with flight refuelling, of any land-based British aircraft—except one—which might be capable of transporting a worthwhile bomb load to enemy targets on the Falklands. The exception was the Vulcan, still untested in actual combat 30 years after the first prototype flew. When the Falklands crisis developed early in April 1982 the remnants of the Vulcan force were concentrated with Nos 44 and 50 Squadrons at Waddington, the third and fourth Waddington units, Nos 9 and 101, being on the point of disbanding.

Without flight refuelling backup by Victor tankers, the Vulcan attacks on targets in the Falklands would have been impossible. This fine shot shows two Victors of the Marham Tanker Wing about to link up for a fuel transfer.

No 44 Squadron was tasked with possible offensive operations over the Falklands, and the crews—drawn from the most experienced of all four Waddington squadrons—came to standby on Thursday April 8, Easter leave having been cancelled. The ten 'fittest' Vulcans were selected from the aircraft pool, and on April 9—Good Friday—Waddington's engineer officer, Squadron Leader Chris Pye, was instructed to restore an air-to-air flight refuelling capability on these machines. This presented several problems, not the least of which was that the flight refuelling probes had been deleted from the Vulcan force some years earlier and the system blanked off at the probe connection. Some of the essential equipment, such as the nose-mounted non-return valves, was still in storage and fairly readily available, but locating the probes themselves was a far from easy task, as the Vulcan-type probe was also urgently needed for mounting on Hercules transports and Nimrod MR 2 maritime patrol aircraft. Squadron Leader Pye and his engineering team rose admirably to the occasion, and in record time a stockpile of probes was built up from time-expired Vulcans which had been allocated to museums or to various airfields for crash rescue training. One probe, for example, came from *XL361*, the damaged Vulcan which had been abandoned at Goose Bay the previous December, while another was 'lifted' from *XM605*, the Vulcan presented to the USAF Museum at Castle AFB. Other probes came from Vulcans at locations such as Catterick; to save time, some of the equipment was ferried to Waddington from locations in the UK by the Jetstreams of the Multi-Engine Training Squadron at RAF Finningley.

Ten Vulcans were quickly re-fitted with the probes, the fuel system tested to 50 psi and ground fuel transfer exercises undertaken as a required step before the aircraft could be declared operational. Intensive training of crews in flight refuelling techniques now began; it was 15 years since Vulcans had practised flight refuelling as a regular exercise, and none of the current crews had ever done it. Over a three-week period, the Vulcans exercised with Victor K 2s of the Marham Tanker Wing off northern Scotland; some bomb-bay modifications were also carried out to enable the Vulcans to accommodate a full load of 21 1,000 lb 'iron bombs' instead of the low-level retarded bombs, which had a different release technique. A further modification involved the installation of a Delco Carousel Inertial Navigation System of the type fitted to British Airways Boeing 747s in five of the Vulcans to assist with long-range navigation over the South Atlantic; the systems were supplied by British Airways and were fitted in Vulcans *XL391*, *XM597*, *XM598*, *XM607* and *XM612*. A sixth Vulcan, *XM654*, was also earmarked to receive the INS equipment, but in the event never took part in the forthcoming operations.

The flight refuelling trials were not without their crop of problems. In some cases it was found that Vulcans receiving fuel suffered fuel spillage around the probe, causing a spray of fuel to float backwards over the nose and render the cockpit windows opaque. Several remedies were tried, including sealing the wiper hole on the cockpit lip, fitting a vortex generator in front of the windscreen and placing a colander around the base of the probe in an attempt to disperse spilt fuel. These refinements helped to reduce the problem, but a complete cure was never found. Yet another task for the Waddington Engineering Wing was to overhaul the Vulcans' Rolls-Royce/Bristol Olympus Mk 103 engines and uprate them to 103 per cent thrust for the operational task in hand.

On April 23 Waddington received a signal from Strike Command HQ asking the Engineering Wing to consider ways of fitting the AN/ALQ-101D electronic counter-measures pod (the 'Dash Ten') to the Vulcan. The Dash Ten was well-proven, having been used for some time by the RAF's Buccaneers, but some means had to be found of hanging it under the Vulcan's wing. This caused some head-scratching, until it was recalled that most B 2s still in service had come off the production line with built-in hardpoints to carry the cancelled Skybolt missile. Even then the problem was not immediately solved, because no one could remember where the hardpoints actually were, and the relevant paperwork had long since gone by the board. So Squadron Leader Pye's men resorted to trial and error, literally prodding at the underside of the Vulcan wing until they found two hard parts, disguised by two small and almost imperceptible fairings whose presence could not be accounted for. Further investigation revealed the long-forgotten hardpoints on every Vulcan except *XM654*, which had been one of the last few B 2s to leave the production line in the days after Skybolt's cancellation, and which consequently had not been modified to carry the missile.

Squadron Leader Pye's next pressing task was to devise some pylons, for none had ever been manufactured for the Vulcan, apart from those fitted to the Skybolt trials aircraft. Searching for suitable material, his team discovered some mild steel 'L'-shaped girders on the Engineering Wing scrapheap. Welded together, these formed the base of the pylon which was to carry the ECM pod. The pylons themselves were made in the local station workshops; these were simple, skeleton-type structures with a leading-edge fairing, and the prototype was built and fitted to a Vulcan in three days. The necessary electrical cables were led through the wing via a series of tubes, never before used, which had originally been intended to feed coolant into the Skybolt missile, while the control panel for the Dash Ten was fitted into the AEO's station by the simple expedient of removing his cool air duct.

At the same time, it had been decided to fit a second locally-built pylon to the hardpoint on the Vulcan's port wing, for reasons of aerodynamic balance and also to carry the AS 37 Martel anti-radar missile, which it was thought might be used to attack enemy radar targets on the Falklands from stand-off ranges. Modifications to the original pylon were carried out, with assistance from British Aerospace, and as before the wiring was led through the unused Skybolt coolant pipes. Two test flights were carried out by Vulcans with Martels on the port wing pylon, one to check aerodynamic characteristics and electrical compatibility, and the other to see how the weapon would function after prolonged flight at high altitude. On this occasion the missile was test-fired after an hour's high-level carriage.

However, for reasons which remain undisclosed, it was decided not to use the Vulcan/Martel combination in anti-radar operations against the Falklands. Instead, the decision was taken to use the American-built AGM-45A Shrike anti-radiation missile. With a speed of 2.0M and a range of about 15 miles, the Shrike carried a 140 lb high-explosive fragmentation warhead and was propelled by a solid-fuel rocket motor. Its operation depended on the carried aircraft being illuminated by ground defence radars, warning of which would be given by the carrier's ESM/ECM receivers; when within appropriate range, the Shrike's sensor heads would be switched on and the missile fired on target acquisition. After launch, the carrier's radar receiver continuously sensed the direction of the radar radiation emitted by the target and issued command signals to the missile's homing guidance system.

It was originally intended to carry one Shrike missile on each of the Vulcan's underwing pylons, but it was subsequently decided to use the twin launcher of the type used by the US Navy's A-6 and A-7 aircraft. This enabled the Vulcan to carry four Shrikes at one time, two under each wing. Some delay was experienced in obtaining the twin launchers, which were not actually fitted and flight tested until the Vulcan force had been deployed to Ascension Island. Other configurations considered at this time included the possible use of Sidewinder AAMs on a twin launcher under the Vulcan's port wing and the use of Paveway laser-guided bombs; trials with the latter were carried out and it was widely rumoured later that the Vulcan had used Paveway in attacks on Port Stanley airfield, the

The Vulcan's last operational role was that of flight refuelling tanker, six aircraft being converted to K 2 standard and operated by No 50 Squadron, Waddington. The photographs here and overleaf illustrate the K 2 in operation.

target being illuminated by suitably-equipped SAS infiltrators, but as far as is known the Vulcans were not employed in this way.

The first three Vulcans were deployed to Ascension Island on April 28, 14 days after their crews had begun flight refuelling training. During this time, each crew had undertaken three day and two night refuellings, the operations being supervised by an Air-Air Refuelling Instructor from the Marham Victor Tanker Wing. These instructors, in fact, accompanied the Vulcans to Ascension and on the subsequent missions, changing seats with the co-pilot (no mean feat in itself on the Vulcan's cramped flight deck) for the link-ups with the tanker aircraft. For a week prior to the deployment to Ascension Island, the Vulcan crews also practised low- and medium-level bombing on ranges in the northern areas of the United Kingdom.

The Vulcan missions flown against Argentine installations on the Falklands were known by the code-name of 'Black Buck', and two aircraft were detailed for each, one as primary and one as reserve. 'Black Buck One', flown on the night of April 30/May 1 1982, involved Vulcans *XM598* (primary) and *XM607* (reserve), although in the event *XM598* developed a fault shortly after take-off and *XM607* assumed the primary role in the mission, which was a free-fall bombing attack from medium level with the twofold objective of rendering the airfield at Port Stanley unusable by Argentine jet fighter and strike aircraft and of creating as much disruption as possible among the enemy ground forces in the area.

The crew of *XM607* comprised Flight Lieutenant Martin Withers (Captain), Flying Officer Peter Taylor (Co-pilot), Flight Lieutenant Bob Wright (Nav Radar), Flight Lieutenant Gordon Graham (Nav Plotter), Flight Lieutenant Hugh Prior (AEO) and Flight Lieutenant Richard Russell (AARI). The aircraft carried a full load of 21 1,000 lb HE bombs fitted with Mk 497 fuzes, some with 30-minute and 60-minute delays.

The Vulcan sortie was supported by 11 Victor tankers, flying in three waves. To conserve fuel, Victors and Vulcan cruised at 260 knots, the tankers flying at their economical cruising altitude of 27,000 ft and the Vulcan at 33,000 ft, where its crew could maintain visual contact with the tanker force. This was some 7,000 ft below the Vulcan's optimum cruise height in its heavily-laden condition and fuel consumption was heavy on the outward leg. The refuelling operation was a masterpiece of planning, with two of the Victor waves topping each other up and the third transferring fuel to the Vulcan, which descended to 27,000 ft for that purpose. As each Victor completed its fuel transfer it broke off and returned to Ascension, until only the Vulcan and two Victors remained.

It was at this point that a serious snag developed. Victor K 2 *XL189* of No 57 Squadron (Squadron Leader Bob Tuxford) was transferring fuel to its companion tanker, which was to have accompanied the Vulcan southwards to make the final transfer, when the aircraft ran into turbulence and contact between probe and drogue was broken. More turbulence was encountered as the Victors tried to re-establish contact, and *XL189*'s drogue fractured the receiver's probe. With the latter inoperative the final part of the refuelling operation would have to be undertaken by *XL189*, so Bob Tuxford switched places with the other Victor and reclaimed some fuel. The other aircraft, unable to receive, then broke off and recovered to Ascension.

Tuxford's next task was to find out if *XL189*'s drogue had sustained any damage, so he signalled *XM607* with a request for a visual inspection. The Vulcan descended and Flight Lieutenant Withers tucked in close to the tanker while the crew tried to inspect the drogue with the aid of the AEO's torch, but they were unable to report by this means that the drogue was still operational. The only alternative method was for *XM607* to link up with the tanker; this was done successfully, and some fuel was transferred before the two aircraft broke contact.

The two crews continued the mission in the comforting knowledge that the final transfer could now be made. Tuxford, however, still had a problem in that he no longer had sufficient fuel reserves to fill the Vulcan's tanks before the final run to the Falklands, as he was supposed to do; *XM607* had used more fuel than planned, and further unscheduled amounts had been used up when the two tankers changed places earlier. On the final link-up, therefore, the two aircraft were compelled to break contact before *XM607*'s tanks were full. In fact, unknown to Martin Withers and his crew, Tuxford had given them some of his own precious reserves; when he turned away after the final contact and set course for Ascension, it was with the knowledge that unless he made rendezvous with another tanker, he would run out of fuel some 400 nautical miles short of his destination. To complicate the problem, he could not break radio silence to warn Ascension of his plight until he heard the code-word from the Vulcan signalling that the attack had been successfully completed. Luckily, Ascension had anticipated his need, and a reserve tanker was waiting to be scrambled when the call finally came, well into a long and agonizing flight north; the contact was made without trouble and *XL189* recovered safely to its base. Bob Tuxford's part in the operation subsequently earned him a well-deserved Air Force Cross.

Meanwhile, Flight Lieutenant Withers and his crew had continued the flight at 31,000 ft after the last contact with the Victor tanker, later coming down to 300 ft over the Atlantic to avoid detection by Argentine radar on the mainland. Flight Lieutenant Russell, the AARI, had now relinquished the co-pilot's seat to its rightful occupant, Flying Officer Taylor, and the two pilots were able to concentrate fully on handling the big aircraft as it ran through strong turbulence at this low altitude. It was a relief when, at about 400 nautical miles from the target, they took the Vulcan up to 10,000 ft, its bombing altitude, for the final run.

This was made on a heading of 235 degrees and *XM607* crossed the Port Stanley runway right on track, thanks to the accuracy of the Carousel INS and the skill of the two navigators. The stick of 21 bombs was released to fall diagonally across the runway, the release occupying five seconds from first to last; one bomb exploded halfway down the runway's length and the remainder caused considerable damage among adjacent aircraft and stores. The bomb run was straightforward, using the NBS. No opposition was encountered, although the AEO's equipment picked up a brief illumination by an Argentine SkyGuard radar. Flight Lieutenant Prior used his Dash Ten and the transmissions ceased.

Immediately after bomb release *XM607* turned on its homeward course, climbing to cruise altitude to conserve fuel. It had originally been planned to descend to 300 ft once again, to escape radar detection and avoid any possible controlled interception by Argentine fighters as the Vulcan cleared the target area, but Flight Lieutenant Withers decided that this would result in dangerously excessive fuel consumption. As it was, *XM607*'s fuel state was 8,000 lb below the planned level as it reached cruise altitude. Withers and the AARI, who had once again taken over the co-pilot's seat, concentrated on finding the most economical power settings as the aircraft headed north; fortunately, contact was made with the rendezvous Victor tanker without undue difficulty, using air-to-air TACAN, DF and the assistance of a Nimrod maritime patrol aircraft. The refuelling operation was not without incident, for a leak developed soon after the link-up, but sufficient fuel was taken on board for *XM607* to recover safely to Ascension Island. It had been airborne for 15 hours 45 minutes. For his skill in successfully completing this, the longest-range bombing operation in history, Flight Lieutenant Martin Withers was awarded the Distinguished Flying Cross.

'Black Buck Two', the second Vulcan bombing attack on Port Stanley airfield, was also carried out by *XM607* on the night of May 3/4 1982, with a different crew: Squadron Leader R.J. Reeve (Captain), Flight Lieutenant D.T. Dibbins (Co-pilot), Flight Lieutenant M.A. Cooper (Nav Radar), Flight Lieutenant J. Vinales (Nav Plotter), Flight Lieutenant B.J. Masefield (AEO) and Flight Lieutenant P. Standing (AARI). Jim Vinales, it will be recalled, was one of the crew of Vulcan *XM610* of No 44 Squadron, which crashed in County Durham in 1971.

On this second operation, *XM607* was once again armed with 21 1,000 lb HE bombs. On this occasion the Stanley runway was not hit, although further damage was inflicted on adjacent installations. Fuel transfers on both the outward and return flights were trouble-free. A third mission, 'Black Buck Three', which also involved a conventional bombing attack, had to be cancelled because of adverse weather conditions—mainly strong headwinds—en route.

The fourth mission, 'Black Buck Four', took off from Ascension on schedule on the night of May 28/29. The Vulcan involved this time was *XM597*, armed with four AGM-45A Shrike anti-radar missiles, and its crew were: Squadron Leader Neil McDougall (Captain), Flying Officer Chris Lackham (Co-pilot), Flight Lieutenant Dave Castle (Nav Radar), Flight Lieutenant Barry Smith (Nav Plotter), Flight Lieutenant Rod Trevaskus (AEO) and Flight Lieutenant Brian Gardner (AARI). The task of *XM597* and its crew was to locate and destroy Argentine radar installations around Port Stanley, but the mission had to be aborted when one of the Victor tankers went unserviceable before the penultimate fuel transfer. All the aircraft involved returned safely to Ascension's Wideawake Field.

The mission was scheduled again for the night of May 30/31 as 'Black Buck Five', with the same aircraft, crew and armament. On this occasion, however, the Vulcan attack was to be co-ordinated with a Harrier strike on Port Stanley airfield. The fact that Shrike missiles were carried externally went a long way towards alleviating the fuel problem, for it enabled two extra tanks, carrying a total of 16,000 lb, to be fitted into *XM597*'s bomb bay, and this reduced the number of refuellings on the outward leg to four. The Vulcan arrived in the operational area on schedule, just before the Harriers made their strike, and while this was in progress *XM597* patrolled at a safe distance while the AEO attempted to locate and identify radar targets with his ECM. Three missiles were launched, but it was impossible to assess results, and after some time *XM597* returned to Ascension, with one fuel transfer en route.

'Black Buck Six' was flown on the night of June 2/3, again with the same aircraft, crew and armament, and was to end in a glare of publicity. *XM597* made a low-level approach to the Falklands operational area at 300 ft, pulling up at a distance of 25 nautical miles from Stanley airfield to let itself be illuminated by defensive radars. There was more than the usual element of risk in this, for the expected Harrier air cover was not available for operational reasons and at this point the Vulcan was vulnerable to interception. The Argentine radar operators appeared to realise what the Vulcan was up to, for as it exposed itself an illumination by a Westinghouse AN/TPS-43 main defence radar suddenly ceased as the equipment was switched off. The Vulcan continued its patrol, its equipment receiving sporadic radar transmissions which were not of sufficient duration for a full lock-on to be achieved. Nevertheless, two Shrikes were launched at radar contacts, and subsequent reports suggested that damage to one main radar antenna had been caused by a missile impacting 80 yards short of it. Proof that the Argentines were aware of the RAF's anti-radar activities came when *XM597*'s AEO detected renewed radar transmissions from the Port Stanley area as the Vulcan was outbound at a range of 125 nautical miles.

So far, apart from the lack of worthwhile targets, there had been no disappointments or

Vulcan XM597, the aircraft that diverted to Rio de Janeiro with a broken refuelling probe during the Falklands operations, landing at Greenham Common in 1983.

frustrations in 'Black Buck Six', and the aircraft received the usual assistance from a Nimrod in making contact with its tanker. It was now, however, that the trouble started. As the Vulcan's probe 'prodded' the tanker's drogue, there was a loud crack as the probe fractured at its weak link without apparent reason and fuel sprayed back over the windscreen, causing an immediate 'white out'. With no possibility of receiving fuel to reach Ascension Island, Squadron Leader McDougall immediately turned west and headed for the one diversion that had been available to the 'Black Buck' crews in the event of trouble—Rio de Janeiro, Brazil.

While the crew set about disposing of certain classified material, McDougall stayed at altitude for economy of fuel and made contact with Rio on the distress frequency at a range of 250 nautical miles. The pilot made a steep, straight-in approach, landing down-wind on an inactive runway. He was only just in time: *XM597*'s tanks held enough fuel for only five more minutes' flying. On the way in, the aircraft's crew had attempted to jettison the Vulcan's two remaining Shrikes, but one had suffered a hang-up and was still on its pylon when the aircraft landed. Once the aircraft had come to a stop the crew acted promptly in covering the missile with items of flying clothing to conceal its nature from the attentions of Brazilian photographers, and afterwards mounted their own watch on the Vulcan with the assistance of Brazilian guards. The missile was removed and *XM597* held at Rio for a week, during which the crew was well entertained and the embarrassment sorted out through diplomatic channels, before being allowed to depart for Ascension on the understanding that she would not be used for further operations against the Falklands.

Three days later, *XM597* flew back to Waddington; her captain, Squadron Leader McDougall, later received a DFC.

There was one more Vulcan operation, 'Black Buck Seven', before hostilities ended on the Falklands. It was flown on June 12 by *XM607*, with Flight Lieutenant Martin Withers and the crew who had carried out 'Black Buck One'. This time, the Vulcan was armed with a mixture of 1,000 lb HE and anti-personnel bombs, fuzed to burst in the air, and the target was enemy troop concentrations holding on around Port Stanley. The operation was held to be a partial success, and all aircraft involved in 'Black Buck Seven' recovered safely to Ascension Island.

It has sometimes been said, since the Falklands Operation, that the results achieved by the Vulcans in no way justified the expense and risk involved in the 'Black Buck' missions. This is untrue. What the Vulcans did—and no other aircraft could have done it, or been in a position to do it, at the time of the first bombing attack—was to deny the use of Port Stanley airfield's runway for a vital period to fast Argentine combat jets. In addition, their operations conspired to shut down vital Argentine radar installations at crucial times, and probably yielded vital information on the effectiveness of stand-off weaponry in the defence suppression role under combat conditions. Indeed, to leave the matter open to some speculation, it may even be that the full story of the Vulcans' activities in the Falklands War has not yet been told.

Of the Vulcan B 2s directly involved in Operation Corporate, *XM597* is still on the Order of Battle at the time of writing (summer 1983). It put in a very nostalgic appearance at the 1983 Greenham Common Air Tattoo, giving the usual superb Vulcan display to the strains of the theme from the TV serial *Harry's Game* over the loudspeakers. *XM607* is now 'gate guardian' at RAF Waddington; *XL391* is at Blackpool Airport, where a preservation group has plans to keep it airworthy; *XM598* was flown to the Cosford Aerospace Museum in January 1983; *XM612* is in the Norwich Aviation Museum; and *XM654*, the aircraft that could not be converted to carry pylons because it had no hard-points, was sold as scrap in December 1982.

On April 30 1982 there was a conference at British Aerospace, Woodford, in which the possibility of using converted Vulcans in the flight refuelling role to assist the Victor tanker force was discussed. On May 4 the go-ahead for six such conversions was received, and on June 23 the first Vulcan tanker conversion, *XH561*, was delivered to No 50 Squadron at RAF Waddington, having flown for the first time five days earlier in its new configuration. Flight Refuelling Ltd undertook some redesign of the standard hose drum unit, enabling it to be mounted inside the Vulcan's former ECM bay in the tail after removal of support structure and additional local strengthening of the airframe. This allowed the installation of three cylindrical tanks in the bomb-bay, instead of the two originally planned. The drogue was housed in a wood-and-metal box structure under the tail cone.

On June 23 1982, the day it arrived back at Waddington, *XH561* successfully carried out its first fuel transfer to a Victor K 2. The other five aircraft returned to service after conversion were *XH558*, *XH560*, *XJ825*, *XL445* and *XM571*, all of them going to No 50 Squadron, which also took on charge *XM597*, *XM652* and *XM655*. No 50 Squadron, therefore, was the last unit to operate the Vulcan. Its 'stop-gap' Vulcan K 2 tanker conversions served until the RAF's VC 10 tankers came on stream with No 101 Squadron in May 1984, when No 50 Squadron disbanded.

For years now, commentators at air displays have been warning us that the Vulcan's distinctive bat-like shape would soon be a thing of the past. Every year, Avro's venerable delta continues to confound them, and will probably continue to do so for several more years to come.

Appendix

Aircraft allocation, service and disposal details

VX770 *Delivered* 30-8-52. *Service* First flight from Woodford; subsequently to A&AEE Boscombe Down for trials. *Remarks* Powered initially by Rolls-Royce Avon RA 3 engines, later by AS Sapphire 6s. Trials aircraft for fuel system, drag measurement and engine handling. Vulcan prototype. *Disposal* Exploded in mid-air and crashed at Syerston, 20-9-58. Crew killed.

VX777 *Delivered* 3-9-53. *Service* A&AEE Boscombe Down; RAE Farnborough. *Remarks* Second prototype Vulcan B 1. High altitude radio and radar trials aircraft. First Vulcan powered by Olympus engines. Damaged in heavy landing at Farnborough, 27-7-54.

Symbolic of the RAF's deterrent power in the mid-1960s, Vulcans of the Waddington Wing formate over Fylingdales.

Converted to prototype Vulcan B 2; first flight in this configuration 31-8-57. Used for aerodynamic trials, 1958–60. *Disposal* Broken up at Farnborough, July 1963, after use in runway experiments.

XA889 *Delivered* 4-2-55. *Service* A&AEE, March 1956. To Patchway in 1957 for Olympus engine development. *Remarks* First production Vulcan B 1; fitted with Olympus 101 engines and auto-stabilisation system. *Disposal* Withdrawn from use and scrapped in 1971.

XA890 *Delivered* 1955. *Service* A&AEE Boscombe Down; RAE Thurleigh; RAE Farnborough. *Remarks* Second production Vulcan B 1. CA radio/radar trials aircraft; carried out blind landing experiments at Thurleigh. Ballistics research aircraft, RAE. *Disposal* withdrawn from use and scrapped in 1971.

XA891 *Delivered* 1955. *Service* A&AEE Boscombe Down; Bristol Siddeley Engines, Patchway; RAE Farnborough. *Remarks* Third production Vulcan B 1. Engine installation development aircraft, Olympus 200. *Disposal* Crashed in Yorkshire, 24-7-59. Crew unhurt.

XA892 *Delivered* 1955. *Service* A&AEE Boscombe Down; to RAF Halton for ground instruction. *Remarks* Fourth production Vulcan B 1. Armament trials aircraft. *Disposal* Instructional airframe, Halton (Serial *7746M*).

XA893 *Delivered* 1956. *Service* A&AEE Boscombe Down. *Remarks* Development aircraft. Used to test electrical systems for Vulcan B 2. *Disposal* Broken up at Boscombe Down. Nose section delivered to 71 MU for display purposes.

XA894 *Delivered* 1957. *Service* A&AEE Boscombe Down. *Remarks* Engine development aircraft. Used as test-bed for Bristol Olympus 22R. *Disposal* Burned out while ground running at Patchway, 3-12-62.

XA895 *Delivered* 16-8-56. *Service* 230 OCU, BCDU. *Remarks* Converted to B 1A. Used to test ECM tail cone. *Disposal* Withdrawn from use 13-1-67 and sold for scrap to Bradbury Ltd, 19-9-68.

XA896 *Delivered* 7-3-57. *Service* 44 Sqn; 230 OCU (from 14-9-61); Bristol Siddeley Engines. *Remarks* Partly converted for use as test-bed for BS100 vectored thrust engine. *Disposal* Withdrawn from use 1966.

XA897 *Delivered* 20-7-56. *Service* 230 OCU; Woodford (for mods); A&AEE Boscombe Down. *Remarks* Aircraft began flight to New Zealand via Aden, Singapore and Melbourne, and return, on 9-9-56. *Disposal* Crashed at London Airport, Heathrow, on 1-10-56. Two survivors, three rear crew plus one passenger killed.

XA898 *Delivered* 3-1-57. *Service* 230 OCU. *Remarks* The only Vulcan B 1 to spend its entire working life as an OCU aircraft. *Disposal* To RAF Halton as instructional airframe (*7856M*) on 25-8-64.

XA899 *Delivered* 28-2-57. *Service* A&AEE Boscombe Down; BLEU Thurleigh. *Remarks* Development aircraft (auto-pilot). First four-engined aircraft to make fully automatic landing, 22-12-59. *Disposal* Instructional airframe (*7812M*).

XA900 *Delivered* 25-3-57. *Service* 230 OCU; 101 Sqn; 230 OCU. *Remarks* None. *Disposal* To RAF Cosford as instructional airframe (*7896M*) on 28-2-66.

XA901 *Delivered* 4-4-57. *Service* 230 OCU; 44 Sqn; 83 Sqn. *Remarks* None. *Disposal* To RAF Cranwell as instructional airframe (*7897M*).

XA902 *Delivered* 10-5-57. *Service* 230 OCU. *Remarks* Damaged in landing accident, 28-2-58. Afterwards used for engine trials (Rolls-Royce Conway and Spey). *Disposal* Withdrawn from use 1963.

XA903 *Delivered* 31-5-57. *Service* A&AEE Boscombe Down; RAE Farnborough. *Remarks* Blue Steel trials aircraft; test-bed for Rolls-Royce RB199 engine. Experimentally fitted with 27 mm cannon installation at A&AEE. *Disposal* To Farnborough, early 1979, for fire fighting.

XA904 *Delivered* 16-7-57. *Service* 83 Sqn; 44 Sqn (from 19-1-61). *Remarks* Converted to B 1A; first B 1A taken on charge by 44 Sqn. Badly damaged in crash landing at Waddington, 28-2-61/1-3-61 (night flying accident). *Disposal* Instructional airframe (*7738M*).

XA905 *Delivered* 11-7-57. *Service* 83 Sqn; 44 Sqn; 230 OCU; 44/50/101 Sqns (Waddington Wing). *Remarks* First Vulcan taken on charge by 83 Sqn. *Disposal* To RAF Newton as instructional airframe (*7857M*).

XA906 *Delivered* 12-8-57. *Service* 83 Sqn; 44 Sqn. *Remarks* Converted to B 1A. *Disposal* Withdrawn from use 10-3-67 and sold as scrap to Bradbury & Co, 6-11-68.

XA907 *Delivered* 29-8-57. *Service* 83 Sqn; 44 Sqn; BCDU. *Remarks* Converted to B 1A. *Disposal* Withdrawn from use 3-11-66; sold as scrap 20-5-68.

XA908 *Delivered* 18-9-57. *Service* 83 Sqn. *Remarks* B 1. Made tour of Central Africa (with *XA904* and *XA911*) in 1958. *Disposal* Crashed in Detroit during visit to USA, 24-10-58. Crew killed.

XA909 *Delivered* 1-10-57. *Service* 101 Sqn; 50 Sqn; 44/50/101 Sqns (Waddington Wing). *Remarks* First Vulcan on 101 Sqn inventory. Converted to B 1A. *Disposal* Destroyed on 16-7-64 while serving in 101 Sqn. Aircraft abandoned over Wales after an engine exploded; crew escaped.

XA910 *Delivered* 31-10-57. *Service* 101 Sqn; 230 OCU; 50 Sqn; 44 Sqn. *Remarks* Converted to B 1A. *Disposal* Instructional airframe (*7995M*).

XA911 *Delivered* 1-11-57. *Service* 83 Sqn; 230 OCU; Waddington Wing. *Remarks* Converted to B 1A. Used as the 'star' of the film *Delta 83*, about the V-Force. *Disposal* Withdrawn from use 9-2-67; sold for scrap 8-11-68.

Pilot's eye-view as a Vulcan approaches Gan in the Indian Ocean on a round-the-world flight.

XA912 *Delivered* 2-12-57. *Service* 101 Sqn; Waddington Wing. *Remarks* Converted to B 1A. *Disposal* Withdrawn from use 9-3-67; sold for scrap 20-5-68.

XA913 *Delivered* 19-12-57. *Service* 101 Sqn; Waddington Wing. *Remarks* Converted to B 1A. *Disposal* Withdrawn from use 21-12-66; sold for scrap 20-5-68.

XH475 *Delivered* 11-2-58. *Service* 101 Sqn; Waddington Wing. *Remarks* Converted to B 1A. *Disposal* Instructional airframe (*7996M*) from 20-11-67.

XH476 *Delivered* 4-2-58. *Service* 101 Sqn; 44 Sqn; Waddington Wing. *Remarks* Converted to B 1A. *Disposal* Withdrawn from use 4-5-67; sold for scrap 21-1-69.

XH477 *Delivered* 17-2-58. *Service* 83 Sqn; 44 Sqn; 50 Sqn. *Remarks* Converted to B 1A. *Disposal* Crashed on low-level exercise over Scotland on 12-6-63; crew killed.

XH478 *Delivered* 31-3-58. *Service* Ministry of Aviation; 44/50/101 Sqns (Waddington Wing); Akrotiri for ground training. *Remarks* Used to test nose-mounted flight refuelling probe. Converted to B 1A. *Disposal* To Akrotiri, Cyprus, for ground training (*MC8047M*).

XH479 *Delivered* 28-3-58. *Service* 101 Sqn; 44/50/101 Sqns (Waddington Wing). *Remarks* Converted to B 1A. *Disposal* To RAF Halton as instructional airframe (*7974M*).

XH480 *Delivered* 22-4-58. *Service* 83 Sqn; 44 Sqn; 44/50/101 Sqns (Waddington Wing). *Remarks* Converted to B 1A. *Disposal* Withdrawn from use 10-11-66; sold for scrap 30-9-68.

XH481 *Delivered* 30-4-58. *Service* 101 Sqn; 44/50/101 Sqns (Waddington Wing). *Remarks* Converted to B 1A. Made tour of South America, 1960, and UK–Australia non-stop flight, 1961. *Disposal* Withdrawn from use 1967; to RAF Cottesmore for fire-fighting, 11-1-68.

XH482 *Delivered* 5-5-58. *Service* 617 Sqn; 50 Sqn; 101 Sqn; 44/50/101 Sqns (Waddington Wing). *Remarks* First Vulcan on 617 Sqn inventory. Converted to B 1A. *Disposal* Withdrawn from use 3-11-66; sold for scrap 19-9-68.

XH483 *Delivered* 20-5-58. *Service* 617 Sqn; 50 Sqn; 44/50/101 Sqns (Waddington Wing). *Remarks* Converted to B 1A. *Disposal* Withdrawn from use 3-8-67; to Manston for fire-fighting.

XH497 *Delivered* 29-5-58. *Service* 617 Sqn; 50 Sqn. *Remarks* While serving in 617 Sqn, this aircraft suffered an accident on 3-7-58. The nosewheel fell off after take-off; rear crew baled out, and pilot landed the aircraft on main wheels and nosewheel strut. Converted to B 1A after repair. *Disposal* Withdrawn from use 17-5-66.

XH498 *Delivered* 30-6-58. *Service* 617 Sqn; 50 Sqn; 44/50/101 Sqns (Waddington Wing). *Remarks* Converted to B 1A. *Disposal* Instructional airframe (*7993M*).

XH499 *Delivered* 17-7-58. *Service* 617 Sqn; 50

Seen through the AEO's periscope, Waddington Wing Vulcans in line astern, October 15 1970.

Sqn; 44 Sqn; A&AEE (Special trials). *Remarks* Converted to B 1A. *Disposal* Withdrawn from use 11-65 (broken up at Bitteswell).

XH500 *Delivered* 15-8-58. *Service* 617 Sqn; BCDU (Special trials); 50 Sqn; 44/50/101 Sqns. *Remarks* First Vulcan to be converted to B 1A standard. *Disposal* Instructional airframe (7994M).

XH501 *Delivered* 3-9-58. *Service* 617 Sqn; 44 Sqn; 44/50 Sqns. *Remarks* Converted to B 1A. *Disposal* Withdrawn from use 3-11-66; sold for scrap 8-11-68.

XH502 *Delivered* 10-11-58. *Service* 617 Sqn; 50 Sqn; 44/50/101 Sqns (Waddington Wing). *Remarks* Converted to B 1A. Last B 1A at Waddington. *Disposal* Flown to Scampton in January 1968 for ground instructional duties; subsequently returned to Waddington for fire fighting.

XH503 *Delivered* 30-12-58. *Service* 83 Sqn; 44 Sqn; 44/50/101 Sqns (Waddington Wing). *Remarks* Converted to B 1A. *Disposal* Withdrawn from use 6-12-66; sold as scrap 8-11-68.

XH504 *Delivered* 30-12-58. *Service* 230 OCU; 44/50/101 Sqns (Waddington Wing). *Remarks* Converted to B 1A. *Disposal* Withdrawn from use 4-1-68; to Cottesmore for fire fighting.

XH505 *Delivered* 13-3-59. *Service* 230 OCU; 617 Sqn; 50 Sqn; 44/50/101 Sqns (Waddington Wing). *Remarks* Converted to B 1A. *Disposal* Withdrawn from use 9-1-68; to Finningley for fire fighting.

XH506 *Delivered* 17-4-59. *Service* 101 Sqn; 617 Sqn; 50 Sqn; 44/50/101 Sqns (Waddington Wing). *Remarks* Converted to B 1A. *Disposal* Withdrawn from use 10-1-68; sold for scrap 8-11-68.

XH532 *Delivered* 31-3-59. *Service* On loan to Controller (Aircraft); 230 OCU; 101 Sqn; 44/50/101 Sqns (Waddington Wing); 19 MU, St Athan. *Remarks* 45th and last production B 1. Converted to B 1A. *Disposal* Withdrawn from use 17-5-66; sold for scrap 8-11-68.

XH533 *Delivered* 26-3-59. *Service* Transferred to Controller (Aircraft). *Remarks* First production Vulcan B 2. First flight on 19-8-58. *Disposal* Broken up at St Athan in 1970.

XH534 *Delivered* 5-12-66 (to RAF). *Service* A&AEE (Development aircraft); 230 OCU; 27 Sqn. *Remarks* Second production B 2. Fitted with Olympus 201 engines and modified ECM tail cone. Converted to B 2A/SR 2. *Disposal* Flown to St Athan on 7-4-81; sold for scrap 16-2-82.

XH535 *Delivered* 27-5-60. *Service* Development aircraft (Ministry of Aviation). *Remarks* B 2. *Disposal* Crashed near Andover, Hants, on 11-5-64 during routine flight from A&AEE. Two pilots ejected, four rear crew killed.

XH536 *Delivered* 16-12-59. *Service* Controller (Aircraft) and Ministry of Aviation (Development aircraft); 9/12/35 Sqns (Coningsby Wing). *Remarks* B 2. *Disposal* Flew into high ground at Fan-Bwlchchwtyth Heddi Senni, 20 miles north-east of Swansea, during low-level navigation exercise on 11-2-66. Crew of five killed.

XH537 *Delivered* 28-5-65 (to RAF). *Service* Development aircraft, Ministry of Aviation; 230 OCU; Scampton Wing (from 1972). *Remarks* Skybolt trials aircraft. B 2 converted to B 2A. *Disposal* Flown from Scampton to Abingdon on 25-3-82 and used for fire-fighting practice.

XH538 *Delivered* Date not known. *Service* Ministry of Aviation; 230 OCU; 27 Sqn; 35 Sqn; 9/44/50/101 Sqns. Transferred from Scampton to Waddington in April 1970, and back to Scampton in April 1971. *Remarks* Blue Steel and Skybolt trials aircraft. B 2 converted to B 2A. *Disposal* Flown from Scampton to St Athan on 11-3-81 and scrapped on 31-8-81.

XH539 *Delivered* Date not known. *Service* Development aircraft, MoA and A&AEE. *Remarks* Blue Steel trials aircraft. B 2. *Disposal* Flown from Boscombe Down to Waddington on 7-3-72 and used for fire-fighting practice.

XH554 *Delivered* 7-4-61. *Service* 83 Sqn; 230 OCU; Scampton Wing. *Remarks* B 2. *Disposal* Flown from Scampton to Catterick on 9-6-81 for crash rescue training with the RAF Fire Fighting and Safety School.

XH555 *Delivered* 14-7-61. *Service* 27 Sqn; 230 OCU; Scampton. *Remarks* B 2. Damaged beyond repair in heavy landing at Finningley in 1968; airframe subsequently used for fatigue destruction testing at HSA Woodford until 1970. *Disposal* Broken up at St Athan, 1971.

XH556 *Delivered* 26-9-61. *Service* 27 Sqn; 230 OCU. *Remarks* B 2. *Disposal* Undercarriage collapsed during engine start at RAF Finningley on 18-4-66 and aircraft sustained Category V damage. Stricken off charge the following day.

XH557 *Delivered* 3-12-65 (to RAF). *Service* Ministry of Aviation; 9/12/35 Sqns (Coningsby); 44/50/101 Sqns (Waddington); 9/35 Sqns (NEAF Bomber Wing); 9/44/59/101 Sqns (Waddington). *Remarks* Bristol Siddeley engine development aircraft (Olympus 201/301). B 2 converted to B 2A. *Disposal* Sold to Bird Group for scrap, 12-82.

XH558 *Delivered* 1-7-60. *Service* 230 OCU; Waddington Wing; 50 Sqn. *Remarks* First B 2 delivered to the RAF (to 230 OCU). Converted to K 2. *Disposal* To RAF Lossiemouth for repaint and removal of K 2 refuelling bin; to RAF Waddington January 1986 to replace *XL426* as display aircraft.

XH559 *Delivered* 8-60 (precise date not recorded). *Service* 230 OCU only. *Remarks* B 2. *Disposal* Flown from Scampton to St Athan in May 1981 and scrapped.

XH560 *Delivered* 1-10-60. *Service* 230 OCU; 12 Sqn; 230 OCU; 27 Sqn; 50 Sqn. *Remarks* First B 2 delivered to 12 Sqn (25-9-62) after reformation. Returned to OCU on 29-11-63 until May 1964, then transferred to 27 Sqn. Converted to K 2. *Disposal* In storage at RAF Marham, 1986.

XH561 *Delivered* 11-60 (precise date not recorded). *Service* 230 OCU; 50 Sqn. *Remarks* B 2. Damaged in landing with undercarriage

A Vulcan pilot tucks in under another aircraft during a line-astern flypast.

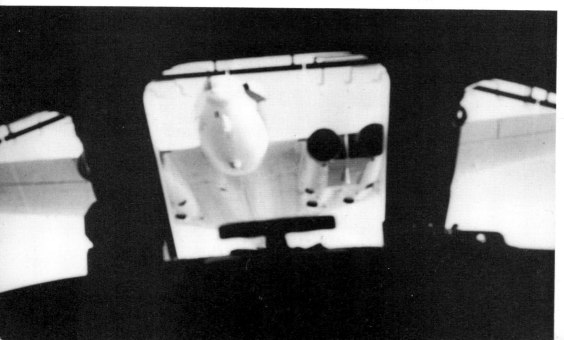

Waddington Wing Vulcans deployed to Butterworth, Malaysia, in June 1968.

up at Finningley on 15-1-65. Converted to K 2. *Disposal* To Fire School, RAF Catterick, 12-6-85 as *8809M*.

XH562 *Delivered* 8-12-60. *Service* 230 OCU; 35 Sqn; 44 Sqn; 230 OCU; 101 Sqn; 50 Sqn. *Remarks* B 2. *Disposal* Flown from Waddington to Catterick on 19-8-82 for use as crash rescue training airframe.

XH563 *Delivered* 23-12-60. *Service* 83 Sqn; 12 Sqn; 230 OCU; 27 Sqn. *Remarks* First B 2 taken on charge by 83 Sqn. Transferred to 12 Sqn on 22-11-62. Electrical systems test aircraft for Skybolt. Converted to SR 2. *Disposal* Withdrawn from use 5-4-82 and placed on display as 'gate guardian' outside Scampton Operations Centre.

XJ780 *Delivered* 13-1-61. *Service* 83 Sqn; 12 Sqn; 230 OCU (from 29-7-65); 27 Sqn. *Remarks* B 2 converted to SR 2. *Disposal* Sold to Bird Group as scrap, 11-82.

XJ781 *Delivered* 22-2-61. *Service* 83 Sqn; 12 Sqn; 230 OCU; 44/50/101 Sqns; 9/35 Sqns (NEAF Bomber Wing, Akrotiri). *Remarks* B 2. *Disposal* On 23-5-73, while visiting Iran, the port undercarriage failed to lower. The aircraft was landed on a foam strip but veered off the runway, tearing off the starboard and nose undercarriage legs. The crew escaped unhurt and the aircraft was stricken off charge on 27-5-73.

XJ782 *Delivered* 1-3-61. *Service* 83 Sqn; 12 Sqn; 230 OCU; 44 Sqn. *Remarks* B 2. *Disposal* Flown from Waddington to Finningley on 4-9-82 and placed on display at Finningley gate.

XJ783 *Delivered* 10-3-61. *Service* 83 Sqn; 9 Sqn; NEAF Bomber Wing; 617 Sqn; 35 Sqn; 101 Sqn. *Remarks* B 2. *Disposal* Sold to Bird Group as scrap, 11-82.

XJ784 *Delivered* 21-12-66 (to RAF). *Service* Ministry of Aviation (Development aircraft); 230 OCU; 9 Sqn; transferred to Akrotiri from Scampton 20-7-70; 50 Sqn; 9 Sqn; 101 Sqn. *Remarks* B 2. *Disposal* Sold to Bird Group as scrap, 12-82.

XJ823 *Delivered* 20-4-61. *Service* 27 Sqn; 35 Sqn; 230 OCU; 44/50/101 Sqns; 9/35 Sqns; 27 Sqn; 35 Sqn; 9/44/50/101 Sqns, Waddington. *Remarks* First B 2 taken on charge by 27 Sqn after re-formation, and also first by 35 Sqn after re-formation. *Disposal* Sold to Mr T. Stoddart, 21-1-83, and flown to Crosby-on-Eden, Carlisle, for display.

XJ824 *Delivered* 15-5-61. *Service* 27 Sqn; 230 OCU; 9 Sqn; 9/35 Sqns (NEAF Bomber Wing); 101 Sqn. *Remarks* B 2. *Disposal* Flown from Waddington to Duxford on 13-3-82 for preservation in the Imperial War Museum collection.

XJ825 *Delivered* 27-7-61. *Service* 27 Sqn; 9 Sqn; 12 Sqn; 35 Sqn; 50 Sqn. *Remarks* B 2, converted to K 2. *Disposal* To RAF Waddington for spares, 8/85. To Battle Damage Repair Flight as *8810M*, January 1986.

XL317 *Delivered* 7-6-62 (to RAF). *Service* Ministry of Aviation; 617 Sqn; Scampton

Wing, 1971. *Remarks* B 2. *Disposal* Flown from Scampton to Akrotiri on 1-12-81 for use with the Akrotiri Engineering Wing as a ground instructional airframe (*8725M*).

XL318 *Delivered* 1-9-61. *Service* 617 Sqn; 230 OCU; 617 Sqn. *Remarks* First B 2 taken on charge by 617 Sqn; also made squadron's last operational sortie, 11-12-81, before disbandment. *Disposal* Dismantled and moved by road (19-2-82–5-3-82) to Hendon for display in the RAF Bomber Command Museum.

XL319 *Delivered* 20-10-61. *Service* 617 Sqn; 83 Sqn; Scampton Wing, 1971; 44 Sqn. *Remarks* B 2. *Disposal* Flown from Waddington to Sunderland on 21-1-82 for display at the North East Aircraft Museum, Sunderland Airport.

XL320 *Delivered* 1-12-61. *Service* 617 Sqn; 27/ 83/617 Sqns (Scampton Wing); 27/617 Sqns; 230 OCU; 617 Sqn; 230 OCU. *Remarks* B 2. *Disposal* Flown to St Athan for disposal on 2-6-81 and sold for scrap 31-8-81.

XL321 *Delivered* 10-1-62. *Service* 617 Sqn; 230 OCU; 35 Sqn; Scampton Wing; 44 Sqn; 50 Sqn. *Remarks* B 2. This aircraft accumulated a total of 6,996 flying hours during its life—more than any other Vulcan. *Disposal* Flown from Waddington to Catterick on 19-8-82 for crash rescue training.

XL359 *Delivered* 1-2-62. *Service* 617 Sqn; 230 OCU; 35 Sqn; Scampton Wing. *Remarks* B 2. *Disposal* Withdrawn from use 3-82 and placed on Scampton fire dump; later (11-82) sold to Bird Group for scrap.

XL360 *Delivered* 1-3-62. *Service* 617 Sqn; 27/ 83/617 Sqns; 35 Sqn; 230 OCU; 44 Sqn. *Remarks* B 2. *Disposal* Flown from Waddington to Baginton/Coventry Airport on 26-1-82 to join Midlands Air Museum.

XL361 *Delivered* 14-3-62. *Service* 617 Sqn; on loan to Ministry of Aviation; 27/83/617 Sqns; 27/617 Sqns; 35 Sqn; Waddington Wing. *Remarks* B 2. *Disposal* Sustained Category 3 damage at Goose Bay, Labrador, while en route Canada–UK. Classed as not worth repairing and abandoned at Goose Bay; stricken off charge 21-12-81.

XL384 *Delivered* 3-62. *Service* 230 OCU; 27/ 83/617 Sqns, Scampton; 83 Sqn to 31-8-69; 27/ 617 Sqns; 230 OCU. *Remarks* B 2. *Disposal* Stricken off charge 14-1-75 following a heavy landing at Scampton in which aircraft was damaged beyond repair. Used for crash rescue training at Scampton (*8585M* and later *8670M*).

XL385 *Delivered* 17-4-62. *Service* Scampton; 9 Sqn; 27/83/617 Sqns. *Remarks* B 2. *Disposal*

Aircraft destroyed by fire at RAF Scampton on 6-4-67. At the start of the take-off run there was an explosion in No 1 engine; debris from the engine ruptured the fuel tanks. Five crew and one air cadet escaped unhurt.

XL386 *Delivered* 11-5-62. *Service* 9 Sqn; Scampton (1971); 83 Sqn to 31-8-69; 44 Sqn; 101 Sqn; 44 Sqn. *Remarks* B 2. *Disposal* Flown from Waddington to Manston on 26-8-82 and handed over to the Central Training Establishment for crash rescue training.

XL387 *Delivered* 1-6-62. *Service* 230 OCU; Waddington Wing; Scampton (1970); 50 Sqn. *Remarks* B 2. *Disposal* Flown from Waddington to St Athan on 25-1-82 and scrapped by 15-12-82.

XL388 *Delivered* 13-6-62. *Service* 9 Sqn; 83 Sqn (to 31-8-69); Scampton; 44 Sqn. *Remarks* B 2. This aircraft carried the name *Mayflower III* and bore ceremonial greetings from the City Council of Lincoln to the Mayor of Lincoln, Nebraska on the 300th anniversary of the original *Mayflower*'s sailing. *Disposal* Flown from Waddington to Honington on 2-4-82 to be used for fire-fighting practice.

XL389 *Delivered* 11-7-62. *Service* 230 OCU; 617 Sqn; 9 Sqn; Scampton (1970); 101 Sqn. *Remarks* B 2. *Disposal* Flown from Waddington to St Athan on 6-4-81 and subsequently scrapped.

XL390 *Delivered* 19-7-62. *Service* 9 Sqn; 27/83/ 617 Sqns; Scampton (1970); 617 Sqn. *Remarks* B 2. *Disposal* Crashed during display practice near Glenview Naval Air Station, California, on 11-8-78. Crew killed.

XL391 *Delivered* 22-5-63. *Service* Ministry of Aviation; BCDU; 9/35 Sqns; 44 Sqn; 101 Sqn. *Remarks* This aircraft was deployed to Ascension Island in May 1982 as part of the 'Black Buck' force involved in air operations against the Falkland Islands. *Disposal* Flown from Waddington to Blackpool Airport on 16-2-83; aircraft preservation group plans to keep it airworthy.

XL392 *Delivered* 1-8-62. *Service* 83 Sqn; Scampton (1971); 35 Sqn. *Remarks* B 2. *Disposal* Flown from Scampton to RAF Valley on 24-3-82 and allocated for fire-fighting training (replaced Shackleton AEW 2 *WL754*, which was to be preserved).

XL425 *Delivered* 30-8-62. *Service* 83 Sqn; Scampton (1972). *Remarks* B 2. *Disposal* Scrapped at Scampton, 13-4-82.

XL426 *Delivered* 12-9-62. *Service* 83 Sqn; Scampton; 50 Sqn. *Remarks* B 2. *Disposal*

Vulcan on detachment to Goose Bay, Labrador.

Used as display aircraft until 1986.

XL427 *Delivered* 1-10-62. *Service* 83 Sqn; Scampton (1971); 83 Sqn (to 31-8-69); 44 Sqn. *Remarks* B 2. *Disposal* Flown from Waddington to RAF Macrihanish, 13-8-82, and used for fire-fighting practice.

XL443 *Delivered* 5-10-62. *Service* 83 Sqn; Scampton (1971); transferred to NEAF from Scampton 11-4-72; 35 Sqn. *Remarks* B 2. *Disposal* Reduced to scrap at Scampton, June 1982, and sold to Bird Group.

XL444 *Delivered* 30-10-62. *Service* 27 Sqn; 27/83/617 Sqns; 230 OCU; 27/83/617 Sqns; 27/617 Sqns; 617 Sqn; 230 OCU; 35 Sqn; 9/44/50/101 Sqns. *Remarks* B 2. *Disposal* Sold as scrap to Bird Group, 12-82.

XL445 *Delivered* 24-11-62. *Service* 27 Sqn, Scampton; 9 Sqn (NEAF Bomber Wing); 230 OCU; 35 Sqn; 44 Sqn; 50 Sqn. *Remarks* B 2 converted to K 2. *Disposal* To BDRF, RAF Lyneham, early 1984. With fire section January 1986 as *8811M*.

XL446 *Delivered* 29-11-62. *Service* 27 Sqn; 44/50/101 Sqns; 230 OCU; Scampton (1970); transferred to NEAF 28-7-82; 9/35 Sqns, Akrotiri; 44/50/101 Sqns; 617 Sqn. *Remarks* B 2. *Disposal* Sold to Bird Group as scrap, 11-82.

XM569 *Delivered* 31-1-63. *Service* 27 Sqn; 44/50/101 Sqns; 9/35 Sqns; 27 Sqn; 9/44/50/101 Sqns; 44 Sqn. *Remarks* B 2. *Disposal* Flown from Waddington to Cardiff Airport on 21-1-83 for display with Wales Aircraft Museum.

XM570 *Delivered* 26-2-63. *Service* 27 Sqn; 617 Sqn. *Remarks* B 2. *Disposal* Flown from Scampton to St Athan on 2-3-81 and sold as scrap on 29-1-82.

XM571 *Delivered* 21-2-63. *Service* 83 Sqn; Scampton; 50 Sqn. *Remarks* B 2 converted to K 2. *Disposal* To Gibraltar 9-5-84: Preserved.

XM572 *Delivered* 1-3-63. *Service* 83 Sqn; 44/50/101 Sqns; 617 Sqn. *Remarks* B 2. *Disposal* Sold to Bird Group for scrap, 11-82.

XM573 *Delivered* 27-3-63. *Service* 83 Sqn; 230 OCU; 44 Sqn. *Remarks* B 2. *Disposal* Withdrawn from use at Offutt Air Force Base, Nebraska, 16-6-82 and presented to the Strategic Air Command Museum.

XM574 *Delivered* 17-6-63. *Service* 27 Sqn; 27/83/617 Sqns; Scampton (1971). *Remarks* B 2. *Disposal* Sold for scrap from St Athan, 29-1-82.

XM575 *Delivered* 21-5-63. *Service* 617 Sqn; 27/83/617 Sqns; Scampton (1970)—27/617 Sqns; 44/50/101 Sqns; 9/44/101 Sqns; 44 Sqn. *Remarks* B 2. *Disposal* Flown to East Midlands Airport on 25-1-83 for display with Leicester Air Museum.

XM576 *Delivered* 6-63. *Service* 27/83/617 Sqns. *Remarks* B 2. *Disposal* During an asymmetric approach to RAF Scampton on 25-5-65 (83 Sqn crew) the aircraft drifted to the left of the runway and crashed while attempting to overshoot. There were no casualties. Aircraft stricken off charge 7-12-65.

XM594 *Delivered* 9-7-63. *Service* 27 Sqn; 27/83/617 Sqns; Scampton (1970); 44 Sqn. *Remarks* B 2. *Disposal* Flown from Waddington to Winthorpe on 19-1-83 for display with Newark Air Museum.

XM595 *Delivered* 20-8-63. *Service* 617 Sqn; 27/83/617 Sqns; Scampton (1970); 617 Sqn; 35 Sqn. *Remarks* B 2. *Disposal* Sold for scrap, 11-82.

XM596 *Delivered* N/A. *Service* Hawker Siddeley Aircraft; RAE. *Remarks* Aircraft not completed;

Above *Strike Command Vulcan detachment at Gan on June 17 1968.* XM598 *is now in the Cosford Aerospace museum.*

Below *This photograph, taken from the cockpit of Vulcan B 2* XM602 *of the Waddington Wing during a trans-Pacific flight in October 1972 (the aircraft is approaching Pago Pago, Samoa) gives a good idea of the restricted view. The whole of the Vulcan cockpit was designed to be blacked out on nuclear sorties.*

Above *Operation Corporate, 1982: A 'Black Buck' Vulcan B2, XM612, taxies past a Wideawake dispersal point.*
Below *Vulcan B 2 XM609 of the Waddington Wing and its crew at Hickam Field, Honolulu, on January 15 1970.*

taken from the production line in 1963 and used as a fatigue specimen to predict Vulcan long-term fatigue life with particular reference to low-level operations. *Disposal* N/A.

XM597 *Delivered* 27-8-63. *Service* 12 Sqn; Waddington Wing; 35 Sqn; 50 Sqn; 9 Sqn; 101 Sqn; 35 Sqn. *Remarks* B 2. First Vulcan to be fitted with passive ECM in fin fairing. Deployed to Ascension Island on 'Black Buck' operation, May 1982, and carried out two defence suppression attacks on Falklands radar installations using Shrike missiles. Made world headlines when forced to divert to Rio de Janeiro, Brazil, on 2-6-82 when flight refuelling probe fractured. *Disposal* To East Fortune 12-4-84; preserved.

XM598 *Delivered* 3-9-63. *Service* 12 Sqn; 44 Sqn. *Remarks* B 2. Deployed to Ascension Island on 'Black Buck' operation, May 1982. Used as reserve aircraft. Should have carried out first bombing attack on Port Stanley airfield, but went U/S. *Disposal* Flown to Cosford Aerospace Museum for display, 20-1-83.

XM599 *Delivered* 30-9-63. *Service* 35 Sqn; 44 Sqn; Waddington Wing. *Remarks* B 2. *Disposal*

Vulcan B 2 XM653 *of the Waddington Wing at El Adem, Libya, on September 19 1967.*

Flown from Waddington to St Athan on 2-6-81 and sold for scrap to Harold John and Co, 29-1-82.

XM600 *Delivered* 2-10-63. *Service* 35 Sqn; 9/12/35 Sqns; 44/50/101 Sqns. *Remarks* B 2. Took part in 'Giant Voice', December 1971. *Disposal* On 17-1-77 a fire in the bomb bay area spread to the port wing. The captain ordered the crew to abandon the aircraft, which crashed ten miles north-east of RAF Coningsby, Lincolnshire. One crew member was injured. Aircraft stricken off charge on 18-1-77.

XM601 *Delivered* 4-11-63. *Service* 9 Sqn. *Remarks* B2. *Disposal* Crashed during overshot from assymetric approach at approach to Coningsby, 7-10-64; crew killed.

XM602 *Delivered* 12-11-63. *Service* 12 Sqn; 101 Sqn. *Remarks* B 2. Took part in 'Giant Voice', December 1971. *Disposal* Flown from Waddington to St Athan and transferred to St Athan Air Museum, 16-3-83.

XM603 *Delivered* 3-12-63. *Service* 9 Sqn; 9/12/ 35 Sqns; 44/50/101 Sqns; 101 Sqn; 44 Sqn. *Remarks* B 2. *Disposal* Flown from Waddington to Woodford on 12-3-82 for preservation by British Aerospace. Has since been restored to its original 'delivery finish' of white overall, and refuelling probe has been removed together with TFR and RWR radars.

XM604 *Delivered* 4-12-63. *Service* 35 Sqn; 9/12/ 35 Sqns. *Remarks* B 2. *Disposal* On 30-1-68, during a routine sortie, a fire in the No 2 engine led to turbine disc separation. The disc entered the bomb bay, severely damaging the flying controls. The Vulcan became uncontrollable and crashed at RAF Cottesmore, Rutland. The pilots ejected but four rear crew (9 Sqn) were killed.

XM605 *Delivered* 20-12-63. *Service* 9 Sqn; 9/12/ 35 Sqns; 44/50/101 Sqns; 9/44/50/101 Sqns; 50 Sqn. *Remarks* B 2. *Disposal* Aircraft flown to Castle Air Force Base, California, arriving on 8-9-81 (44 Sqn crew) for presentation to USAF Museum for permanent display.

XM606 *Delivered* 20-12-63. *Service* 12 Sqn; 9/12/35 Sqns; loaned to Ministry of Aviation; 44/50/101 Sqns; 9/44/50/101 Sqns. *Remarks* B 2. While on loan to MoA, carried out low-level trials from Akrotiri, Cyprus, in 1966 to test new TFR equipment. *Disposal* Flown to Barksdale Air Force Base, Louisiana, on 9-6-82 and presented to the 8th Air Force Museum.

XM607 *Delivered* 31-12-63. *Service* 35 Sqn; 101 Sqn; 44 Sqn. *Remarks* B 2. Deployed to Ascension Island on 'Black Buck' operation, May 1982, and carried out three bombing attacks on Port Stanley Airfield. *Disposal* 'Gate guardian' aircraft at RAF Waddington, 1983.

XM608 *Delivered* 28-1-64. *Service* 9 Sqn; 9/12/ 35 Sqns; 44/50/101 Sqns; 9/44/50/101 Sqns. *Remarks* B 2. *Disposal* Flown from Waddington to St Athan, April 1981. Reduced to scrap and sold December 1982.

XM609 *Delivered* 28-1-64. *Service* 12 Sqn; 9/12/ 35 Sqns; 44/50/101 Sqns; 9/44/50/101 Sqns. *Remarks* B 2. *Disposal* Flown from Waddington to St Athan in March 1981 and reduced to scrap by 31-8-81.

XM610 *Delivered* 11-2-64. *Service* 9 Sqn; 9/12/ 35 Sqns; 44/50/101 Sqns. *Remarks* B 2. *Disposal* On 8-1-71, during climb-out from a low-level exercise over Northumberland, No 1 engine exploded and the port fire-warning lights illuminated. The fire persisted and control became difficult. The crew abandoned the aircraft successfully and the Vulcan crashed near Wingate, County Durham. Two crew members (44 Sqn) were injured.

XM611 *Delivered* 13-2-64. *Service* 9 Sqn; 9/12/ 35 Sqns; Waddington Wing. *Remarks* B 2. *Disposal* Flown from Waddington to St Athan on 28-1-82 and subsequently scrapped.

XM612 *Delivered* 2-3-64. *Service* 9 Sqn; 9/12/ 35 Sqns; 44/50/101 Sqns; 44 Sqn. *Remarks* B 2. Deployed to Ascension Island, May 1982, for 'Black Buck' operation. Used as reserve aircraft. *Disposal* Flown from Waddington to Norwich Airport on 30-1-83 to join City of Norwich Aviation Museum.

XM645 *Delivered* 11-3-64. *Service* 9/12/35 Sqns; 44/50/101 Sqns; 230 OCU; transferred from Scampton to Waddington April 1971; 44/ 50/101 Sqns; 9/35 Sqns; 9 Sqn. *Remarks* B 2. *Disposal* On 14-10-75, the aircraft undershot the runway at RAF Luqa, Malta, and the port undercarriage leg was pushed up into the wing, starting a fire as the aircraft bounced back into the air. While climbing to give the rear crew a chance to bale out, the fire caused an explosion. The captain and co-pilot ejected as the aircraft broke up, but five other crew members were killed. A woman civilian on the airfield was killed by falling wreckage and two civilians were injured.

XM646 *Delivered* 7-4-64. *Service* 12 Sqn; 9/12/ 35 Sqns; NEAF Bomber Wing, Akrotiri; 9/44/ 50/101 Sqns. *Remarks* B 2. *Disposal* Flown from Waddington to St Athan on 26-1-82 and subsequently scrapped.

XM647 *Delivered* 15-4-64. *Service* 35 Sqn; 9/12/ 35 Sqns; NEAF Bomber Wing; 9/44/50/101 Sqns; 44 Sqn. *Remarks* B 2. *Disposal* Flown from Waddington to Laarbruch, Germany, on 17-9-82 and used for fire-fighting training.

XM648 *Delivered* 5-5-64. *Service* 9 Sqn; 101 Sqn; 44 Sqn. *Remarks* B 2. *Disposal* Reduced to scrap at Waddington and sold to the Bird Group, 12-82.

XM649 *Delivered* 13-5-64. *Service* 9 Sqn; 9/12/ 35 Sqns; 44/50/101 Sqns. *Remarks* B 2. *Disposal* Flown from Waddington to St Athan and sold as scrap to the Bird Group, 2-12-82.

XM650 *Delivered* 27-5-64. *Service* 12 Sqn; 44/50/101 Sqns; 9/44/50/101 Sqns. *Remarks* B 2. Took part in 'Giant Voice', December 1971. *Disposal* Flown from Waddington to St Athan on 16-3-83 for reduction to scrap.

XM651 *Delivered* 19-6-64. *Service* 12 Sqn; 50 Sqn. *Remarks* B 2. *Disposal* Sold as scrap to the Bird Group, 11-82.

XM652 *Delivered* 14-8-64. *Service* 9 Sqn; 44

Sqn; 35 Sqn; 50 Sqn. *Remarks* B 2. *Disposal*
All but approx 27 ft of nose scrapped. Nose
section purchased from a Sheffield scrap yard
by Tim Wassell of Burntwood, Staffs, in
1985.

XM653 *Delivered* 3-9-64. *Service* 9 Sqn; 44/50/
101 Sqns; 9/44/50/101 Sqns. *Remarks* B 2.
XM653 was the first Vulcan B 2 to be withdrawn
from use in the progressive rundown of the V-
Force from 1980. *Disposal* Flown from
Waddington to St Athan on 18-12-80 and sold
for scrap on 28-7-81.

XM654 *Delivered* 22-10-64. *Service* 12 Sqn; 101
Sqn; 9/44/50/101 Sqns; 35 Sqn. *Remarks* B 2.
Took part in 'Giant Voice', December 1971.
Disposal Sold as scrap to the Bird Group, 12-82.

XM655 *Delivered* 20-11-64. *Service* 9 Sqn; 44
Sqn; 50 Sqn; 101 Sqn; 44 Sqn. *Remarks* B 2.
Disposal Sold to Roy Jacobsen for display at
Wellesbourne Mountford as *G-VULC*. Sold
3-9-85 as *N655AV*, but still at WM in August
1986. Started up and taxied around airfield
17-8-86.

XM656 *Delivered* 14-12-64. *Service* 35 Sqn;
9/12/35 Sqns; 44/50/101 Sqns; 9/44/50/101
Sqns; 35 Sqn. *Remarks* B 2. *Disposal* Sold as
scrap to the Bird Group, 30-3-83.

XM657 *Delivered* 12-64. *Service* 35 Sqn; 44
Sqn; 9/44/50/101 Sqns. *Remarks* B 2. Last production Vulcan and the last B 2 to be delivered.
Disposal Flown from Waddington to Manston
on 5-1-82 for fire-fighting practice.

The Vulcan's last operational role was that of flight refuelling tanker, six aircraft being converted to K 2 standard and operated by No 50 Squadron, Waddington.

Of related interest...

HAWKER HUNTER

This lavishly illustrated volume is both a tribute to a fine machine, and a superlative reference source. **Francis Mason** traces the aircraft's history from interceptor, to ground attack fighter and advanced trainer; recalls its unique export success; and analyses its structure and flying characteristics. *The Hunter — most beautiful of all jet fighters — lovingly reviewed.*

LIGHTNING

Bryan Philpott. First flown in 1957 and still in active service, the Lightning was the first supersonic aircraft designed and built in Britain. This book details the aircraft's development and success — and shows how, but for Government vacillation, the Lightning, with its great overseas sales potential, could have re-vitalised the British military aircraft industry.

METEOR

Bryan Philpott — who flew Meteors in the RAF — presents a detailed study of the development and service career of Britain's first operational jet. Interceptor, night fighter and ground-attack aircraft, the Meteor saw combat in World War 2 and Korea. Many drawings and photographs, some in colour.